Modelling Norms

Corinna Elsenbroich • Nigel Gilbert

Modelling Norms

Springer

Corinna Elsenbroich
Department of Sociology
Centre for Research in Social Simulation (CRESS)
University of Surrey
Guildford, UK

Nigel Gilbert
Department of Sociology
Centre for Research in Social Simulation (CRESS)
University of Surrey
Guildford, UK

ISBN 978-94-007-7051-5 ISBN 978-94-007-7052-2 (eBook)
DOI 10.1007/978-94-007-7052-2
Springer Dordrecht Heidelberg New York London

Library of Congress Control Number: 2013943121

Printed on acid-free paper

Springer is part of Springer Science+Business Media (www.springer.com)

Acknowledgements

This book took a little longer than expected but books, it seems, have their own schedule, independent of that of the authors, publishers or funders. It is impossible to thank everyone who has contributed directly or indirectly to the work but some people should be explicitly mentioned. The writing of the book was funded by the UK Economic and Social Research Council through the National Centre for Research Methods within a project called Simulation Innovation: A Node. One of the aims of the project was to develop and disseminate agent-based modelling as a method in the social sciences, and that is also the aim of this book, specifically in relation to modelling norms. We thank the ESRC for funding this exciting and important project. As in all projects, many things in addition to research need to be done and we thank Lu Yang especially for handling the organisational issues for us so competently.

We also thank the editorial team at Springer for their patience and help in copy editing the book.

Some people have contributed rather directly to the book through collaboration. We thank Maria Xenitidou for her expertise in social psychology, Piter Dykstra for the development of the model in Chap. 12 and Harko Verhagen for collaboration about collective intentionality. We thank Rainer Hegselmann for commenting on a draft. We are grateful to our colleagues in CRESS, the Centre for Research in Social Simulation, for their companionship and encouragement. Our thanks also go to two anonymous referees whose comments improved the book a lot. All remaining faults and inaccuracies are our own.

Contents

Chapter 1
Introduction

Man is a mediocre egoist; even the most cunning thinks his habits more important than his advantage.

Friedrich Nietzsche

"Life is what you make it." Although we probably often feel creatures of circumstances, this proverb contains an important insight into the human condition: humans have agency, humans can make decisions about their actions. But how do humans make decisions? What motivates them? Why do different people make different decisions in very similar circumstances? And why do people make similar decisions in vastly different circumstances? These questions about human motivations, decisions and behaviours, and the role of circumstances, lie at the heart of the social and behavioural sciences.

The research question "Why do some people commit crimes?" asks why some people break the rules of their own society. Asking this question seems to suggest that non-criminal behaviour is a kind of default that needs no explanation. The question "Why do people cooperate?" asks why people behave in a way that might be detrimental for themselves but beneficial for society. The question seems just as legitimate as the question about crime but suggests that defection, or criminal behaviour, is the default. Which is the right question to ask? Which behaviour is the default? The answer is 'neither'. Both questions are perfectly legitimate. The interesting thing about human behaviour is that *all* behaviour needs to be explained. What is seen as default behaviour and what as explanandum depends solely on the vantage point of the research(er).

Both vantage points above relate to the topic of social norms or normative behaviour. Why people commit crimes, i.e. contravene social norms, is a question of criminology. Why people adhere to norms is a question of sociology/social psychology. In the end these two questions can be combined into one: the question of human behaviour in relation to *social norms*, i.e. either adhering to them or contravening them. This overarching question lies at the heart of the social sciences and is called *inter alia* the structure-agency problem, the micro-macro problem or

C. Elsenbroich and N. Gilbert, *Modelling Norms*, DOI 10.1007/978-94-007-7052-2_1,

the individual-collective behaviour problem. We look at the question of social norms from both sides, discussing theories and models of cooperation in Chap. 2 and crime in Chap. 3.

But first of all we introduce social norms, run through some methodological issues around studying micro and macro phenomena in the social sciences and discuss the possibility of analytical social science.

1.1 Social Norms

Social norms govern most of our life. Although we might be conscious of some norms, like queuing politely for the bus in England, most of our behaviour is relatively automatic, like getting dressed before leaving the house. We would not think of transgressing certain norms, whilst we delight in transgressing others. We would not spit into a stranger's face unprovoked or wear our underpants on our head. But we might delight in crossing a red pedestrian light in Germany where it is the norm to wait at the lights, even if there is no car in sight. So, why do we do what we do? And what are the consequences of many people doing as they do?

This is what this book is about. We will look at questions of deliberate action, social influence, conformity, obedience and compliance and how individual behaviours affect social outcomes and vice versa. We will discuss these questions first from a theoretical perspective in Chaps. 2 and 3, introduce the method of agent-based modelling in Chap. 4 and spend the remainder of the book looking at models explaining different aspects of normative behaviour.

Why do people do what they do? The first answer to this question is usually, 'because they want to'. Although this might sound a little flippant, this answer is a serious contender as an explanation. It is the explanation favoured by individualism, although it is usually phrased in rather more formal terms. Individualist approaches to the question of human behaviour start from two premises: (a) individuals have preferences and (b) individuals try to maximise their own utility. Preferences are simply preferences for certain states of the world over other states. I prefer to have cake to being hungry. I also prefer cake to an apple although I prefer the apple to being hungry. Given these preferences I will act in such a way as to get the cake. If cake is impossible I will try to get the apple. Individualism asserts that agents will do whatever guarantees the best outcome for themselves, they are selfish utility-maximisers. Intuitively this makes sense and it can explain a lot of human behaviour, particularly the bad bits. However, some behaviour is rather more tricky to explain within this framework. Let's try out some examples:

Why do people pay on public transport? On many public transport systems one can get away without buying a ticket. Ticket inspections are relatively rare so that paying the fine if one is caught usually amounts to less than paying every time one takes a ride. Buying a ticket is detrimental to an agent's utility and yet, most people buy tickets.

Why do people give money to charity? Charitable organisations receive a lot of donations from all strata of society. Whilst we might say that rich people can easily give some money away, poor people also donate despite it costing them a lot more in relative terms. There is usually no public recognition for the donation nor any direct benefit to the donator. Donating to charity is detrimental to an agent's utility and yet, many people donate.

Why do people join a trade union? Joining a trade union means paying a membership fee. Trade unions bring advantages such as negotiated pay and work conditions. But workers that are not members of a trade union also benefit from the negotiated pay and work conditions. So, although trade unions provide a benefit for their members, non-members benefit from the trade union negotiations and do not have to pay a membership fee. Thus joining a union is detrimental to an agent's utility and yet, many people join unions.

People seem to do things although they are detrimental to their personal utility. Different explanations are put forward as to why they do. People might buy a transport ticket as it is embarrassing to be caught without. People might donate to charity as it makes them 'feel good'. People might join the trade union because they feel the duty to contribute rather than free-ride. These sentiments are not explicable by individualism.

So people might still do what they want to do but what they want to do seems to be more complicated than simple personal preferences and utility maximisation. An alternative explanation of human behaviour is a structuralist approach in which human action is explained by the social structures in which it occurs. The embarrassment we feel being caught, the joy we feel helping others, the duty we feel to contribute, come from the social structures we live in and we have been socialised into. This structuralist approach, although explaining a lot of social behaviour, has a terrible side-effect: Suddenly people no longer do what they want to do but they are made to act by structures. People lose their agency in the mire of social structures that constrain behaviour. This can be called the *Paradox of Agency*, that on the one hand, individual preferences are not enough to explain the range of behaviours found in the world but social structures seem too coercive, leaving no space for any individual agency.

Our second question was, what are the consequences of many people doing as they do? If all your colleagues are members of the union, you might be more inclined also to join the union. If everybody cancelled their membership of the union, the union would cease to exist. The old slogan 'Imagine There Is a War and No One Turns Up!' comes to mind. Many people behaving in the same or similar way brings about social phenomena such as social institutions (trade unions, war), fashions and fads (suits and ties), traditions (Easter egg hunts, birthday parties, Sunday roasts), conventions (driving on the right side of the road) and even new objects (money, wedding rings, crowns). These behavioural regularities are often called 'social norms'.

We will encounter many definitions of a social norm in the following chapters. We will see that all the definitions capture something relevant about social norms but we will also see in Chap. 10 that each definition fails to cover certain other aspects.

One reason for this difficulty in pinning down a definition of social norms is that norms function on different levels. A social norm might define a society (national stereotyping), demarcate 'groups' within a population (Mods and Rockers), be used as an instrument of power and coercion (Patriarchy), be the reason for an individual's action (conformity, compliance), or many other things. It makes a difference in the definition of a social norm whether we apply it to an aggregate, where it is a behavioural regularity, or to an individual, where it is a rule of conduct.

Social norms also need to be contrasted to moral and legal norms. All three provide rules of conduct but the source of the rules is subtly different.

Definition 1.1.1. A social norm is a rule of conduct derived from a social behavioural expectation.

Definition 1.1.2. A moral norm is a rule of conduct derived from a moral value.

Definition 1.1.3. A legal norm is a rule of conduct derived from the code of law.

The source of moral rules is a set of moral values, the source of legal rules a set of laws. Is it fair to contrast these two sources to social expectations? After all, moral rules are not free from social influence and what is the code of law if not enshrining social values? Although there is certainly social influence on laws and mores, the social influence is not direct as in the case of social norms. The immediacy of social influence can be used as a distinguishing mark of normative behaviour (Elsenbroich and Xenitidou 2012).

1.2 How to Study Social Norms

The study of norms has become more and more interdisciplinary over the past century. Whilst it used to be the prerogative of moral philosophy, psychology and sociology, norms are now a prevalent concept in economics, politics, computer science, logic, artificial intelligence, communication theory and evolutionary biology. Neo-Darwinian theories explain altruism as a phenotype of the selfish gene so that altruism becomes a mechanism that has evolved to increase the chances of gene survival through the generations (Dawkins 1976). Psychological research on norms reaches from assessing hormonal influences on behaviour (Fairchild et al. 2008) to motivation and identity studies (Turner 1996). In computer science norms have informed the subfields of deontic logic, argumentation theory, Artificial Intelligence, human-computer interaction, etc. In economics, norms have been used to explain (away) preferences but also to widen the scope of the *homo economicus* (Ellickson 1998).

In this book we are concerned with a particular methodology applied to the study of social norms, the methodology of agent-based modelling. Agent-based modelling has possibly been the most radical methodological revolution in the social sciences of the past 50 years. We will discuss agent-based modelling in more detail in Chap. 4. It is sufficient for now to know that agent-based modelling is a computer simulation method for the social sciences. It allows the dynamic representation of (social) processes. An agent-based model can be used to explore experimentally the influences and interdependencies of different parameters on a (social) phenomenon.

1.3 Theoretical Social Science

How can computer simulations help us understand anything about the real world? The social sciences, like the natural sciences, should be based on empirical findings. Comte, grandfather of sociology, called the new science 'social physics' and Durkheim saw it as the natural extension of the natural sciences into the realm of the social. Empiricism and data are important in the natural sciences, at least since Bacon's *Novum Organon*. Nowadays, natural scientists rarely go out into the real world to collect data, rather they stay in and generate data under highly controlled conditions in laboratories. This process is called experimentation and it is the backbone of natural science. The social sciences, on the other hand, are dominated by data gathering in the real world. Whether using interviews, focus groups, surveys, observations, or text analysis, social scientists collect data rather than generate it. Nevertheless, although scarce, experimentation does exist in the social sciences. Experimental economics mainly investigates the soundness of assumptions of game theory, asking subjects for their decisions in artificial social setups. Social psychology conducts experiments into the social influences between people.

However, although there is (some) experimentation at the micro level, i.e. small scale, often dyadic, interactions between people, there is no macro experimentation. There are many reasons for this. There are ethical reasons not to experiment on human beings.[1] The experimentation on humans in concentration camps during the second world war led to a code of ethics enshrined in the Nuremberg Code, containing ten points covering minimal mental and physical suffering, informed consent and maximal reduction of risk. A second problem for the social sciences is the reflexivity of the subjects of study. For example informed consent poses a problem for the social sciences as disclosure of the experimental setup might change the behaviour of people. Had Milgram (1973) informed his 'teachers' that no actual electro shock was administered to the subject, could the experiment have shed any light on human behaviour?[2] A third problem is that social systems are too large and/or too complex to experiment on. A society just does not fit into a laboratory. (For a more detailed discussion, see for example Hollis 1994, Chaps. 3 and 9).

Do the social sciences need experimentation? The answer to this question depends on what is seen as the goal of the social sciences. For some the purpose

[1] See for example http://listverse.com/2008/09/07/top-10-unethical-psychological-experiments/

[2] See Sect. 2.2.4 for a summary of the experiment.

of the social sciences is to represent the social world, to gain (deep) understanding of the meanings of social interactions and to provide a 'thick description' of human behaviour, Geertz (1973). For others the aim of social science is generalisation, perhaps not to the point of finding laws, but at least statistical general statements. Corresponding to these are two kinds of methods. Qualitative analysis, focused on deep understanding of specific small scale samples of social actors and phenomena but not focused on explanation or generalisation, and quantitative methods, mainly statistical analysis, focused on explanation and generalisation.

A third conception of the aim of the social sciences is analytic sociology (Hedström and Swedberg 1998). Here the goal of the social sciences is to find the underlying mechanisms of social phenomena. Rather than staying at the level of specific description or statistical generalisation, the aim is to uncover the 'nuts and bolts' of the social world, to extract the causal relationships (Elster 1989).

Experiments are vital for the investigation of mechanisms. Social scientists using quantitative methods often make causal claims such as "socio-economic deprivation *causes* low attainment in pupils". However, they do not explain low attainment, they merely present evidence for a link between the variables "socio-economic deprivation" and "low attainment". Elucidating a mechanism means to open the black box of a statistical correlation and show *how* an effect is produced. We cannot gain causal knowledge from statistical knowledge directly, or, as Cartwright (1989) puts it, "no causes in, no causes out". And whilst statistical analysis gives us associations of variables over a static population, it does not tell us what happens in a dynamic setting, or statistical "[a]ssociations characterize static conditions, while causal analysis deals with changing conditions." (Pearl 2003, p. 104).

If the social sciences are seen as descriptive and interpretative there is no need for experimentation; observations and recording of data is sufficient. If the goal of the social sciences is, however, to investigate the mechanisms underlying social phenomena, experimentation becomes paramount. In this book we will discuss computer simulation as an appropriate method for the investigation of mechanisms. Computer modelling sounds a lot like armchair philosophising rather than the empiricism a proper science demands. In the following section we look at the use of 'armchair science', i.e. not leaving one's armchair but conducting science rather than 'mere' philosophising. The traditional method of armchair science is thought experimentation. As we will see, thought experimentation has been very important to the natural sciences and we argue that computer simulation is a form of thought experimentation for the social sciences.

1.3.1 Thought Experiments

Rather surprisingly, armchair science has often been at the heart of scientific advances. The instrument of armchair science is the thought experiment, a form of 'what-if' reasoning. Kühne (2005) points to the difference between the "old", intuitive method of explaining the world employed by Aristotle (e.g. the Aristotelian

Law of Free Fall), which Kühne describes as 'picturing nature', to the 'new' method which tries to 'reconstruct nature' using idealisation, non-intuitive premises and superimposition of simpler facts (e.g. Galileo's law of inertia). Traditional social science is similar to the Aristotelian method whereas analytic sociology advocates a paradigm shift towards reconstruction.

As the name *thought experiment* suggests, a thought experiment is an experiment happening purely in thought, or in the 'laboratory of the mind' as Brown (1991) catchily calls it. Examples of thought experiments run through the ages of scientific enquiry, from Galileo's tied together stones, Newton's Bucket, Einstein's Train to Schrödinger's Cat.

For example Galileo's thought experiments on motion undermined prevailing paradigms (although they were not accepted until much later). The then common conception of a body's motion originated from Aristotle's natural philosophy which proposed that bodies have *natural speed*, with heavier bodies moving faster than lighter bodies. But what happens if two bodies are tied together? Galileo (1628/2010) executes a thought experiment in a dialogue between Salvati and Simplicio

> Salvati: If we take two bodies whose natural speeds are different, it is clear that on uniting the two, the more rapid one will be partly retarded by the slower, and the slower will be somewhat hastened by the swifter. Do you not agree with me in this opinion?
>
> Simplicio: You are unquestionably right.
>
> Salvati: But if this is true, and if a large stone moves with a speed of, say, eight, while a smaller stone moves with the speed of four, then when they are united, the system will move with a speed of less than eight. Yet the two stones tied together make a stone larger than that which before moved with a speed of eight: hence the heavier body now moves with less speed than the lighter, an effect which is contrary to your supposition. Thus you see how, from the assumption that the heavier body moves faster than the lighter one, I can infer that the heavier body moves more slowly... And so, Simplicio, we must conclude therefore that large and small bodies move with the same speed, provided only that they are of the same specific gravity.

This thought experiment gives us a good idea of how rationalisation alone can convey knowledge about empirical matters. From the hypothesis that two bodies have different speeds, Galileo asks the question what happens if they are tied together. If the two bodies have different *natural speeds* the slower body has to slow down the heavier body. But the tied together bodies constitute a new single body, heavier than either of the original bodies, which, according to the theory of *natural speeds* has to fall faster. This contradiction shows that the theory of *natural speeds* cannot be true.

The history of science is full of breakthroughs resulting from what can be seen as pure armchair science. This is somewhat at odds with the idea of an experimental science in which nature is the arbiter of truth, not reasoning, and thought experimentation is not without its critics. One major debate is between a Platonic (Brown 2004a,b) and an empirical interpretation of thought experiments (Norton 2004a,b). Brown's position is that thought experiments actually reveal nature because of the possibility of the mind to "peek at the platonic heavens" (Brown

2003). Empiricism is not enough to understand nature making rationalisation an essential part of scientific methodology. Norton's position on the other hand is that thought experiments are "nothing but" arguments. This means that thought experiments do not contain new informative content but are purely deductive. This stands in contrast to what Kühne (1995) calls the 'paradox of thought experiments', as it seems to be the case that they do in fact lead to new empirical insights meaning they cannot be deductive.

Brendel (2004) argues against Brown's Platonism and holds with Norton that thought experiments can be *reconstructed* as arguments, but that their function is more than just that of an argument. Instead, in their execution they are what Dennett (1995) calls *intuition pumps*. The difference between a formal argument and an intuition pump is that the latter does not have to state and reveal all the premises necessary to reach a certain conclusion. On the contrary, as Dennett (1984) states "intuition pumps are cunningly designed to focus the reader's attention on 'the important features, and to deflect the reader from 'bogging down in hard-to-follow details'." This omission of 'irrelevant premises' is on the one hand the strength of thought experiments, as they tap into intuition directly, but at the same time a danger as this omission can lead to abuse.

What makes a good thought experiment? Einstein and Infeld (1938) cite Galileo's thought experiment of a cart on a frictionless plane to show uniform motion in the absence of external forces. This thought experiment superimposes the single factors of force and motion and reconstructs phenomena like friction and inertia. Intuitively, a thought experiment can be described as a hypothetical reconstruction of reality by singling out simple features and superimposing them, reading off their interactions.

The discussion on thought-experiments is often divided into thought-experiments in the natural sciences (Brown 1991; Norton 2004b; Kühne 2005) and thought-experiments in philosophy (Cohnitz 2006); the former clearly juxtaposed to the experimental natural sciences, the latter more in line with an interpretation of thought-experiments as (counterfactual) arguments.

1.3.2 Thought Experiments in the Social Sciences

As we have seen above, there is plenty of high quality literature on thought experiments in the natural sciences (Kühne 2009 for an excellent overview and Brown 1991; Kühne 1995, 2005; Norton 2004b; Brendel 2004 for further philosophical discussion). Another field of study in which thought experiments are prevalent is philosophy itself, in particular in ethics (e.g. survival lottery, Harris 1975), philosophy of mind (e.g. brain-in-vat, Putnam 1982), philosophy of language (e.g. the Chinese Room, Searle 1984) and questions of material or personal identity (e.g. the ship of Theseus, Neurath 1921).[3] The social sciences have thought

[3]For a full analysis of thought experiments in philosophy see Cohnitz (2006).

experiments such as Hume's *Specie-Flow* economy, the Prisoner's Dilemma, Rawls' *Veil of Ignorance* and Hardin's *Tragedy of the Commons*, to name some famous ones, but they are few and far between. We will discuss two in more detail as they exemplify the common kinds of thought experimentation in the social sciences.

1.3.2.1 Hume's Specie-Flow Mechanism

Hume (1752) presents a thought experiment about the flow of money (specie) between economies. Imagine four fifth of the money in Britain to be destroyed over night. What would happen to the economy? Hume argues that commodity and labour prices would fall sharply to accommodate the lack of currency. That in turn would mean that other nations would increase buying British goods as they were comparatively cheap and within due course money would flow back into the British economy. This in turn would lead to increased commodity and labour prices until the trading economies are in equilibrium again. Similarly, if money was multiplied fivefold overnight, prices would increase sharply so that goods from other nations would become more and more attractive, leading to the money flowing out of the British economy.

Hume concludes his thought experiment as follows:

> Now, it is evident, that the same causes, which would correct these exorbitant inequalities, were they to happen miraculously, must prevent their happening in the common course of nature, and must for ever, in all neighbouring nations, preserve money nearly proportionable to the art and industry of each nation. *Of the Balance of Trade* (Hume 1752)

The purpose of the scenario is to show that it is not the absolute quantities of money that matter in an economy but the relative proportions of prices and money and to point to the importance of industry and people rather than the importance of money.

1.3.2.2 Hardin's Tragedy of the Commons

The Tragedy of the Commons (Hardin 1968) is a well known application of rational choice theory to a common good. Imagine a common, a land for everyone to graze their livestock on. One day a herdsman thinks that he should add an animal to his stock. After all, more animals will bring him more money. The herdsman is aware of the possibility of overgrazing but reasons that the increase of that risk by him adding one animal is minute, a fraction of the utility gained by the added animal. The problem is that each and every herdsman should reason this way, thus rapidly leading to overgrazing.

This scenario explores the interdependence of individual utility and common good. The scenario has rational choice theory as a background, asserting that each herdsman would make the decision to add one animal after another to his herd. Without this assumption the tragedy of the commons vanishes. Hardin uses the tragedy to argue against applications of commons in any area of life and for regulation and private ownership.

Hume's specie-flow describes the interdependence of money, prices and wages. It stays at the level of institutional facts and their interaction without having to touch on human decision making. This kind of thought experiment is mainly used in economics where institutions are more clearly defined than in other social sciences.

Hardin's Tragedy of the Commons explores the interdependence of individual utility maximisation and social utility maximisation. The decision that maximises the individual's utility leads in the long run to a collapse of utility for all. This thought experiment is an example of many relying on rational choice and game theory.

The two kinds of social science thought experiments can be summarised as either analysing the interdependence of institutions or exploring the macro effects of individual decisions. But what happens when we add tariffs to Hume's flow of money? Exchange rates? Cartels? Debt? Soon the analysis of institutional interdependencies becomes too complex to execute in the mind. Similarly for the case of the other kind. In order to get interesting results from rational choice theory or the prisoner's dilemma we need large numbers of agents repeatedly interacting. We can no longer execute experiments in thought, instead we analyse scenarios mathematically, with differential equations and equilibria. These in turn no longer lay open what the causal mechanisms underlying the phenomena are and we are back to square one where we can no longer uncover mechanisms.

1.3.3 Thought Experiments and Agent-Based Modelling

So the main barrier to thought experiments in the social sciences, at both the institutional facts and the individual facts levels, is the complexity of the interactions needed to generate interesting social phenomena. In this section we introduce agent-based modelling as a method of thought experimentation for the social sciences. We have discussed two kinds of thought experiments in the social sciences in Sects. 1.3.2.1 and 1.3.2.2, one investigating the interaction of institutions, the other based on simple scenarios built on rational choice theory. These two examples showed that only relatively simple interactions can be modelled in thought experiments before they quickly become too complicated to think through. Let us see how we can enhance the 'laboratory of the mind' with the virtual laboratory of computer simulations.

Agent-based modelling has been a ground breaking methodological innovation, introducing a new, model-centred epistemology into the social sciences. Agent-based models are computer programs consisting of a number of autonomous, heterogeneous agents interacting with an environment and with each other. The environment in an agent-based model can represent a geography of resources (e.g. houses, food), a social space (e.g. networks), or something more abstract like an opinion or information space. Agents move about in space, both changing the space (e.g. consuming resources) and reacting to it (e.g. moving towards the nearest resource). Agents also interact with each other, e.g. exchanging information or imitating one another. Given these ingredients, many macro phenomena can be generated from the interactions of agents at the micro level. Agent-based models have successfully been employed in the study of complex social phenomena including opinion dynamics, technology adoption, markets, social networks and segregation.

Agent-based models allow the superimposition of several single facets of reality for reconstruction (Stöckler 2000), making them more similar to thought experiments than other simulations. This somewhat simplifies the justification and validation of agent-based models. Whilst other simulation methods (see Chap. 4) define a complete system in advance and compare the simulation outcomes to empirical data, agent-based-simulation models might be constructed by step-by-step enrichment (Gilbert and Troitzsch 2005). Starting from very few parameters, other factors can be added one by one and at each point, the results can be scrutinised for validity (Gilbert 2008). This reflective process of enrichment allows maximal control over parameters thus preserving intellectual surveyability.

A well-known example of an agent-based model is a model of ethnic segregation discussed in Schelling (1971) (see Chap. 4 for more detail). Schelling wondered about the persistence of segregation in American cities. Imagine agents randomly allocated to the patches on a grid. The agents come in two colours, red and green. Agents have a threshold for how many neighbours (the adjoining patches) of the other colour they tolerate. If the number of other coloured agents exceeds this threshold, the agent moves to an arbitrary other patch on the grid. Schelling initially executed this set of agent interactions on a checkered board by hand. He found that segregation resulted even with agents having very weak preferences for similarity.

There are many computer implementations of this thought experiment as agent-based models (for one example see Wilensky 1997). Although even the initial experiment executed by hand on a checkered board showed the rough results of segregation resulting from weak similarity preferences, in the computer implementation we can vary the parameters (such as the density of agents, the number of neighbours considered and the agents' tolerance thresholds) and see the respective influences of these variables and their interdependencies. For example we can identify a 'tipping point' of the tolerance threshold at about 30 % when the degree of segregation shoots up from the initial 50 % to between 75 and 80 %. Also, segregation gets worse as the density of agents decreases. This is a good example of a virtual experiment. There is a limited number of variables the interaction of which is investigated by systematic variation.

There will never be a city where the decision to move is made at random given a certain percentage of other-coloured neighbours by all agents just as there will never be a frictionless horizontal plane with a cart with frictionless wheels (as in Galileo's thought experiment). What Galileo's thought experiment and agent-based model have in common, and what makes them good examples of their kind, is that they take simple intuitive concepts, like *force, tolerance* and *movement* and present an idealised reconstruction of reality to expose presumed (or hypothetical) underlying mechanisms (Stöckler 2000).

Although agent-based models can be seen as the thought experiments of the social sciences, there is one caveat. Whilst thought-experiments are easily described, can be reconstructed as arguments and are 'intuition pumps', i.e. have great intellectual simplicity, agent-based models are mostly complex and often intellectually opaque. The complexity is exactly the point of agent-based models: we compute because we cannot think it out. But this leads to the following problem: thought experiments are either justified by empirical validation (a crucial experiment) or, more often, by coherence with background knowledge (Kühne 1995). Both justifications are relatively simple in the case of though experiments due to the very simplicity they display. For agent-based models neither justification is easy due to the intellectual opacity resulting from their computational complexity. Empirical validation poses grave problems with all kinds of possibilities for error, and the coherence argument fails as we no longer have the transparency of all the assumptions and their interactions. Still, given the problems of experimentation and the limitations of thought experiments in the social sciences, agent-based modelling seems a promising methodology for the experimental exploration of social dynamics.

1.4 Summary

In this book we set out to do three things. Firstly we want to clarify the discussion of social norms in the social sciences, focussing on sociology and criminology. By tackling the questions of deviant behaviour and cooperative behaviour as a single question of human behaviour relating to social norms we unify two hitherto separate research strands. Uncovering the underlying mechanisms of behaviour in relation to social norms will contribute to both sociology and criminology.

Secondly we propose agent-based modelling as a method to study the mechanisms underlying social norms (and other social macro-phenomena). Given the possibility of specifying agents at the individual level with macro phenomena emerging through repeated actions and interactions in a simulation, mechanisms can be investigated dynamically.

Thirdly we advance the study and modelling of social norms by extending current models of social norms. We present three models to that effect. The first situates agents in a social network, encoding group membership aspects of normative behaviour. The second implements argumentation, encoding communication aspects of normative behaviour. The third implements moral decision making, encoding value aspects of normative behaviour.

In the first two chapters we discuss how normative and deviant behaviour is theorised and modelled in sociology and criminology. This sets the theoretical backdrop for the clarification of the concept of social norms and provides the theories on which agent-based models of social norms can be built. We then introduce agent-based modelling and discuss some epistemological challenges of this new methodology in Chap. 4. In Chaps. 5–9 we discuss existing agent-based models of normative behaviour. In Chap. 10 we consider the achievements and shortcomings of existing models in the light of the theoretical discussion in the beginning of the book. In Chaps. 11–13 we present extensions to existing models. In Chap. 15 we conclude and propose a paradigm change in the modelling of social norms, away from the strong individualism characterising all the models discussed in the book towards a genuinely social, collectively minded agent.

References

Brendel, E. (2004). Intuition pumps and the proper use of thought experiments. *Dialectica, 58*(1), 89–108.

Brown, J. R. (1991). *Laboratory of the mind: Thought experiments in the natural sciences*. London/New York: Routledge.

Brown, J. R. (2003). Why empiricism won't work. *Proceedings of the Philosophy of Science Association, 2*, 271–279.

Brown, J. R. (2004a). Peeking into plato's heaven. *Philosophy of Science, 71*, 1126–1138.

Brown, J. R. (2004b). Why thought experiments do transcend empiricism. In C. Hitchcock (Ed.), *Contemporary debates in the philosophy of science* (pp. 23–43). Malden: Blackwell.

Cartwright, N. (1989). *Nature's capacities and their measurement*. New York: Oxford University Press.

Cohnitz, D. (2006). *Gedankenexperimente in der philosophie*. Paderborn: Mentis.

Dawkins, R. (1976). *The selfish gene*. New York: Oxford University Press.

Dennett, D. (1984). *Elbow room: The varieties of free will worth wanting*. Cambridge: MIT.

Dennett, D. (1995). Intuition pumps. In J. Brockman (Ed.), *The third culture: Beyond the scientific revolution* (pp. 180–197). New York: Simon and Schuster.

Einstein, A., & Infeld, L. (1938). *The evolution of physics*. London: Cambridge University Press.

Ellickson, R. C. (1998). Law and economics discovers social norms. *Faculty Scholarship Series* (Paper 407). http://digitalcommons.law.yale.edu/fss_papers/407.

Elsenbroich, C., & Xenitidou, M. (2012). Three kinds of normative behaviour: Minimal requirements for feedback models. *Computational and Mathematical Organization Theory, 18*(1), 113–127.

Elster, J. (1989). *Nuts and bolts for the social sciences*. Cambridge/New York: Cambridge University Press.

Fairchild, G., van Goozen, S., Stollery, S. J., Brown, J., Gardiner, J., Herbert, J., & Goodyer, I. M. (2008). Cortisol diurnal rhythm and stress reactivity in male adolescents with early-onset or adolescence-onset conduct disorder. *Biological Psychology, 64*(7), 599–606.

Galileo, G. (1628/2010). Dialogues Concerning Two New Sciences. Digireads.com.

Geertz, C. (1973). *The interpretation of cultures*. New York: Basic Books.

Gilbert, N. (2008). *Agent-based models: Number 153 in quantitative applications in the social sciences*. Los Angeles: Sage Publications.

Gilbert, N., & Troitzsch, K. G. (2005). *Simulation for the social scientist* (2nd ed.). Maidenhead/New York: Open University Press.

Hardin, G. (1968). The tragedy of the commons. *Science, 162*(3859), 1243–1248.

Harris, J. (1975). The survival lottery. *Philosophy, 50*, 81–87.

Hedström, P., & Swedberg, R. (1998). *Social mechanisms: An analytical approach to social theory*. Cambridge/New York: Cambridge University Press.

Hollis, M. (1994). *The philosophy of social science*. Cambridge/New York: Cambridge University Press.

Hume, D. (1752). Political discourses. In C. U. P. Knut Haakonssen (Ed.), *Politicial essays* (1994th ed.). Edinburgh: A. Kincaid and A. Donaldson.

Kühne,. U. (1995). Thought experiments and the inference to a coherent explanation. In *Volume of Abstracts. 10th International Congress of Logic, Methodology and Philosophy of Science*, Florence (p. 238).

Kühne, U. (2005). *Die Methode des Gedankenexperimnents*. Suhrkamp Verlag.

Kühne, U. (2009). A short history of the method of thought experiments in science. In *Thought Experiments: A Workshop*, Toronto.

Milgram, S. (1973). The perils of obedience. *Harper's Magazine*, 62–77.

Neurath, O. (1921). *Anti-spengler*. München: G.D.W. Callwey.

Norton, J. (2004a). On thought experiments: Is there more to the argument? Proceedings of the 2002 Biennial Meeting of the Philosophy of Science Association. *Philosophy of Science, 71*, 1139–1151.

Norton, J. (2004b). Why thought experiments do not transcend empiricism. In C. Hitchcock (Ed.), *Contemporary debates in the philosophy of science* (pp. 44–66). Oxford: Blackwell.

Pearl, J. (2003). Statistics and causal inference: A review. *Sociedad de Estadistica e Investigacion Operativa Test, 12*(2), 101–165.

Putnam, H. (1982). *Reason, truth and history*. Cambridge: Cambridge University Press.

Schelling, T. (1971). Dynamic models of segregation. *Journal of Mathematical Sociology, 1*, 143–186.

Searle, J. (1984). *Minds, brains and science: The 1984 Reith lectures*. Cambridge: Harvard University Press.

Stöckler, M. (2000). On modeling and simulation as instruments for the study of complex systems. In M. Carrier, G. J. Massey, & L. Ruetsche (Eds.), *Science at century's end*. Pittsburgh: University of Pittsburg Press/Universitaetsverlag Koblenz.

Turner, J. C. (1996). Some current issues in research on social identity and self-categorization theories. In N. Ellemers, R. Spears, & B. Doosje (Eds.), *Social identity*. Blackwell.

Wilensky, U. (1997). *NetLogo segregation model* Technical report, Center for Connected Learning and Computer-Based Modeling, Northwestern University, Evanston.

Chapter 2
Theorising Norms

Using the word weird implies that there is a norm.

Robyn Hitchcock

This chapter looks at theories of social norms. The problem of social norms is how to explain why humans behave pro-socially at a cost to themselves. How the micro-level, the individual, and the macro-level, society, are linked is at the heart of sociology. Historically its study was divided into rather extreme positions of individualism and structuralism. This chapter explores this theoretical landscape and prepares the ground for the models discussed in the book.

In the introduction we discussed the structure/agency problem of the social sciences. Most people will agree that individuals exist. But there seems to be something social, 'over and above' just individuals. Nobody will deny the existence of some social facts. There are clearly attributes of societies that we can describe, quantify and study such as 'hierarchies' and 'networks'. There are also facts about societies such as 'equality' or 'freedom'. What is contentious about such social facts is their causal influence and their ontological independence from individuals. In the next section we will see that a range of coherent views on the causal nature of social norms is possible.

2.1 Sociological Theories of Social Norms

Social norms are the backbone of sociology. In Table 2.1 we give a quick historical overview of some influential positions on social norms. This is not a complete set of views but gives an overview. We discuss the three most important positions, Positivism, Functionalism and Individualism, in more detail below.

C. Elsenbroich and N. Gilbert, *Modelling Norms*, DOI 10.1007/978-94-007-7052-2_2,

Table 2.1 Soundbites on social norms

Sociologist (Position)	Social norms ...
Comte (Positivism)	... are the influence of individuals over each other
Marx (Dialectic Materialism)	... are outcomes of property relationships
Durkheim (Positivism)	... have strong causal status, coercing individual behaviours
Simmel (Anti-positivism)	... are behaviour patterns agents can conform or deviate from
Weber (Anti-positivism)	... are causes of social actions
Parsons (Functionalism)	... are the regulatory patterns to ensure social order
Giddens (Structuralism)	... are both motivation for and consequence of individual action
Elster (Rational Choice)	... work through shame and guilt rather than reward and punishment
Coleman (Individualism)	... are the result of iterated interactions of individuals
Ullmann-Margalit (Game Theory)	... are Nash equilibria in coordination games
Bicchieri (Game Theory)	... are situation frames triggering scripts of behaviour

2.1.1 Positivism and Social Facts

The roots of sociology are positivist, following Comte's desire to establish a social science as a logical continuation of the natural sciences. The goals are description and prediction of the social world. After Comte's positivism, Emile Durkheim (1895) set out to establish scientific sociology at the end of the nineteenth century. His claim about social facts is a radical one. For him social facts exist over and above individuals. They have an autonomous ontology and are the causes of people's behaviour, or in Durkheim's words, they have *coercive power*. Social facts are the blueprint for agents' behaviour.

Durkheim reached a conclusion about the existence of social facts from his assumption that moral (non-selfish) behaviour was not explicable otherwise. The only way to resolve the selfish/social problem was that society is an entity, over and above the sum of individuals.

> If we cannot be bound by duty except to conscious beings and we have eliminated the individual, there remains as the only other possible object of moral activity the *sui generis* collective being formed by the plurality of individuals associated to form a group... We arrive then at the conclusion that if a morality, or system of obligations and duties, exists, society is a moral being qualitatively different from the individuals it comprises and from the aggregation from which it derives. (Durkheim 1895, p. 25)

Morality has become a less and less relevant concept in sociology but the idea of 'social facts' is stronger than ever, as we will see at various points in this book. For Durkheim social facts are *sui generis* facts, independent of the behaviours of individuals. They are what holds society together. They are usually non-physical but can have a physical instantiation. For example money is a physical social fact as is a flag or a wedding ring: without their social meanings they would simply be a piece of metal or paper, a piece of cloth and a ring of (precious) metal.

One kind of social fact is a social norm. Norms are behavioural regularities in a society as well as being behavioural expectations. Violation of expected behaviour is often punished, either directly or by ostracism from the group that subscribes to the norm. Thus social norms have a coercive effect on the behaviour of individuals.

The ontological assertion of the independence of social facts has a methodological consequence. For Durkheim social facts result from other social facts.

> The determining cause of a social fact must be sought among the antecedent social facts and not among the states of the individual consciousness. (Durkheim 1895)

This means that investigating the social world cannot be reduced to investigating individuals and their behaviour. Sociology is an independent science with its own domain, that of social facts, and not reducible to the individual facts studied in psychology.

2.1.2 Anti-positivism and Verstehen

Often the terminology of social norms is associated with the anti-positivist turn in sociology at the turn of the twentieth century. Social norms can be seen as the cultural phenomena that need *verstehen*, i.e. understanding, rather than being the basis for a set of generalisable, ahistorical, universal laws. According to anti-positivism, social science is not about the description and prediction of social phenomena, but about understanding (*verstehen*). The term *verstehen* goes back to the historian Droysen (1858) who made a distinction between nature and history, where explanation is the method of the former and interpretation that of the latter. The philosopher Dilthey (1883, 1900) further developed the concept, focussing on the first person participatory perspective from which people experience themselves and their social world. Given the importance for interpretation at the individual level, he argued that social phenomena can only be interpreted by studying this subjective perspective.

The hermeneutic approach to social phenomena was further developed by Max Weber (1973, 1984), whose philosophy was opposed to the positivist positions of Comte and Durkheim as well as Marxist economic determinism. For Weber, the goal of sociology is to discover the meanings of social actions (Detel 2008). A social action is a behaviour of an agent brought about by its interpretation of other agents' behaviours. Thus, to understand social actions we need to understand these interpretations.

According to Weber, the social sciences need to diverge from the natural sciences and become interpretative and participatory rather than observational and experimental. Social action becomes the unit of analysis, with meanings, symbols and social norms at the heart of what needs to be understood. However, Weber also acknowledges the hypothetical character of the results from the "operation called Verstehen" (Abel 1948), stating that "...even when they are of utmost 'evidence' are only hypotheses in the first place: They need to be verified [sic!] with principally the same means as any other hypothesis." (Weber 1973, p. 437)

For social norms this means that one should focus less on the regularity and predictability of behaviour and more on the influence that normative criteria have on individuals' conceptualisations of their (social) environment.

2.1.3 Functionalism and Structure

Functionalism pervaded sociology for the second half of the twentieth century. Prominent thinkers include Herbert Spencer, Talcott Parsons and Robert Merton. Functionalism can be seen as the methodological consequence of Durkheim's social ontology combined with an anti-positivist methodology. It analyses society through the functions and functional interdependence of its constituent parts, which are norms, customs, traditions and institutions. The question is no longer the individualist question, why does the selfish human behave morally (socially), but becomes the question of the existence of social order. In a very simplified form, the functionalist answer is that social order exists to ensure the survival of society. Functionalism has been criticised as a conservative ideology, asserting the status quo by identifying the existing structures and institutions as necessary for the survival of society.

Herbert Spencer's functionalism is modelled on the biology at the time with evolutionary theory providing the most important principles for the analysis. Just like organisms in the wild, societies face the possibility of extinction by forces similar to natural selection, demanding that societies adapt constantly. The selection pressures are both internal and external and brought about mainly by population changes. Spencer (1897) identifies *aggregation, differentiation* and *integration* as the universal dynamics governing the universe and *inter alia* society. Matter aggregates to form more complex entities which differentiate, and integrate with the environment. Environmental pressures might lead to the dissolution of these complex structures. In terms of society, the forces underlying these processes are for example demographic change and migration. Adaptations to the environment can be beneficial or detrimental. There are three general ways to deal with societal selection pressures:

1. *Regulatory*: rules of social control, cooperation and coordination.
2. *Resources*: ways and means of producing and allocating resources such as food, services and ideas.
3. *Logistics*: ways and means of distributing resources.

Although this direct transfer of the dynamics of evolutionary biology onto society is no longer *en vogue*, the use of evolutionary principles to explain social phenomena flourishes in fields such as neo-darwinism (Schelkle et al. 2000), evolutionary economics (Hanusch 2008), evolutionary game theory (Vincent and Brown 2005) and in complexity theory (Frenken 2005) and we will discuss an evolutionary model of social norms in Sect. 6.1.2.

Parsons' structural functionalism has been one of the most influential sociological theories. Despite being a holistic position, his starting point is the dyad rather than society as a whole (Parsons 1937). In dyadic interactions individuals have to make action choices constrained by physical and social factors. Social constraining factors ensue from the expectations that each individual has of the other with these expectations informed by the norms and values of the specific society.

Also Merton advocated the functional analysis of the social world rather than a focus on individual motives, with shared values underlying the explanation of how societies and institutions work. He was, however, also critical of some of the functionalist assumptions. His main critical contribution is the existence of dysfunctional structures and institutions. Dysfunctional structures and institutions can either be general, or functional for some and dysfunctional for others. In Merton's strain theory the different functionality of social structures for different groups in society is used for the explanation of crime (Merton 1938). By no longer asserting all institutions and structures as positive, Merton's functionalism overcomes the criticism of supporting the status quo.

2.1.4 Individualism and Rational Choice

Rational choice is a model of human behaviour based on classic utilitarian notions of pleasure seeking and pain avoidance as developed for example by Bentham (1823). Pleasure and pain have since been replaced by the concept of *payoff*. In the von Neumann and Morgenstern (1944) tradition, choice is modelled solely on the probabilities of obtaining payoffs, the product of which is the *utility* of an action. A *rational agent* is defined as a utility maximiser, i.e. from several possible courses of actions the agent will choose the one with the highest utility. Although widely accepted in economics, other social sciences have been more reluctant to take up rational choice theory (see McCarthy 2002 for a comprehensive discussion). In sociology the paradigm of individual choice was largely ignored and it took until the late 1950s for the development of rational choice theory to take off in the form of *Exchange Theory*, e.g. Homans (1958) and Blau (1964). Exchange theory conceptualises social interactions as exchanges of social currency. More recently, the work of Coleman (1990) carried the beacon of rational choice theory forward for the analysis of social phenomena.

There are some general assumptions underlying rational choice theory:

- Humans are goal oriented and fully intentional.
- Humans have a set of preferences or utilities which are hierarchically ordered (in a partial order).
- To decide on an action, humans calculate the maximal utility outcome with respect to their preference hierarchy.

All of these assumptions are controversial. Are humans really goal orientated? Many behaviours do not seem to fit this assumption. Is there really a partial order of preferences? Some decisions seem far too complex to be conceptualised in a simple partial order, as captured in the idiom 'comparing apples and oranges' which points to the incommensurability of two categories. The third assumption might be the most controversial. There are two main lines of criticism. We see plenty of evidence against the assumption that agents necessarily maximise their utility, i.e. behave in a selfish way, for example, when we see parents interacting lovingly with their children or firemen running into a burning building. The world is full of examples of seemingly altruistic behaviour which have to be explained by a theory that assumes selfishness. The second criticism concerns what is often referred to as *perfect rationality*. That means that the agent has complete information and unlimited computational power to assess all outcomes and calculate all utilities. This is obviously a false assumption as no-one has complete information about possible actions and outcomes. Despite its empirical inadequacy, the assumption was famously defended by Friedman (1953), saying that a theory should not be judged by the realism of its assumptions but by its predictive power. That means what matters is not whether humans actually are perfectly rational decision makes but whether phenomena can be modelled *as if* they were.

Although neo-classical economics is a relative success story in terms of prediction, the rational agent seems to be less useful in other social sciences. *Perfect rationality* has been ameliorated to become *bounded rationality* (Simon 1982) suggesting that, rather than calculating the full array of options, agents employ *heuristics* to make decisions. The agent is no longer assumed to have perfect information, memory and computational power. This changes the study of decision making considerably. If perfect rationality is assumed, a decision is only dependent on the preference relation. Once perfect rationality is removed, agents with the same preference relation might choose different outcomes. There are many factors that might then play a role, such as computational ability and the choice of heuristics. In the computational sciences, in particular distributed artificial intelligence, the idea of "bounded rationality" has been used for the construction of the Belief-Desire-Intention (BDI) agent (Bratman 1987) (See Chap. 4 for a discussion of BDI agents). Largely based on a folk-psychological idea of how people make decisions, the BDI agent decides on a course of action according to its beliefs, desires and intentions. These three concepts map loosely onto the parameters of a utility function with the intention being the goal, desires being the preference ordering and beliefs being the probabilities of the outcomes. What is more important here, though, is that the search is no longer for an equilibrium but for the actual decision mechanism. For both the bounded rational agent and the BDIagent, the preference relation becomes secondary whilst the heuristics, strategies and computational power come to the fore in the analysis of decision making. This is called *procedural rationality* (Rubinstein 1998, p. 22).

In the social sciences rational choice theory has long been met with scepticism. After all, according to rational choice, decisions are made in a social void, reducing the social to individual calculation. The most prominent proponent of rational choice

		Player 2	
		Stay quiet	Confess
Player 1	Stay quiet	1, 1	0, 5
	Confess	5, 0	3, 3

Fig. 2.1 Prisoner's dilemma payoff matrix

theory in sociology is undoubtedly James S. Coleman (1964, 1990). Working on the mathematisation of sociology all through his career, rational choice was at the centre of all his work. To bring rational choiceout of its purely individualistic pit, he later developed concepts such as 'social capital', a highly influential notion in research fields such as social network analysis. Social capital is a person's ability to draw on productive social connections.

2.1.5 Social Interactions as Games

Game theory is the "social interaction" version of rational choice theory, i.e. rational choice applied to social situations, or, in game theory parlance, *strategic interactions*. The most famous game is the Prisoner's Dilemma. Imagine two people, Bonny (Player 1) and Clyde (Player 2), who are caught committing a crime together. Both are individually offered the same choice, to confess and bear witness against the other in the ensuing trial, or to stay quiet. The reward for confession is to go free while the other agent serves the full 5 year sentence. However, if both confess, both go to prison for 3 years. If both stay quiet, both go to prison for a minor conviction for 1 year. Figure 2.1 shows the Prisoner's Dilemma payoff matrix. It is in the interest of each of the prisoners to defect, i.e. to confess and go free. But because *both* agents have the same strictly best response to the strategic choice of the opponent player, i.e. have a dominant strategy, both confess and both go to prison for 3 years.

The Prisoner's Dilemma has only one Nash equilibrium, but it is a suboptimal one.[1]

The Prisoner's Dilemma is just one among many social dilemmas with a structurally similar general payoff matrix.[2]

This payoff matrix expresses a Prisoner's Dilemma if

$$T_i > R_i > P_i > S_i \text{ for } i = 1, 2.$$

[1]A Nash equilibrium is a solution to a game, such that no player can improve its payoff by unilaterally changing its strategy.

[2]In the example in Fig. 2.1, the numbers represent years in jail so that lower numbers represent higher payoffs.

		Player 2	
		Cooperates	Defects
Player 1	Cooperates	R_1, R_2	S_1, T_2
	Defects	T_1, S_2	P_1, P_2

Fig. 2.2 A generalised payoff matrix

		Player 2	
		Stag	Hare
Player 1	Stag	9,9	0,8
	Hare	8,0	7,7

Fig. 2.3 Payoff matrix for stag hunt

Other games can be expressed using different relationships between the payoffs. The following relation is for a game called "stag hunt", the "cooperation game" or the "assurance game". Similar in structure to the Prisoner's Dilemma, there is a definite advantage for both players to cooperate rather than defect but, unlike the Prisoner's Dilemma, there is no dominant strategy, since cooperation is the best reply to cooperation and defection to defection.
The general relationship of payoffs for the stag hunt game (Fig. 2.2) is:

$$R_i > T_i > P_i > S_i \text{ for } i = 1,2.$$

The example goes back to Rousseau (1755) and is discussed in detail by Aumann (1976) and Harsanyi and Selten (1988). Rousseau describes a situation where joint cooperation is required for two hunters to catch a stag. Catching a hare, on the other hand, does not need the other's cooperation. However, if both defect, there is a chance of hunting the same hare making success for each less likely. Both cooperating and both defecting are Nash equilibria, meaning there is no dominant strategy (Fig. 2.3).

Another simple coordination game, often called the "battle of the sexes" is expressed by the payoff matrix shown in Fig. 2.4. A couple want to go out in the evening but they have not agreed where to go. He prefers the opera, she prefers football, but both prefer to do something together than to do it alone. Unlike the Prisoner's Dilemma and Stag Hunt, here the players have different preferences. The generalised matrix of this coordination game has a different symmetry axis, as can be seen in Fig. 2.4. Because of the different preferences, the action that is cooperation for player 1 is defection for player 2, i.e. player 1 goes where it does not want to go and player 2 goes where it wants to go anyway.

		Player 2	
		Cooperates	Defects
	Defects	R_1, P_2	S_1, S_2
Player 1			
	Cooperates	T_1, T_2	P_1, R_2

Fig. 2.4 A generalised payoff matrix for the battle of the sexes

		Player 2	
		Football	Opera
	Football	3,2	0,0
Player 1			
	Opera	0,0	2,3

Fig. 2.5 Payoff matrix battle of the sexes

		Player 2	
		Football	Opera
	Football	3,2	1,1
Player 1			
	Opera	0,0	2,3

Fig. 2.6 Payoff matrix battle of the sexes with asymmetric preferences

In this case, if both cooperate, i.e. both go where the other player wants to go, they end up in different places and, given their preference for spending the evening together, their payoff is 0. The same for both defecting, i.e. both going where they want to go (Fig. 2.5).

In general the relationship between the payoffs is:

$$R_i > P_i > T_i = S_i \text{ for } i = 1,2$$

An alternative representation, which takes into account the different preferences even more strongly, is shown in Fig. 2.6. In this matrix the worst case occurs if both end up alone in the wrong place, i.e she goes to the opera and he to football. The battle of the sexes can thus be expressed as

$$R_i > P_i > S_i \geq T_i.$$

All these games are coordination or cooperation games and they have been used extensively to model the emergence of social norms. This especially true of the Prisoner's Dilemma (Sects. 6.1.1 and 6.1.2 describe the use of the iterated Prisoner's Dilemma in agent-based models of the emergence of social norms).

The literature on applying these stylised games of strategic interaction to model aspects of social life is vast. Lewis (1969) is an early application to the study of social norms. For Lewis, convention is an arbitrary solution to a coordination problem, brought about by repeated strategic interactions (games). Ullmann-Margalit (1978) analyses the emergence of social norms from the assumption of selfish behaviour, describing norms as solutions to social dilemmas.

People are repeatedly faced by socially problematic situations, social dilemmas. The repeated application of the same (or similar) solutions can lead to the emergence of a social norm, i.e. a behavioural regularity. From this perspective, norms are Nash equilibria to coordination or cooperation games. Bicchieri (1993) expounds on the equilibrium account of social norms. Bicchieri (2006) takes the idea of social norms and strategic interactions further, developing an account of social norms guiding responses to social coordination and strategic interaction problems. Agents are confronted with a social scenario which activates a 'script', a generalised response. Iteration of these scripts in similar situations lead to the emergence of social norms. This account is sensitive to the problem of 'framing' a social situation (see also Sect. 2.2.4). Although adherence to social norms can be operationalised as simple coordination and cooperation, *any* behavioural regularity can be explained, such as driving on the left or right, or wearing a hat to a wedding. One might argue, however, that some social norms have a different underlying mechanism in which not just a social norm but a pro-social norm evolves. Bicchieri argues along these lines (Bicchieri 2006, p. 217), saying that pro-social norms need to be analysed differently. Instead of social dilemmas, she turns to games explicitly designed to elucidate moral norms such as equality and fairness.

We discuss the "ultimatum game" as an example of a game to investigate fairness and equality (Güth et al. 1982). Although there are others, such as "divide the cake" or the "dictator game", the ultimatum game has become the most used example, almost on a par with the Prisoner's Dilemma. Unlike the above games, players move sequentially, the second player reacting to the first player's move.[3] Two players divide a windfall W of unit size 1. The players move sequentially and take on the roles of either proposer P or responder R. P offers a share of W to R. R decides whether to accept or reject W. If R accepts, W is divided according to P's offer; if R rejects, neither gets anything.

The rational strategy in the ultimatum game is for P to offer as little as possible. The rational strategy for R is to take any offer greater than zero. Experimental evidence, however, shows that this is rarely the case, (Fig. 2.7), which shows that both offer and rejection thresholds in all countries are much higher than rationality suggests. Also, they are variable, the rejections in particular varying hugely from country to country. Experimental game theory seems to open more questions than it solves.

---

[3]The coordination and cooperation games above can also be expressed sequentially (extensive form), but as there is no knowledge of the other player's move, a sequential representation makes no difference to the game.

	Mean offer	Mean reject
Austria	39.2	16.1
Chile	34	6.7
Ecuador	34.5	7.5
France	40.2	30.7
Germany	36.7	9.5
Indonesia	46.6	14.6
Israel	41.7	17.7
Japan	44.7	19.3
Yugoslavia	44.3	26.7
Kenya	44	4
Netherlands	42.2	9.3
Peru	26	4.8
Spain	26.6	29.2
Sweden	35.2	18.2
Tanzania	37.5	19.3
UK	34.3	23.4
US East	40.5	17.2
US West	42.6	9.4

Fig. 2.7 An international comparison of offers and rejects in the ultimatum game (Taken from Oosterbeek et al. 2004, p. 177)

Comparing rational and evolutionary dynamics on a number of games, Skyrms (2000) shows that fair strategies can evolve. Using replicator dynamics on a population with a distribution of different strategies, it can be shown that many initial distributions lead to the proliferation of fairness (see Alexander 2009 for an excellent exploration of evolutionary game theory.)

Game theory is one of the most important formal approaches to the study of social norms. But pure game theory, in particular experimental game theory, opens many new questions. Reinterpreting game payoffs as evolutionary fitness, evolutionary game theory shows that both simple behavioural regularities and pro-social norms can survive selection against more defective strategies (Skyrms 1996). As an explanation for the apparent non-rationality of offers and rejections in Fig. 2.7 several explanations have been proposed. Above we discussed Bicchieri's normative framing approach (Bicchieri 2006), where behavioural heuristics are employed to make decisions. Other approaches explaining the discrepancy between perfect rationality and experimental outcomes are Gigerenzer and Selten's (2001) work on bounded rationality, proposing different psychological heuristics for decision making, and approaches specifically amending the preferences of people by motivational variables constraining utility maximisation, such as altruism (Levine 1998), fairness (Rabin 1993) or intrinsic aversions to inequality (Falk et al. 2008). An approach that uses both evolutionary dynamics and psychological components is the indirect evolutionary account of Güth and Kliemt (1998) who develop a model for the evolution of trust. As a paradigmatic example this uses the Trust Game.[4] In addition to the evaluation of payoffs, a motivational component m is introduced, which divides the population into trustworthy and non-trustworthy types. Rather than using direct replicator dynamics on the level of strategies, strategies become more frequent by agents actively adopting more successful ones, i.e. implementing learning.

All these explanatory hypothesis have some intuitive appeal but it is not clear what a criterion might be to decide for one rather than another, i.e. the actual psychological foundations of the apparent irrationality.

2.2 Psychological Theories of Social Norms

Social norms are not only the subject matter of sociology. Psychology is also interested in norms from several different perspectives. Important aspects of social norms in psychology are how norms are internalised, how they connect to feelings like shame and guilt, and how they are linked to empathy and moral reasoning. This is mainly studied in individual psychology which we discuss in the following section. Afterwards we turn to social psychology. Social psychology is less interested in the mechanisms of internalisation and more concerned with mechanisms of social influence, i.e. how social norms exert their 'coercive power' on individual behaviours.

2.2.1 Developmental Psychology and Internalisation

Childhood is seen as the main period of norm internalisation. The period from childhood through adolescence to adulthood is the period of *socialisation*, i.e. the period in which social norms, values and mores are instilled in the person. There are two obvious reasons why childhood is particularly important: (a) the child is initially only aware of its own needs and has to learn the needs of others (b) learning is much easier in childhood than in adulthood, partly due to a more active mind and partly due to a lack of preformed structures. There is a third reason: children have less power and are thus easier to control and form. It is, however, also clear that norm internalisation is not confined to childhood but continues through a person's life, albeit with less necessity (once a set of norms is internalised and the social surrounding is relatively stable there is no need for new internalisation) or at a slower rate (radical changes in society or migration into a new society might demand the internalisation of new norms but there is ample evidence that this becomes harder with age).

[4]The trust game is a sequential game in which a proposer's trusting first move can be exploited by the move of a second player.

2.2.2 Cognitive Developmental Psychology

Normative behaviour is one of the main areas of research in developmental psychology. The theories of Piaget, Kohlberg and Vygotsky are the major positions on the development of social and moral behaviour. Piaget's theory of cognitive development was one of the most influential psychological theories of its time. According to Piaget, a child goes through a set of stages of cognitive development that are fixed in order but not in how long they take. The four stages are:

1. *Sensory-motor Stage* (0–2 years): Children experience the world through the five senses, at first stationary, then moving around. During the sensorimotor stage children are egocentric, meaning they cannot perceive the world from others' viewpoints. During this stage the child has simple motor reactions to sensory input, first reacting only to internal inputs, (hunger, tiredness, etc.) later adding external inputs (social interaction, moving about). Simple habits are formed from the coordination of simple stimulus reactions.
2. *Preoperational Stage* (2–7 years): This stage is characterised by *magical thinking*, inferring causal relationships from correlations and the weakening of egocentrism. Children cannot yet reason logically.
3. *Concrete Operational Stage* (7–11 years): Children can now reason logically but stay on a rather concrete level and often need practical aides for reasoning tasks.
4. *Abstract Operational Stage* (11–16): Children develop abstract reasoning capacity and can reason logically without aides.

During the first two stages, the sensory-motor stage and the pre-operational stage, a child is completely egocentric, meaning they cannot perceive the world from another's viewpoint although this egocentricity weakens during the second phase (ages 2–7). Piaget's theory of a child's socialisation is a theory of moral development. Rather than equating cultural norms with moral norms, i.e. moral norms are learned by cultural transmission, Piaget proposed that children construct their moral norms from their interactions with the world, thus emphasising the importance of peers rather than just authority figures. A child's socialisation does not progress through fixed stages (except for the move from egocentricity to sociocentricity) but is connected to cognitive development. Piaget does, however, recognise different kinds of moral regulation, from the initial anomy (non-regulation by others or the self) during the egocentric phase to heteronomy (regulation by others) to autonomy (self-regulation). Note that heteronomy and autonomy are not necessarily successive stages of development. He identified the former as a socialisation achieved by coercion and punishment, the latter by following self-constructed rules and principles.

Kohlberg's (1976) developmental theory is directly concerned with morality. His theory is an extension and refinement of Piaget's socialisation theory but without being tied as strongly to a hierarchy of cognitive development. Kohlberg's six stages are divided into three levels where the levels correspond somewhat to Piaget's.

Level I Pre-conventional Level

- **Stage 1 Punishment and Obedience:** Bad things are punished and should be avoided. The reasoning at this stage is solely influenced by authority ruling. Bad behaviour is behaviour designated as bad by authority and it gets punished; thus it should be avoided.
- **Stage 2 Instrumental Relativism:** At this stage children understand that not all decisions are fully determined but that different viewpoints are possible. The inference from this new relativism is that one might as well do what is good for oneself. In addition to selfish behaviour this brings about reciprocal behaviours as children start understanding patterns such as "You scratch my back, I'll scratch yours." Reciprocity is however perceived concretely and as a one-to-one interchange.

Level II Conventional Level

- **Stage 3 Interpersonal Relationships:** At this level children understand that good behaviour pleases others. Good boy/girl is defined as having good intentions, motives and feelings towards others. The moral scope is relatively narrow, consisting of relationships such as family and close friends.
- **Stage 4 Law and Order:** Children start to understand laws as necessary to hold a community together. They argue that laws must not be broken. This stage could easily be confused with Stage 1 in which children also argue that laws must be obeyed but the reasoning is relevantly different. Whereas in Stage 1, laws must be obeyed as one is punished otherwise, in Stage 4 laws must be obeyed for the good of society.

Level III Post-conventional, Autonomous or Principled Level

- **Stage 5 Social-Contract and Utilitarianism:** Children, at this stage young adults, understand that laws are there as a result of and to enforce a social contract. Actions are evaluated against principles like utilitarianism and ideas of general fairness.
- **Stage 6 Universal Ethical Principles:** This stage goes even beyond the evaluation of actions against utilitarianism and fairness to the evaluation of the principles themselves.

Whilst Piaget's developmental stages are cognitive, Kohlberg focusses more on behaviour, stressing regulation by others and self-regulation. He analyses moral reasoning rather than behaviour (in fact, discrepancies are often found between a person's moral reasoning and their actual behaviour). Kohlberg's stages fulfil three formal criteria. Each stage is *qualitatively different* from the others. They are also *structured wholes*, meaning they are general patterns of thought applied consistently to moral problems rather than singular responses. Finally, the stages appear in *invariant sequence*, i.e. progression is fixed from one stage to the next without a stage being jumped. The stages are *hierarchically integrated*. This means that someone at Stage 4 can understand Stage 3 reasoning but will no longer employ it in their own moral decision making. And finally, the stages are a *universal sequence*, meaning they are identical in all cultures.

According to Kohlberg, not all people reach the highest stages. In a cross cultural comparison of moral reasoning he found that most middle class suburban Americans reach Stage 4 whereas most members of smaller, more tribal societies reason at Stage 3. His explanation was that moral reasoning is culturally determined and in tightly knit societies there is little need for stages beyond 3 or maybe 4.

Kohlberg's work has been criticised on several counts. Firstly it seems that the progression of development is not as linear as Kohlberg asserts. Test subjects seem to show signs of regression from higher to lower levels. Similarly, the discrepancy between reasoning and action choices questions the meaningfulness of assigning a level of moral reasoning to a subject. The cross cultural findings are seen as highly controversial. The hierarchical order of the Stages suggests that lower stages represent lower development leading to a view of some cultures as less developed than others. Kohlberg's research was mainly based on a male sample. Since a large percentage of women score at Stage 3, emphasising the relationship and empathy aspects of morality rather than abstract principles, his analysis has been accused of being sexist. The critique is in turn accused of overemphasising sex differences in moral reasoning (Gilligan 1982). Despite these criticisms, Kohlberg's moral development stages are still recognised as a major achievement.

Accumulating anomalies regarding the stage concept of moral development, mainly showing that the stringent hierarchy idea cannot be upheld, led to a less hierarchical theory. Turiel's *Domain Theory* distinguishes the development of moral and conventional behaviour and finds that actions from these different domains are interpreted according to different principles (see Turiel 1983). Moral actions are right or wrong regardless of the existence of a rule, and are evaluated according to principles of welfare, fairness and harm. Rightness or wrongness of conventional actions is evaluated purely by whether the action is covered by a rule or not, not by their effect. Having morality and convention develop in parallel rather than according to a single hierarchy inspired many important educational frameworks about how to foster healthy development. Separating the domains makes it possible to account for inconsistency of judgements in different contexts, for the display of moral reasoning in children much younger than could be expected from Kohlberg's theory and for the disregard of social norms whilst upholding moral norms, e.g. in adolescents.

2.2.3 Social Developmental Psychology

A major systematic position critical of Piaget's and by extension Kohlberg's theories is Vygotsky's theory of moral development. While Piaget and Kohlberg do not see the moral development of the child in complete social isolation, the developmental stages are not strongly socially determined and cognitive development is largely focussed on the individual. Vygotsky on the other hand sees social embedding as essential to both moral and cognitive development. An infant's inabilities never occur in social isolation but infants are part of dyads (or triads) in which their lack of skills are supplemented by more skilled individuals. In and through this social embedding the infant learns new skills, cognitive and social. His developmental theory is called *cultural mediation* the theory is not restricted to infancy. On the contrary, life is a continuation of the internalisation of social and cultural goods. Important are the *Zone of Proximal Development*, roughly the expanding developmental horizon of a child. As development progresses the child gets more and more independent and able to execute more actions unaided. Children can actively be supported in their development by *scaffolding* in which the level of support is adapted to the child's performance. Moral and social development are simply part of the general development of a child acquired by the same kind of learning and assisted in the same way by the social setting.

2.2.4 Social Psychology and Social Norms

We have already had an encounter with social psychology in the form of Vygotsky's criticism of cognitive developmental psychology. Here we look at social psychology more generally. Social psychology departs from individual psychology in treating the 'social' as the key element. According to social psychology, psychological processes are both social and cognitive. Social processes are the ways in which perceptions, thoughts, emotions, memories, motives and actions are influenced by other people such as friends, personal relationships or family. Cognitive processes are the ways in which perceptions, thoughts and memories guide our understanding of the world.

The study of norms and normative behaviour in social psychology is a branch of social influence research–research into the ways people affect the thoughts, feelings and behaviours of others. Social cognition perspectives on social influence, using experimental (and, later, field) methods, have dominated the study of norms. The classic experimental studies lead to a tripartite classification of adherence to social norms into *conformity, obedience* and *compliance*. Although social psychology is a theoretically rich and varied social science discipline, the categorisation of normative behaviour into conformity, obedience and compliance has a relatively wide reach within the theoretical landscape (see *inter alia* Franzoi 2000; Myers 2002; Hewstone et al. 2008). It is based on the conclusions of many studies in experimental social psychology that focussed on the ways in which individuals influence one another in group situations (e.g. Sherif 1936; Asch 1952; Milgram 1973).

Conformity refers to yielding to perceived group pressure by copying the behaviour and beliefs of others (Franzoi 2000). An agent conforms if it simply follows the behaviour of other agents. An agent can conform to a majority or a subgroup of the population. We drive on the left hand side of the road when in Great Britain but on the right on the European continent. We might wear bumbags and socks when on holiday in Italy just like other tourists or wear sunglasses and black like the Italians do. In either case, we conform to a subset of the population.

Conformity research has its foundations in Sherif's *Norm Development Research*, which consisted of lab experiments on optical illusions (the Autokinetic Effect) without prior information or a frame of reference. The conclusion drawn was that where reality is ambiguous and fluid, people develop and internalise shared 'frames of reference' in order to introduce order, stability and coherence into their relations with the stimulus world and each other (Sherif 1936); also see the discussion in Turner (1991). This research emphasised the development of norms as a consequence of informational influence, i.e. the desire to obtain useful/accurate information and, thus, achieve a correct or appropriate result.

Asch (1952) disagreed with the idea that group influence is arbitrary and hypothesised that when reality is not ambiguous and individuals are presented with facts, they would not conform to a developing consensual norm but will remain independent. In his *Line Judgment Experiments* he showed (in one third of the trials) that norms are not shared frames of reference but group evaluations of what is right and wrong. Conforming to these norms involves converging individual perceptions and behaviour to that of the group. In other words, Asch's work underlined the element of group pressure in the formation of and conformity to a norm (Sherif 1936). This research emphasised the tendency to conform in order to gain social acceptance and avoid social rejection or conflict.

More recent research has concluded that over time social norms become associated with specific settings. The situation acts as a stimulus, 'activating' remembered mental representations of normative behaviours (e.g. Stereotype Activation) (Dijksterhuis and Bargh 2001; Aarts and Dijksterhuis 2003). These are also called 'situational' norms and are activated in anticipation of entering a particular—already experienced—situation, e.g. being quiet when entering a place of prayer or a library. This research stressed how social norms become diffused and thus normative behaviour itself becomes routine, being executed without involving conscious thought.

Obedience refers to the performance of an action in response to a direct order or command. An agent obeys a norm if there is an authority enforcing the norm, e.g. by punishment. The punishment can be applied by a small group or even a single person with authority, for example, the police or a father. We do not jump a red light when driving because we are afraid of being caught and fined by the police. Punishment can also be applied by ostracism by the agent's community.

The classic research on obedience is Milgram (1973), which consisted of lab experiments involving subjects role-playing 'teachers' and 'learners'. Physical punishment in the form of electric shocks was administered by teachers to learners when instructed by the experimenter. The 'learners' played an act of being shocked but did not receive real shocks. The experiments indicated the pervasiveness of social power and status in situations of obedience. Authority, such as playing the role of experimenter, increases the likelihood that commands will be obeyed.

Obedience is treated as a demand on the agent to make a binary choice. If the external pressure becomes too high and is exercised by a more 'powerful' agent, the agent will change its behaviour and obey the norm. The agent needs to understand the cost of defying a norm, i.e. the possibility of punishment. Nothing seems to change in the agent between the pre-norm adoption and post-norm adoption state (see Milgram 1973; cf. Gibson and Haritos-Fatouros 1986). Norm adherence is fully determined externally; once the external threat is gone, the individual will cease to adhere to a norm. Analyses of norms that assume that agents follow the mechanism of obedience are theories based on a Hobbesian conception of a selfish individual that needs to be constrained by society.

Compliance refers to acting publicly in accord with a direct request or suggestion. An agent complies with a norm if it follows it whilst being able to consider other behaviours. To comply contains the element of decision, e.g. to comply to something now but not later or to comply to something superficially but not *really*. Often compliance is associated with *publicly* acting in a certain way whilst retaining one's personal values. We might comply with wearing a suit to work although we would never wear formal clothes otherwise.

Compliance is often treated as deliberate social influence (Hewstone et al. 2008) in the sense that individuals make conscious and deliberate attempts to gain the social approval of others. Factors that foster compliance are positive moods (likelihood of compliance when in a good mood), reciprocity (the expectation that one should return a favour or a good deed), and giving reasons (explanations that make requests reasonable). All come with the precondition of equal social status amongst the individuals who interact, as otherwise compliance might reduce to obedience (Franzoi 2000; Moscovici 2000). Compliance entails an assessment of the situation, thus individuals behave as participants rather than recipients in social encounters.

In experimental terms, compliance is a more complex form of norm adherence than the other two. When conforming, the agent's mental change is complete, i.e. one norm is replaced by another. When obeying only the behaviour changes in this particular situation but the norms remain the same. Compliance involves the possibility of gradual change. The concession of the individual to social pressure while attempting to maintain their individual values may have the effect of gradually changing their values. Compliance demands representations of the world 'given compliance' and the world 'without compliance' and involves agents making behaviour choices that are sensitive to the context. It also demands intentionality; the agent deliberately decides whether to comply with a norm or not. The interplay of these representations and the intentionality and context-sensitivity of behaviour choices is where the interesting feedback between individual and society lies.

We will come back to this distinction later in Chap. 10 when we discuss theories of normative behaviour for agent-based modelling.

2.3 Formalisations of Social Influence

So far we have looked at theories of social norms. In this section we look at some formalisations. The distinction between the two is not sharp. The three formalisations are the theory of reasoned action, social impact theory and social network analysis.

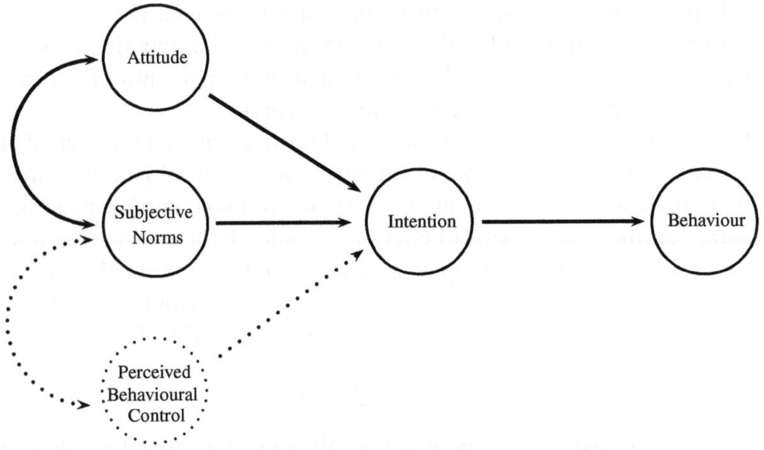

Fig. 2.8 The theory of reasoned action and the theory of planned behaviour

2.3.1 The Theory of Reasoned Action

Ajzen and Fishbein's *theory of reasoned action* is a predictive model of behavioural intention and attitude. Whereas previous research made weak correlative links between attitude and behaviour, the theory of reasoned action is a causal action theory. Situated in social psychology, it posits that an action decision is informed by an individual's attitude together with some social influence factors. It is an empirically corroborated theory with many applications. According to the theory of reasoned action, two parameters fully determine the choice for every intentional action (Fig. 2.8).

1. The attitude A of an agent towards an act o;
2. Subjective norms SN about the performance of o.

The attitude is calculated almost like a traditional utility function,

$$A(o) = \sum b_i \times e_i \quad (2.1)$$

where b_i are the beliefs about an act o, i.e. the subjective probability that it will lead to the desired outcome, and e_i is an evaluation of the outcome, i.e. its preferability. The subjective norms are constituted by what 'significant others' think about the performance of o. The measure is composed of

$$SN(o) = \sum n_i \times m_i \quad (2.2)$$

where n is the strength of a normative belief of a significant person for α and m $\alpha's$ motivation to comply with beliefs of that person, i.e. the significance of the other. These two dimensions are then integrated into an equation to calculate the *behavioural intention* (BI) of an agent α to perform o.

In the Theory of Planned Behaviour, a fourth component is added, that of *perceived behavioural control.* Perceived behavioural control is a measure of how far an agent feels in control of a situation. There are two components to perceived behavioural control: c is a control belief, as revealed by a question such as 'How often do you encounter unanticipated demands on your time?', and p is the perceived power of the control belief, for example 'If I encountered unanticipated events that placed demands on my time it would make it difficult to…'.[5]

$$PBC(o) = \sum c_i \times p_i \tag{2.3}$$

These measures are then combined into the following equations for calculating the behavioural intention of an agent. The equation according to the theory of reasoned action is:

$$BI_\alpha(o) = w_1 \sum b_i \times e_i + w_2 \sum n_i \times m_i, \tag{2.4}$$

The equation for the Theory of Planned Behaviour has the term for perceived behavioural control added:

$$BI_\alpha(o) = w_1 \sum b_i \times e_i + w_2 \sum n_i \times m_i + \sum c_i \times p_i, \tag{2.5}$$

Both the theory of reasoned action and Theory of Planned Behaviour have been used widely in empirical studies of behaviours including the use of the contraceptive pill, alcohol consumption, teenagers' sexual activity and consumer choices.

The theory of reasoned action is a very important model for the analysis of social norms as it explicitly formalises how norms influence an individual's actions. By taking the judgements of others into account the individual's decision is not only informed by its personal attitude. The theory of reasoned action thus provides a formalisation of the dynamics underlying the influence of social norms and proposes the need to embed the agent into a social framework by highlighting the importance of 'significant others'.

2.3.2 *Social Impact Theory*

Social impact theory is a mathematical formalisation of how agents are influenced by other agents, what *impact* they have on others (Latané 1981). The three constituents of social impact theory are *social forces, the psychosocial law* and *the number of targets*.

---

[5]Both questions are taken from the Theory of Planned Behaviour questionnaire at http://people.umass.edu/aizen/tpb.html

Social force is a function of three elements, the number (N) of agents exerting impact, their immediacy (I) and their strength (S). Each one contributes to the impact of an event. Each element can be given numerical values and the final social impact is a function of the values S,I and N. N, the number of people, is easily measured. I, the immediacy of the event, is its recency and whether there are other events possibly intervening. These other events could be contradictory events or detracting events. S, the strength of the impact, results from the importance or power of the source(s). The importance partly results from relational factors between the agents, such as previous and possible future relationships, and partly from absolute factors such as age, class, and status.

$$I_1 = f(SIN) \tag{2.6}$$

The psychosocial law states that the impact increases with increasing numbers of sources but at a reducing rate. The biggest difference is between zero and one source, with diminishing returns as the number increases.

$$I_2 = sN^t, \tag{2.7}$$

for some scaling factor s and some constant power t, where t is less than 1.

The strength, immediacy and number of targets, i.e. the number of individuals involved in an event, also influence the impact in the reverse way of the strength, immediacy and number of sources.

$$I_3 = 1/f(SIN) \tag{2.8}$$

This phenomenon is also called the *diffusion of responsibility* and can be observed in emergency situations (Latané and Darley 1970).

Overall impact is defined as the sum of Eqs. 2.6–2.8. Social impact theory as described above is the calculation of the impact of a specific event on a set of targets. It is a generalisable theory but with the possibility of specific applications and falsifiable predictions and retrodictions obtained from Eqs. 2.6–2.8. However, the measurement of the S, I are not exact enough to completely determine outcomes. Also agents may differ in their susceptibility to social impact. Nonetheless, it is a useful theory for the exploration of social situations with some empirical corroboration.

Latané himself developed a dynamic social impact theory (Latané 1996). Rather than assessing a particular single event, the dynamic version explores the diffusion of beliefs through social systems. Dynamic social impact theory sees society as a self-organising complex system in which social structure emerges from iterated interactions of agents and their respective impacts on beliefs and attitudes. Through its immediacy postulate, dynamic social impact theory can explain the emergence of local cultures (influence nearby greater than from far away). The process of consolidation leads to the formation of subcultures on the fringes of majority groupings.

Table 2.2 Major concepts of social network analysis

Concept	Definition
Dyad	A pair of actors plus the (possible) ties between them
Triad	A triple of actors plus the (possible) ties between them
Density	Ratio of number of actual ties over all possible ties
Degree	Number of ties of a node
Eigenvector centrality	Assignment of relative scores based on connections to high-scoring nodes increasing a node's score more than connections to low-scoring nodes
Assortativity	Nodes with many ties are linked to nodes with many ties
Clustering	How far some nodes are more closely connected to each other than the rest of the networks

In Sect. 8.2.4 we will see a computer implementation of social impact theory in which these dynamics are explored further.

2.3.3 Social Network Analysis

Social network analysis is a subfield of mathematical sociology focussing on the social organisation of agents in networks (see Wasserman and Faust 1994). Social networks consist of *nodes* and *ties*, nodes being agents and ties relationships between agents. The nodes can be any kind of agent, individuals, households, companies or countries. Ties can be of different strengths, can be static or dynamic (new ties being established and old ties broken) and can be directed or undirected (e.g. friendship is often seen as an undirected tie whereas 'best friend' is directed as it is not necessarily a symmetric relationship). Nodes are usually homogenous, only differentiated by the number/strength of ties with which they are connected. Often the term 'social capital' is used to interpret the social embedding of individual agents (e.g. Granovetter 1973, 1983; also see Lin 1999 for a review). Social network analysis diverges from traditional sociology by focussing on the relationships between agents rather than individual agent attributes (Table 2.2).

Social network analysis has proven useful for explaining many social phenomena. In a popular publication of social network analysis (Christiakis and Fowler 2009) show how characteristics like obesity and happiness spread through social networks. This strong dependence of people's behaviour and their friends (and their friends' friends and their friends' friends' friends…) makes social network analysis an important model for the study of social norms. As often with structural approaches to human decision making, individual agency is somewhat underemphasised as the structure of the network is the main explanans.

Social influence network theory is another, and rather different, mathematical social theory resulting from the combination of social psychology and mathematics (e.g. Friedkin and Johnsen 1999). Opinion or attitude changes are calculated by averaging opinions within groups. Agents start out with their own opinion. The average of all opinions within a group is called a "norm" opinion. Agents modify their opinion by averaging their initial opinion with the norm opinion.

In contrast, in social network analysis it is the structure of the network that is the unit of analysis. Attributes of the nodes are purely relational. In social influence network theory it is the existence of specific ties that modifies the attitudes and beliefs of agents (nodes) in the network. The distribution of attitudes in the network is more important than the formal network structure. We will see a network implementation in Chap. 11.

2.4 Conclusion

The theoretical landscape of social norms is rich and varied. Different disciplines approach social norms from different vantage points. Attempts at providing a classification of norms repeatedly fail (Morris 1956; Verhagen 2007). This is clearly a problem when it comes to modelling norms, for which one needs to be clear what is being modelled, for the construction as well as for the validation of the model.

The second problem we encountered is how to study social norms. Can they be reduced to individual behaviours, e.g. to rational choices, or do they have to be studied independently within a web of social facts and social structures.

In the next chapter we look at a specific kind of normative behaviour namely criminal behaviour. This will give us an area with a more defined behaviour for modelling but we will see that similar problems of definition are pervasive also in crime research. In Chaps. 5–9 we discuss models of normative behaviour originating from different theoretical perspectives. In Chap. 10 we tackle the problem of norm classification head on, providing the necessary theoretical backdrop for the newer models of social norms discussed towards the end of the book.

References

Aarts, H., & Dijksterhuis, A. (2003). The silence of the library: Environmental control over social behavior. *Journal of Personality and Social Psychology, 84*(1), 18–28.

Abel, T. (1948). The operation called Verstehen. *American Journal of Sociology, 54*(3), 211–218.

Alexander, J. (2009). Evolutionary game theory. In E. N. Zalta (Ed.), *The Stanford encyclopedia of philosophy* (Fall 2009 ed.). http://plato.stanford.edu/archives/fall2009/entries/game-evolutionary/

Asch, S. E. (1952). *Social psychology*. Englewood Cliffs: Prentice-Hall.

Aumann, R. J. (1976). Agreeing to disagree. *Annals of Statistics, 4*, 1236–1239.

Bentham, J. (1823). *Introduction to the principles of morals and legislation*. Oxford: Clarendon Press.

Bicchieri, C. (1993). *Rationality and coordination*. Cambridge/New York: Cambridge University Press.

Bicchieri, C. (2006). *The grammar of society: The nature and dynamics of social norms.* New York: Cambridge University Press.
Blau, P. M. (1964). *Exchange and power in social life.* New York: Wiley.
Bratman, M. E. (1987). *Intention, plans and practical reason.* Cambridge: Harvard University Press.
Christiakis, N., & Fowler, J. (2009). *Connected.* New York: Little, Brown and Company Hachette Book Group.
Coleman, J. S. (1964). *Introduction to mathematical sociology.* New York: The Free Press of Glencoe.
Coleman, J. S. (1990). *Foundations of social theory.* Cambridge: Harvard University Press.
Detel, W. (2008). On the concept of basic social norms. *Analyse & Kritik, 30*, 469–482.
Dijksterhuis, A., & Bargh, J. A. (2001). The perception-behavior expressway: Automatic effects of social perception on social behavior. *Advances in Experimental Social Psychology, 33*, 1–40.
Dilthey, W. (1883). *Einleitung in die Geisteswissenschaften: Versuch einer Grundlegung fir das Studium der Gesellschaft und der Geschichte* (4th 1957 ed.). Stuttgart/Gottingen: Teubner/Vandenhoeck & Ruprecht 4.
Dilthey, W. (1900). Die entstehung der hermeneutik. In *ilhelm Dilthey: Gesammelte Schriften Band 5* (pp. 317–338). Stuttgart/Gottingen: Teubner/Vandenhoeck & Ruprecht.
Droysen, J. G. (1858). Grundriss der Historik. In *Johann Gustav Droysen: Historik. Vorlesungen tiber Enzyklopddie und Methodologie der Geschichte* (4th 1960 ed., pp. 328–331). Darmstadt: Wissenschaftliche Buchgesellschaft.
Durkheim, E. (1895). *The rules of sociological method.* New York: Free Press.
Falk, A., Fehr, E., & Fischbacher, U. (2008). Testing theories of fairness—intentions matter. *Games and Economic Behavior, 62*, 287–303.
Franzoi, S. L. (2000). *Social psychology* (2nd ed.). New York: Brown & Benchmark.
Frenken, K. (2005). *Innovation, evolution and complexity theory.* Cheltenham: Edward Elgar Publishing.
Friedkin, N. E., & Johnsen, E. C. (1999). Social influence networks and opinion change. *Advances in Group Processes, 16*, 1–29.
Friedman, M. (1953). *Essays in positive economics.* Chicago: University of Chicago Press.
Gibson, J. T., & Haritos-Fatouros, M. (1986). The education of a torturer. *Psychology Today, 20*, 50–58.
Gigerenzer, G., & Selten, R. (2001). Bounded rationality: The adaptive toolbox. Cambridge/MA: MIT Press.
Gilligan, C. (1982). *In a different voice: Psychological theory and women's development.* Cambridge: Harvard University Press.
Granovetter, M. S. (1973). The strength of weak ties. *American Journal of Sociology, 78*(6), 1360–1380.
Granovetter, M. S. (1983). The strength of weak ties: A network theory revisited. *Sociological Theory, 1*, 201–233.
Güth, W., & Kliemt, H. (1998). The indirect evolutionary approach: Bridging the gap between rationality and adaptation. *Rationality and Society, 10*, 377–399.
Güth, W., Schmittberger, R., & Schwartze, B. (1982). An experimental analysis of ultimatum bargaining. *Journal of Economic Behavior and Organization, 3*, 367–388.
Hanusch, H. (2008). *Evoutionary economics.* Cambridge University Press.
Harsanyi, J. C., & Selten, R. (1988). *A general theory of equilibrium selection in games.* Cambridge: MIT.
Hewstone, M., Stroebe, W., & Jonas, K. (Eds.). (2008). *Introduction to social psychology: A European perspective* (4th ed.). Oxford: Blackwell.
Homans, G. C. (1958). Social behavior as exchange. *American Journal of Sociology, 63*, 597–606.
Kohlberg, L. (1976). Moral stages and moralization: The cognitive-developmental approach. In T. Likona (Ed.), *Moral development and behavior: Theory, research and social issues.* Holt: Rinehart and Winston.
Latané, B. (1981). The psychology of social impact. *American Psychologist, 36*(4), 343–356.

Latané, B. (1996). Dynamic social impact: The creation of culture by communication. *Journal of Communication, 46*(4), 13–25.
Latané, B., & Darley, J. M. (1970). *The unresponsive bystander: Why doesn't he help?* New York: Appleton-Century Crofts.
Levine, D. K. (1998). Modeling altruism and spitefulness in experiments. *Review of Economic Dynamics, 1*, 593–622.
Lewis, D. (1969). *Convention: A philosophical study*. Oxford: Blackwell.
Lin, N. (1999). Social networks and status attainments. *Annual Review of Sociology, 25*, 467–487.
McCarthy, B. (2002). New economics of sociological criminology. *Annual Review of Sociology, 28*, 417–442.
Merton, R. K. (1938). Social structure and anomie. *American Sociological Review, 12*, 99–107.
Milgram, S. (1973). The perils of obedience. *Harper's Magazine*, 62–77.
Morris, R. T. (1956). A typology of norms. *American Sociological Review, 21*, 610–613.
Moscovici, S. (2000). *Social representations: Explorations in social psychology*. Cambridge: Polity Press in association with Blackwell Publishers.
Myers, D. G. (2002). *Social psychology* (7th ed.). New York: McGraw-Hill.
Oosterbeek, H., Sloof, R., & ven de Kuilen, G. (2004). Cultural differences in ultimatum game experiments: Evidence from a meta-analysis. *Experimental Economics, 7*, 171–188.
Parsons, T. (1937). *Struture of social action*. New York: McGraw Hill.
Rabin, M. (1993). Incorporating fairness into game theory and economics. *American Economic Review, 83*(5), 1281–1302.
Rousseau, J. J. (1755). Discours sur l' origine d' inegalite parmi les hommes [discourse on the origin of inequality among men]. In *Oeuvres Completes* (vol. 3). Paris: Edition Pléiade.
Rubinstein, A. (1998). *Models of bounded rationality*. Cambridge: MIT.
Schelkle, W., Krauth, W.-H., Kohli, M., & Elwert, G. (Eds.). (2000). *Paradigms of social change: Modernization, development, transformation, evolution*. Frankfurt/New York: Campus Verlag/New York: St. Martin's Press.
Sherif, M. (1936). *The psychology of social norms*. New York: Harper and Raw Publishers.
Simon, H. A. (1982). *Models of bounded rationality*. Cambridge: MIT.
Skyrms, B. (1996). *Evolution of the social contract*. Cambridge/New York: Cambridge University Press.
Skyrms, B. (2000). Game theory, rationality and evolution of the social contract. *Journal of Consciousness Studies, 7*(1–2), 269–284.
Spencer, H. (1897). *First principles*. New York: D. Appleton and Company.
Turiel, E. (1983). *The development of social knowledge: Morality & convention*. New York: Cambridge University Press.
Turner, J. (1991). *The structure of sociological theory*. Belmont: Wadsworth Publishing.
Ullmann-Margalit, E. (1978). *The emergence of norms*. Oxford: Clarendon Press.
Verhagen, H. (2007). Normtypographies. In G. Boella, L. van der Torre, & H. Verhagen (Eds.), *Normative multi-agent systems*, Number 07122 in Dagstuhl seminar proceedings, Dagstuhl. Wadern: Internationales Begegnungs- und Forschungszentrum für Informatik.
Vincent, T. L., & Brown, J. S. (2005). *Evolutionary game theory, natural selection and Darwinian dynamics*. Cambridge/New York: Cambridge University Press.
von Neumann, J., & Morgenstern, O. (1944). *Theory of games and economic behaviour*. Princeton: Princeton University Press.
Wasserman, S., & Faust, K. (1994). *Social network analysis: Methods and applications*. Cambridge/New York: Cambridge University Press.
Weber, M. (1973). Über einige Kategorien der verstehenden Soziologie. In *Max Weber: Aufsätze zur Wissenschaftslehre*. Tubingen: J.C.B. Mohr—Paul Siebeck.
Weber, M. (1984). *Soziologische Grundbegriffe* (6th ed.). Tübingen: UTB/Mohr Siebeck.

Chapter 3
Theorising Crime

Bank robbery is an initiative of dilettantes. Real professionals open a bank.

Berthold Brecht

This chapter applies theories of social norms to the question of criminal behaviour. We discuss rational choice and deterrence models, environmental criminology and sociological theories such as Sutherland's differential association theory and Hirschi's social bond theory.

In the previous chapter we introduced the research question 'Why do people cooperate?'. Normative behaviour was seen as the behaviour that needed explaining, the assumption being that selfish behaviour is the default. In this chapter we look at the flip-side of the coin, assuming that normative behaviour is the default and what needs explaining is why people commit crime.

But what is crime? Crime is the violation of society's legally enshrined norms. The following presents a range of sociological theories of crime (see also Carrabine et al. 2004).

1. **Crime as Normal:** Rather than condemning crime this view asserts that crime is a normal part of society and serves functions within social organisation and thus cannot be eliminated. Crime should be studied by mapping its functions within societies. Example: *functionalism* (Durkheim 1895).
2. **Crime as Conflict:** Crime is a result of specific conflicts within a society. These conflicts result from power differences within society, in particular class. Crime should be studied by investigating the social divisions, power relationships and (economic) interests within society. Example: *Marxist criminology* (Dahrendorf 1959).
3. **Crime as *Anomie*:** Crime is the result of tensions, stresses and strains within society, leading to the breakdown of norms and social organisation. Crime should be studied by looking at the tensions and strains in society. Example: *strain theory* (Merton 1938).

C. Elsenbroich and N. Gilbert, *Modelling Norms*, DOI 10.1007/978-94-007-7052-2_3,

4. **Crime as Urban Problem:** Crime is seen in relation to modern city life. Cities generate enclaves of sub-cultures, defining their own values, languages, norms and fashions. Some of these sub-cultures are criminal. Crime should be studied by studying the ecology of crime. Example: *Chicago School* (McKenzie 1924).
5. **Crime as Choice:** Crime is a result of a calculation in which committing a crime has higher utility than not committing a crime. Crime should be studied using rational choice theory with a focus on how to reduce the utility of crime. Example: *rational choice theory* (Becker 1968).
6. **Crime as Environmental:** A generalisation of the Chicago School ecology approach. Crime is a result of environmental factors presenting the possibility of crime (temptations). It should be studied looking at environmental factors. Example: *environmental criminology* (Brantingham and Brantingham 1991).
7. **Crime as Social Learning:** Crime is a form of socialisation in a criminal environment. Through social learning and cultural transmission criminal values and skills are learned. Crime should be studied by looking at life histories and people's construction of meaning and values. Example: Sutherland's *differential association theory* (Sutherland 1947).
8. **Crime as Detachment:** Crime is a result of too weak a bond to groups with law abiding values and behaviours. Social controls break down if the individual is not bound by society. Crime should be studied by looking at social exclusion and the breakdown of social bonds. Example: Hirschi's *social bond theory* (Hirschi 1969).
9. **Crime as Lack of Self-Control:** Crime is the result of a lack of self-control. The lack of self-control in an individual is the result of insufficient parenting in early childhood. Crime should be studied by studying the socialisation of children. Example: *general theory of crime* (Gottfredson and Hirschi 1990).
10. **Crime as Moral Decision Making:** Committing a crime is a breaking a social norm (as defined in law). A crime is committed when an agent perceives crime as an action alternative in a situation and there are no external (e.g. deterrence) or internal (e.g. self-control) constraints. Crime should be studied analysing specific actors in specific situations. Example: *Situational Action Theory* (Wikström et al. 2012).

These theories can be divided into internal theories of crime focussed on the criminal (5, 7, 8, 9) and external theories of crime focussed on the environment (1, 2, 3, 4, 6). Internal theories analyse specific attributes of the offender, such as socio-economic factors, class, self-control, and the decision mechanisms that lead to criminal behaviour, whilst external theories explain criminal behaviour by pointing to external factors that are supposed to determine criminal behaviour (social and physical environment). Situational Action Theory bridges this divide, combining individual and environmental parameters into a specific action theory of crime.

Thus, when it comes to explaining criminality, there are two choices to be made. First, are criminals fundamentally different from non-criminals or are they essentially the same? Second, if criminals are different, are they different intrinsically (personality, psychology, morality) or extrinsically (economic or social influences), see Fig. 3.1.

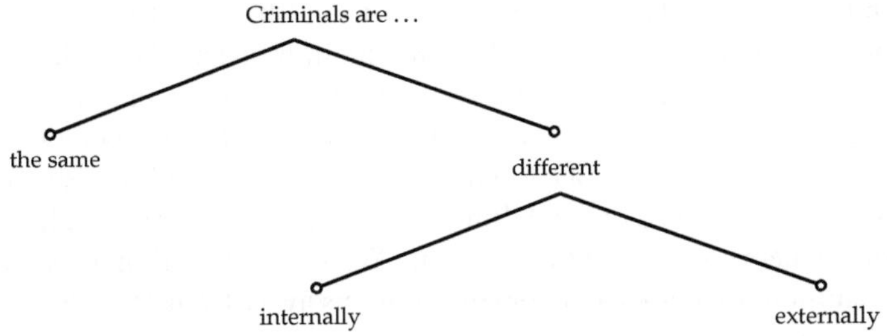

Fig. 3.1 What is a criminal?

The criminal is seen as essentially the same as others in rational choice theory of crime (Becker 1968), routine activity theory (Cohen and Felson 1979), situational crime prevention (Clarke 1997) and environmental criminology (Brantingham and Brantingham 1991). All of these theories put the cause of crime into the environment, although with slightly different emphases. For example for rational choice theory, crime is simply a calculation between the likelihood of being caught, the severity of punishment, and the payoff of a crime. For environmental theories, it is the actual physical environment presenting opportunities that leads to crime. In addition to examining these theories, we discuss two mathematical models of crime, the first a model of criminal population dynamics (Ormerod et al. 2001), the second a statistical model of the development of crime hotspots (Short and Dorsogna 2008).

If we start from the position that the criminal is somehow different from the non-criminal, we need to put our finger on the specific differences. For example, Miller and Lynam (2001) examine the applicability of four different personality models to the criminality of an individual. These are the five-factor model (FFM; McCrea and Costa 1990), the PEN model (Eysenck 1977; Carrasco et al. 2006), Tellegen's three-factor model (Tellegen 1985), and Cloninger's temperament and character model (Cloninger et al. 1993). They find that a strong case can be made for relating personality to criminality. In addition to the correlations of personality and anti-social behaviour, the authors point out that potential importance of personality to criminology given the longitudinal stability of personality. Also, personality traits such as *agreeableness* and *self-control* are direct measures of theoretical constructs in criminological theories such as Gottfredson and Hirschi's (1990) General theory of crime and can thus be used for empirical assessment of these theories.

The third option is to consider criminals to be different from non-criminals, but assume that the differences arise from extrinsic factors, the rightmost branch in Fig. 3.1. Examples of such theories of crime are social disorganisation theory (Shaw and McKay 1931), differential association theory (Sutherland 1947) and social bond theory (Hirschi 1969). Differential association theory asserts that criminality is learned from interactions with others in the same way as other socialisation processes (see Sect. 3.4.1). This stands in contrast to Hirschi's social bond theory (Gottfredson and Hirschi 1990). Social bond theory sees criminals as having weaker social bonds and being less able to keep up friendships. Because they have only weak bonds, delinquents are only able to maintain transient friendships with other criminals, leading to the observed phenomenon of clustering. The weakness of social bonds leads to delinquents having a lower stake in society (less social bonding) and are thus more prone to violate social norms and laws (see Sect. 3.4.2).

As this book is focussed on modelling normative behaviour we shall only discuss in detail those theories relevant to modelling. We start with rational choice theory as its use in criminology marks a major shift in focus away from offender pathology to the offender as a 'consumer', deciding to commit a crime because it is the action alternative with the highest utility. We continue with theories of environmental criminology as they are the backdrop to much crime simulation. Finally we discuss socialisation theories of crime, Sutherland's differential association theory, Hirschi's social bond theory and the general theory of crime. Consideration of Situational Action Theory are delayed to Chap. 13, where we also present an agent-based implementation of this theory.

3.1 Individual Based Theories of Crime

Most traditional theories look for the explanation of crime in criminals themselves. The idea is that criminality is inherent in the individual. This could be in hormones, the mind, personality, brain, or genes. Such theories of crime are non-sociological (i.e. strictly focussed on the individual) and positivist (i.e. science will discover the causes of crime). Probably the oldest individual based theory of crime is the demonological approach, deriving from religious and supernatural beliefs where the criminal is a sinner, tempted or possessed by the devil. Temptation also plays a role in the classical school of crime in which it is assumed that crime is the result of hedonism. Relying on the *felicity calculus* of utilitarianism (i.e. 'maximise pleasure, minimise pain'), the individual has to be reined in by punishment that makes crime not pay. We will discuss deterrence theories and rational choice theory (the modern incarnation of the felicity calculus) in more detail below. The most prevalent individual based theories nowadays are based on a 'crime as sickness' view. Whether the origin is seen in mental illness, genetic disorder, hormonal imbalance or physiological differences, the criminal is 'unhealthy'. As these theories are non-social, they do not fit to our conceptualisation of crime as the flipside of normative behaviour and we will not discuss these theories further. For more on crime pathology and its relation to crime policy, see Rimke (2011).

There is, however, one influential individual based theory of crime that needs mentioning and this is Gottfredson's and Hirschi's general theory of crime. As we will see later, Hirschi's early work contended that crime was the result of the weak social bonds of criminals leading them not to be bound by society's rules (see Sect. 3.4.2). Later he distanced himself from this view and, together with Gottfredson, developed a theory of crime based on the assertion that the root cause of crime is a person's low self-control. Crimes are defined as "acts of force or fraud undertaken in pursuit of self interest" (Gottfredson and Hirschi 1990, p. 15). Although the general theory of crime uses the individual based property of self-control for the explanation of crime, it also has a social aspect as it contends that self-control is the result of the proper socialisation of individuals in childhood and is thus a theory of the internalisation of social norms. We will discuss a norm internalisation model in Chap. 9 and use the concept of self-control for a model of crime as moral decision making in Chap. 13.

3.2 Deterrence Theories

Deterrence theories of crime, as the name suggests, focus on the failures to deter of the criminal from committing a crime. Deterrence theories are based on rational choice theory, which we briefly discussed in the previous chapter. The goal is to make "crime not pay" by increasing the cost of crime, i.e. the punishment. The application of rational choice theory brought about a conceptual shift in criminology, away from the focus on individual based explanations of crime.

Often seen as the starting point of the economic, and hence rational choice, analysis of crime is Becker (1968) which presents a model of criminal decision making based on perfect rationality. In Becker's model, the combination of the probability p of getting caught combined with the severity S of the sentence compared to the benefits B of the crime are what influences an offender's decision.

$$EU = f(B,p,S) \tag{3.1}$$

If we increase either p or S (or reduce the benefit B), the expected utility, EU, will decrease and the criminal will have less interest in committing the crime. Becker's intent is not to model the actual decision mechanism of the criminal, i.e. the *procedural rationality*. His intention is to model crime as a rational endeavour, showing that the decision to commit a crime does not need a pathology but is based on exactly the same kind of cost-benefit analysis as non-criminals employ for making decisions.

In the formalisation above, the deterrent is the product of p and S, equating an increase in probability of capture to an increase in the severity of punishment. Given the goal of cost effective deterrence and their mathematical equivalence in the utility function, Becker focuses on the severity of punishment rather than the increase of the probability of capture as severe sentences are more cost effective for society than costly increases in, for example, more police presence. Long incarceration is also costly but Becker argues for high monetary fines as the most effective deterrent. However, psychological theories do not corroborate this equivalence hypothesis. For example the study published in Witte (1980) found that there is a significant psychological difference between p and S with a higher probability of being caught being a much more effective deterrent.

Mehlkop and Graeff (2007) develop an action-theoretic extension to Becker's model.

$$EU = f(q, B, p, S) \tag{3.2}$$

where q is the subjective probability of successfully carrying out the crime. They discuss normative and social dimensions of rational choice theory modelling. Some other models based on perfect rationality, but not solely interested in deterrence, are available. For example Pyle (2000) devised a more complex utility function which incorporates the allocation of time to legal and illegal activities. His model then links the decision to commit a crime to the agent's position in the labour market. Although this approach is more contextual, links between crime and the economy are at best tenuous (Bandyopadhyay et al. 2011).

The distinguishing feature of rational choice theory in criminology is that it sees the criminal simply as "another consumer". According to rational choice theory the expected utility of crime is simply greater for criminals than others. The question remains why the utility is so relevantly different for different agents. Often the utility function is amended by more and more variables, "refining" the choice of the agent. Once separate parameters skewing the utility function have to be taken into account, the questions of traditional criminology creep up one-by-one. Is it the socio-economic conditions of the offender raising the benefit from crime? Is it a psychological disposition that makes the criminal evaluate the probability of getting caught differently?

3.3 Environmental Crime

We are all aware of the warning signs not to leave shopping in the car, not to get our mobiles out in public and to carry laptop computers in inconspicuous bags. We see white vans with signs saying "no tools are left overnight" or security vans asserting that the drivers have no access to the money safe. These are all crime prevention measures based on the belief that crime can be prevented by reducing opportunity.

Like rational choice, environmental theories of crime deviate considerably from traditional criminology, no longer focussing on the characteristics and dispositions of the offender but instead on the external parameters that lead to crime. Clarke (1997) states that "...explaining crime has been confused with the problem of explaining the criminal". He reminds us that in a detective novel, the criminal can only be convicted if she has both a motive *and an opportunity*. Whilst traditional criminology focusses on the motivation of offenders, environmental theories are concerned with the opportunities for crime. Routine activity theory explains crime as 'the convergence of a motivated offender, a suitable victim and a lack of a guardian', (Cohen and Felson 1979). In the right (or rather wrong) situation, anyone could be the victim of crime and anyone could be the offender.

Environmental theories of crime can be seen as putting flesh on the bones of the abstract concepts *probability* and *severity* of rational choice theory. Where rational choice theory states that beliefs and preferences determine the utility function of an agent, environmental theories show where the beliefs and, to a lesser extent, preferences come from. Which situation presents an opportunity to a motivated criminal becomes an analysis of the interaction between guardianship (opportunity) and desire to commit a crime (utility of the outcome). Where Becker argues that the deterrence of crime is important, environmental theories look at the exact circumstances, situations and environmental constellations leading to criminal offences. Their focus is thus on the external parameters without much interest in the choice mechanism as such.

The environmental view of crime has been picked up by crime simulations. It has, by definition, the ingredients of agent-based models, i.e. an environment (a dark underpass, a broken CCTV camera, an exposed mobile) and a social interaction (the victim holding the mobile, a crowd of people, a policeman). Indeed, the first agent-based models are simulations of this kind. One example models the interaction between criminals and police presence by defining a population consisting of cops, robbers and victims, specifying the conditions under which a crime is committed (e.g. victim and robber 'meet' and no cop is present) and seeing how the relative numbers of cops and robbers influence crime rates (Groff and Birks 2008). Similar dynamics are used to analyse the spatial distribution of crime, such as the emergence of crime hotspots (Bosse et al. 2008). The most recent innovation in artificial crime modelling is to integrate real geographies into the simulations, thus modelling the spatial factors of crime. Examples of state of the art implementations can be found in Szakas et al. (2008) and Liu and Eck (2008). Below we discuss an environmental simulation model in more detail.

An implication of environmental theories of crime is that everyone in the same situation would commit the crime. This sounds preposterous at first. However, there are two interpretations of *same situation*.

1. Anyone in the same circumstances and with the same socio-economic, psychological, etc. ... profile would commit the crime. This interpretation is trivial if it means that identical agents in identical situations would perform identical actions. Alternatively there must be something to distinguish two agents in the same situation, e.g. socio-economic or psychological factors. But once we are looking for these factors, we are back to the offender profiling that traditional criminology is concerned with. This interpretation contradicts the assumption that only the external circumstances are relevant for the explanation of crime.
2. Anyone who *perceives the situation* as the same would commit the same crime. For example, we might think that everyone passing a car with a handbag on the passenger seat, seeing the bag, wanting it and thinking it unlikely to get caught etc. will smash the window and snatch the bag. However, one person might think they will get caught, another might think that there will be nothing valuable in the bag. This is exactly what rational choice theory stipulates as the mechanism of criminal decision making and it reduces to saying that if two agents have the same expected utility function they commit the crime.

By opting for the second interpretation we subscribe to a rational choice foundation for environmental theories of crime.

We shall now discuss four well-known environmental theories. The first two are routine activity theory (Cohen and Felson 1979) and environmental criminology (Brantingham and Brantingham 1991). These two are the more ecological theories of crime and have direct simulation applications. In Sect. 3.3.3 we discuss a third environmental theory, Situational Crime Prevention (Clarke 1997), which is more focused on agent decision making. Finally, the Broken Window Theory (Wilson and Kelling 1982) stipulates that a decline in social norms is a consequence of an area deteriorating slowly, starting with minor demeanours but soon spiralling out of control.

3.3.1 Routine Activity Theory

As stated above, environmental theories are the antithesis of traditional criminology. Whilst criminology in the past analysed the psychological dispositions or the socio-economic conditions of an offender to explain crime, environmental approaches look at the environmental structures conducive to crime, such as space, time, opportunity or guardianship. The forerunner of this externalisation of criminal behaviour is routine activity theory (Cohen and Felson 1979). Routine activity theory states that a crime has three ingredients: a motivated offender, a suitable target and the absence of a capable guardian who could prevent the crime. There is no interest in *why* the offender is motivated. A crime occurs simply due to the convergence of these three conditions in time and space.

Routine activity theory is based on sociological work on human ecology (Hawley 1950) focusing on the importance of space and time for societal interactions. For example fights in market squares in British cities are a phenomenon resulting from pubs closing at 23:00 and hundreds of drunken people assembling in a small space. Single person households and women's participation in the labour market are conducive to daytime burglary with more empty houses presenting more opportunities, (Clarke 1997). We discuss an agent-based model of routine activity theory in Sect. 5.2.

3.3.2 Environmental Criminology

Environmental criminology (Brantingham and Brantingham 1991) is a spatial or geographical extension of routine activity theory. Taking the convergence of offenders, victims and guardians as the necessary condition for crime, environmental criminology looks at spatial distributions and displacement patterns. Environmental criminology proposes five components that together constitute the necessary and sufficient conditions for a crime. These five components are space (geography), time, offender, and target. Similar to routine activity theory, environmental criminology sees the convergence of an offender and a target as the root cause of crime. It adds the dimensions of a spatial setting, which includes attributes of the space itself that might be crime inducing, such as an underpass, and a time (at night the underpass is dark).

The focus of environmental criminology is on the space and time of crimes. Environmental criminologists are interested in the design and use of space, as shown by traffic flows and street design. One innovation in environmental criminology is the use of maps as data for crime analysis, mapping crime scenes to analyse the impact of the environment.

Implementation of simulations in geographical information systems (GIS) has advanced this field of environmental criminology rapidly over the past decade. We discuss a model in some detail in Sect. 3.5.1.

3.3.3 Situational Crime Prevention

Whilst environmental criminology is a geographical follow-on theory of routine activity theory, situational crime prevention (Clarke 1997) is a decision theory follow on. Situational crime prevention also focuses on external opportunity structures, availability of targets, lack of guardianship etc. But, whilst both routine activity theory and environmental criminology leave the motivation of the offender as a black box, situational crime prevention combines the routine activity theory origins of human ecology and rational choice theory in criminology. It is based on a theory of offender's decision making (Clarke and Cornish 1985; Cornish and Clarke 1987) that is sensitive to specific variables of the crime and offender. For example, situational crime prevention differentiates between starting and continuing to commit crimes and between different crimes such as robbery, burglary and murder.

The starting point for situational crime prevention is a rational choice theory of crime. Later it was distinguished from rational choice theory and named the *reasoning criminal approach* (see McCarthy 2002 for a more detailed discussion). Although the mechanism is still a weighing up of the costs and benefits of a criminal action, the focus is on the preferences that inform the decision. Cornish and Clarke argue that criminology has had a far too deterministic focus.

> [...] the resulting accounts of criminal behaviour have still tended to suggest deterministic models in which the criminal appears as a relatively passive figure; thus he or she is seen either as prey to internal or external forces outside personal control, or as the battlefield upon which these forces resolve their struggle for the control of behavioural outcomes. (Clarke and Cornish 1985, p. 148).

With rational choice theory being a general theory of decision making, Cornish and Clarke argue for the analysis of crime becoming more particularised. When analysing the choices to commit a crime, what they call the *choice points* of a burglary will be very different from those of a violent murder. Even the choice

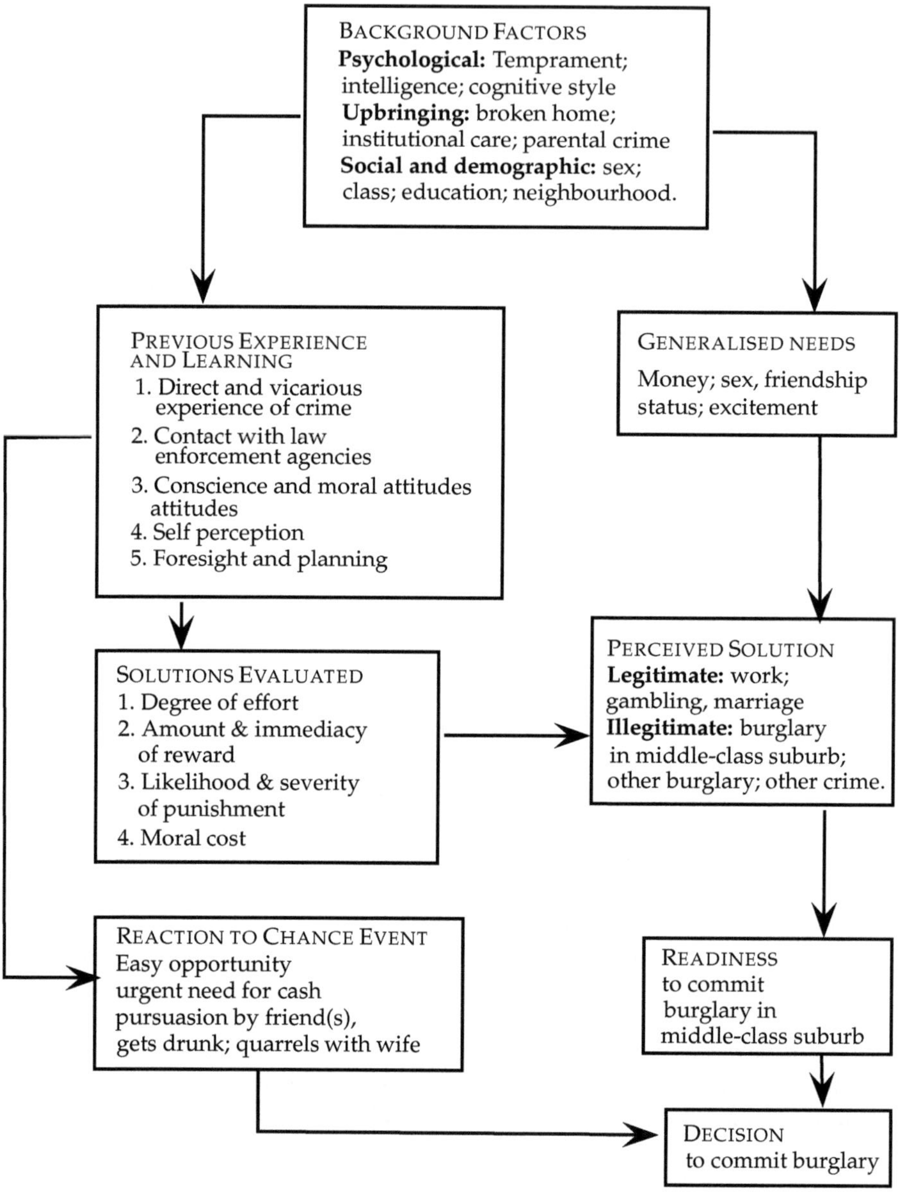

Fig. 3.2 Cornish and Clarke: Initial involvement model. (Example: burglary in a middle-class suburb from Cornish and Clarke (1986, p.3))

points between the decision to commit a general burglary and the decision to burgle 'this specific house' need to be differentiated. The authors also point at a distinction between the decisions of starting, continuing and desisting from crime. The decision graph in Fig. 3.2 shows the decision points for the initial involvement in crime. The authors argue that only when we understand the actual mechanisms involved in the choices can we hope to produce effective policies for crime prevention. For analysing the decisions taken by criminals, Cornish and Clarke rely on self-report data from criminal offenders. Although this type of data comes with caveats, it is the only data we can draw on for a general theory of criminal decision making.

The rational choice approach can be described as an on/off switch; if and when the utility of committing a crime exceeds the disutility of punishment, a crime is committed. Cornish and Clarke's framework is like a complex set of dials and switches, in which different fine tuning leads to the decision to commit a crime. Many different parameters are taken into account, such as an agent's opportunity, psychology and background. Other factors are *needs* and *previous experiences*. The interesting and novel part of the decision framework is that these externalities are filtered through a reasoning procedure, the *perceived solution* box. This box lists the options that the agent sees as available for need satisfaction. The perceived solutions are directly influenced by the needs and the *solutions evaluated*, which in turn are influenced by the previous experiences. The evaluated solutions are closely related to the utility function of the economic analysis, containing the costs and benefits of the criminal act. Some social variables are integrated in this approach, such as the 'broken home', the 'neighbourhood' and the contact with 'law enforcement agencies'.

From this detailed decision diagram it is easy to see a theory of crime prevention developing. Each decision point is a possible policy intervention. Situational crime prevention, as the name suggests, focuses on the situational variables of crime, and aims to propose interventions that increase criminals' efforts and risk. Some of the recommendations can be seen in Table 3.1.

3.3.4 Broken Windows and Zero Tolerance

Another environmental theory of crime is the *broken window theory* (Wilson and Kelling 1982). It describes the dynamics behind an area becoming crime prone. Wilson and Kelling, based partly on Zimbardo's 1969 experiments, contend that environmental disorder can lead to the rapid decline of an area and that the best way to prevent crime is to keep an area orderly, e.g. cleaning up graffiti, repairing broken windows and dealing with 'undesirables' quickly. Broken window theory is based on differentiating agent types. Harcourt (2001) distinguishes two dimensions of agents (Table 3.2).

Broken window theory has been one of the major theoretical foundations of policy implementations in both the United States and Britain, (e.g. Guiliani's 'Zero Tolerance' clear-up of New York). Broken window theory's success lies in this intuitive appeal to a simple mechanism of deterioration and neighbourhood change and its easy translation into policy applications. It makes intuitive sense that the deterioration of neighbourhoods due to disorder might facilitate the influx of crime. However, empirical support is scant and plenty of data

Table 3.1 Situational crime prevention policy interventions (Cornish and Clarke 2002)

Increase the effort	Harden targets (e.g. immobilisers in cars) Control access to facilities (e.g. entry phones) Screen exits (e.g. tickets needed) Deflect offenders (e.g. separate female toilets) Control tools/weapons (e.g. photos on credit cards)
Increase the risk	Extended guardianship (e.g. neighbourhood watch) Assist natural surveillance (e.g. improved street lighting) Reduce anonymity (e.g. taxi driver IDs) Utilise place managers (e.g. support whistle blowers) Strengthen formal surveillance (e.g. CCTV in town centres)
Reduce the rewards	Conceal targets (e.g. motorcycle covers) Remove targets (e.g. removablc car radios) Identify property (e.g. vehicle licensing) Disrupt markets (e.g. checks on pawn brokers) Deny benefits (e.g. graffiti cleaning)
Reduce provocations	Reduce frustration and stress (e.g. soothing lighting) Avoid disputes (e.g. reduce crowding in pubs) Reduce emotional arousal (e.g. prohibit peadophiles working with children) Neutralise peer pressure (e.g. 'it's ok to say no') Discourage imitation (e.g. rapid vandalism repair)
Remove excuses	Set rules (e.g. hotel registration) Post instructions (e.g. 'No parking') Alert conscience (e.g. 'shoplifting is stealing') Assist compliance (e.g. litter bins) Control drugs/alcohol (e.g. breathalysers in pubs)

Table 3.2 The four agent types of broken window theory (Harcourt 2001, p. 25)

	Regulars	Strangers
Ordered	Decent folk	Visitors
Disordered	Drunks and derelicts	Criminals

contradicts broken window theory (cf. Taqi-Eddin & Macallair 1999). Given the empirical evidence that neighbourhoods do not necessarily deteriorate due to minor demeanours and disorderliness together with evidence that public order policing is not the most effective way to allocate scarce resources to prevent crime (Harcourt 1998, 2001; Harcourt and Ludwig 2006) the continuing success of broken window theory is interesting. Broken window theory stipulates that an area's decay leads to a decline in adherence to social norms, that is, a norm change without any inter-agent transmission of norms because the decline is introduced purely environmentally.

3.4 Sociological Theories of Crime

In this section we look at theories that explain crime by social rather than environmental influences. We start with differential association theory, a theory that can be seen as a social ecology theory. Sutherland, associated with the Chicago School, saw crime as a set of values and skills acquired by social learning just like any other set of values and skills. People's value systems are made by the community they are socialised in. The second theory we discuss is Hirschi's social bond theory, a social control theory that asserts that crime is the result of the weak social bonds of the criminal to groups and institutions (e.g. family), resulting in the criminal not feeling the need to adhere to the z norms and laws of society.

3.4.1 Differential Association Theory

Differential association theory (Sutherland 1947) is a theory of socially determined criminality. Rather than a pathological, biological or economic explanation of crime, all prevalent at the time, differential association theory saw the difference between criminals and non-criminals as lying in the social associations in which people are embedded. Through tight knit social association with people defying the law, people's values adjust to be in turn more law defying, thus making criminal activity more likely. By excess exposure to definitions favourable to violation of the law people become delinquent. People thus become criminals through the social influence of other people. Differential association theory has a set of basic principles:

1. *Criminal behaviour is learned.* Negatively, this means that criminal behaviour is not inherited, as such; also, the person who is not already trained in crime does not invent criminal behaviour, just as a person does not make mechanical inventions unless he has had training in mechanics.
2. *Criminal behaviour is learned in interaction* with other persons in a process of communication. This communication is verbal in many respects but includes also "the communication of gestures".
3. *The principal part of the learning of criminal behaviour occurs within intimate personal groups.* Negatively, this means that the impersonal agencies of communication, such as picture shows and newspapers, play a relatively unimportant part in the genesis of criminal behaviour.
4. *When criminal behaviour is learned* the learning includes (a) techniques of committing the crime, which are sometimes very complicated, sometimes very simple; (b) the specific direction of motives, desires, rationalizations, and attitudes.
5. *The specific direction of motives and drives is learned from definitions of legal codes as favorable and unfavorable.* In some societies an individual is surrounded by persons who invariably define the legal codes as rules to be observed, whereas in others he is surrounded by persons whose definitions are favorable to the violation of the legal codes. In our American society these definitions are almost always mixed, and consequently we have culture conflict in relation to the legal codes.

6. *A person becomes delinquent because of an excess of definitions favorable to violation of law* over definitions unfavorable to violation of law. This is the principle of differential association. It refers to both criminal and anti-criminal associations and has to do with counteracting forces. When persons become criminals, they do so because of contacts with criminal patterns and also because of isolation from anti-criminal patterns. Any person inevitably assimilates the surrounding culture unless other patterns are in conflict; a Southerner does not pronounce "r" because other Southerners do not pronounce "r." Negatively, this proposition of differential association means that associations which are neutral so far as crime is concerned have little or no effect on the genesis of criminal behaviour. Much of the experience of a person is neutral in this sense, e.g., learning to brush one's teeth. This behaviour has no negative or positive effect on criminal behaviour except as it may be related to associations which are concerned with the legal codes. This neutral behaviour is important especially as an occupier of the time of a child so that he is not in contact with criminal behaviour during the time he is engaged in neutral behaviour.
7. *Differential associations may vary in frequency, duration, priority, and intensity.* This means that associations with criminal behaviour and also associations with anti-criminal behaviour vary in those respects. Frequency and duration as modalities of associations are obvious and need no explanation. Priority is assumed to be important in the sense that lawful behaviour developed in early childhood may persist throughout life, and also that delinquent behaviour developed in early childhood may persist throughout life. This tendency, however, has not been adequately demonstrated, and priority seems to be important principally through its selective influence. "Intensity" is not precisely defined, but it has to do with such things as the prestige of the source of a criminal or anti-criminal pattern and with emotional reactions related to the associations. In a precise description of the criminal behaviour of a person these modalities would be stated in quantitative form and a mathematical ratio be reached. A formula in this sense has not been developed, and the development of such a formula would be extremely difficult.
8. *The process of learning criminal behaviour by association with criminal and anti-criminal patterns involves all of the mechanisms that are involved in any other learning.* Negatively, this means that the learning of criminal behaviour is not restricted to the process of imitation. A person who is seduced, for instance, learns criminal behaviour by association, but this process would not ordinarily be described as imitation.
9. *Though criminal behaviour is an expression of general needs and values, it is not explained by those general needs and values since non-criminal behaviour is an expression of the same needs and values.* Thieves generally steal in order to secure money, but likewise honest laborers work in order to secure money. The attempts by many scholars to explain criminal behaviour by general drives and values, such as the happiness principle, striving for social status, the money motive, or frustration, have been and must continue to be futile since they explain lawful behaviour as completely as they explain criminal behaviour. They are similar to respiration, which is necessary for any behaviour but which does not differentiate criminal from non-criminal behaviour.

(Sutherland 1947, pp. 5–7)

Differential association theory explains crime entirely by social interaction, including communication and learning. Biological inheritance, the economic situation and macro-societal phenomena like power or exclusion play no role in the explanation of crime. We will return to differential association theory in Chap. 11 where we discuss a social network model of juvenile delinquency.

3.4.2 *Social Bond Theory*

Social bond theory is a social control theory of crime where the decision space of a person is limited by its social bonds. Social control theories argue that the social embeddedness of a person constrains their actions and encourages them not to commit crimes. Whereas previously discussed theories explain why people commit crimes, i.e. see crime as the abnormal behaviour, social control theories takes crime as the default behaviour. The question is no longer why people commit crimes, but why some people *do not* commit crimes. This is an essentially Hobbesian view of humanity, where only a social contract can make coexistence in a society possible by resolving the conflicts arising from different people's needs.

Hirschi's *Causes of Delinquency* (1969) is one of the most influential social control theory publications. He specifically hones in on the idea of social bonds as the reason why people behave normatively. A weakening of social bonds is the main cause of criminality. His important contribution is to provide an alternative to the then pervasive strain and cultural conflict theories, where race, ethnicity or class are taken as explanatory variables and criminal behaviour is thought to be caused by group specific subcultural values. Hirschi argues that it is not subcultural values that cause crime. In his theory, there is one shared value system for all. The distinguishing parameter between criminals and non-criminals is a variance in the embeddedness within that value system. The variance, in turn, is explained by a variance in the strength of social bonds. Four components are important for the maintenance of healthy social bonds:

1. Attachment: The strength of attachment to other people (e.g. family, peers). An agent more attached to others is less likely to behave deviantly.
2. Commitment: The fear of breaking the law. The more agents previously invested in conventional behaviour, the higher the price for deviance and the less likely they are to break the law.
3. Involvement: The degree of involvement in conventional activities. The more involved agents are in conventional activities, the less time they will have for deviant behaviour ("idle hands are the devil's workshop").
4. Belief: The belief in a common value system. The more agents believe in shared values, the less likely they are to deviate from these values.

Hirschi also contributes an analysis of the peer effect on youth delinquency. One of the most consistent findings in criminology is the clustering of delinquent peers. Hirschi's stand is that it is not the association with the peers that is the root cause of this phenomenon but that those youths are socially unattached. Thus, rather than network influences raising the level of delinquency, it is the lack of network links that causes delinquency.

Theories that lend some theoretical support to this hypothesis are Reckless' (1961) invocation of *self-concept* and *self-image* as an explanation for resilience to crime, even in a highly criminogenic environment with self image being connected to parental ties, as well as Toby's (1957) use of a *stake in conformity* to explain why some youths can successfully be isolated from criminal tendencies.

Gibbs (1989), although strongly supporting the idea of *social control* as an important variable for criminal behaviour, criticises Hirschi for not clearly defining the concept. Gibbs delineates the concept of social control from other forms of external controls. Social control is the attempt by one or more individuals to manipulate the behaviour of another individual or individuals by or through a *third party*. The third party is the important concept which enshrines the *social* aspect of social control. Hirschi is interested in social bonds themselves and sees these bonds as sufficient for control. Gibbs argues that social bonds might make control more effective but the bonds are not the control itself.

Another control theory of delinquency is Matza's *Neutralisation theory* (Matza 1964, p. 181), a theory of how individual agency supersedes social bonds. It proposes five reasoning techniques with which individuals cut the tie between themselves and society or between themselves and their crime. These techniques enable delinquents to break 'the moral bind to law'.

> 1. *The denial of personal responsibility.* 'Of course I am delinquent. Who wouldn't I be, coming from my background?' neutralising personal responsibility by citing circumstances.
> 2. *The denial of harm to anyone.* In this pattern of neutralisation, stealing a car is only borrowing it; truancy harms no-one and drug use 'does not hurt anyone but me'.
> 3. *The delinquent denies that the person injured or wronged is really a victim.* 'The assaulted teacher was unfair', the victim of a mugging was 'only queer' and the gang youth assaulted was 'out to get me'.
> 4. *The delinquent condemns the condemners.* 'Society is much more corrupt than I am.'
> 5. *Delinquent group or gang loyalties supersede loyalty to the norms of an impersonal society.* 'When I stabbed him, I was only defending my turf.' The youth places his gang or delinquent group above the law, the school, society.
>
> (Carrabine et al. 2004, p. 61)

Neutralisation shows how social norms can be negated by an individual.

The above theories suppose that there is one majority normative system and that criminals deviate from it in the full knowledge what is right and wrong. An alternative theory is Kobrin (1951). Kobrin puts forward an analysis of conflicting values in delinquency areas.

> [...] observations suggest that delinquency is widely diffused in the urban high rate areas and therefore represents normative behaviour which, like all normative behaviour, generates a systematic scheme of values and institutional forms for its expression. [...] a significantly large number of boys in these areas are free of the kind of involvement in delinquent practices which ordinarily results in the acquisition of a police record or in the development of adult criminality. With respect to the careers of these individuals it seems necessary to assume the ultimate dominance of the norms of conventional society. Thus, a duality of conduct norms in the high rate areas rather than the hegemony of either conventional or criminal value systems may be regarded as the fundamental sociological fact in the culture of these communities.
>
> (Kobrin 1951, p. 193)

Although there are high crime rates in certain areas, there are still many living in those areas that do not commit crimes as well as many that cease over time to commit crimes. This means that we cannot divide the world into different normative areas. Rather we have people interacting with both conventional and criminal norms simultaneously. This theory describes a fluid conception of delinquency in which the agent plays different roles at different times and in different social constellations.

3.5 Models of Crime

Just as the previous chapter discussed some formalisations of normative behaviour we shall conclude this chapter with some models of crime. Apart from economics, criminology is the social science that has most embraced mathematical methods. In contrast to economics, it has also embraced simulation methods more than any other social science. The first model we consider is based on routine activity theory and simulates the emergence of crime hotspots using offender behaviour (routines), victim vulnerability and risk. The second is a model of how population dynamics might influence crime rates.

3.5.1 *Criminal Hotspots*

The following model will give us a feel for crime simulations. In Short et al. (2010) a model is developed to analyse the conditions of emergence, spread and dissipation of criminal hotspts. The authors develop a set of partial differential equations linking the development of spatio-temporal variables of crime spots with offender behaviour. Potential crime targets are distributed in space with each spatial location having an associated risk, a field $A(x,t)$. Risk is calculated by the following equation,

$$\delta B/\delta t = \nu D \bigtriangledown^2 B - \omega B + \kappa \rho A \tag{3.3}$$

where $A^0(x)$ is a static spatial risk component with $B(x,t)$ providing the dynamics. $\rho(x)$ is the density of criminal agents at location x and κ the growth in risk at the rate ρA. The idea of κ is that offenders are 'pulled back' to locations where they previously committed a crime. D is a diffusion coefficient, where $\nu \in [0,1]$ stands for a near repeat factor of a crime, i.e. close neighbourhoods of crime are more likely to be affected, and ω describes the decay of risk over time at location x.

The density of offenders is operationalised by the following equation. Some assumptions are made about offender behaviour, such as that offenders choose the criminal opportunities close to home and having targets with high vulnerability, here expressed as 'high risk'.

$$\delta \rho/\delta t = \nu D \overrightarrow{\bigtriangledown}[\overrightarrow{\bigtriangledown}\rho - 2\rho \overrightarrow{\bigtriangledown} lnA] - \rho A + \gamma \tag{3.4}$$

Offenders move up gradients of lnA or diffuse in the absence of a risk gradient; $\vec{\nabla}$ is the gradient operator. Offenders exit the system at rate ρA and new ones are introduced at a constant rate per unit area γ.

The behavioural assumptions of near repeat offending, risk assessment, staying close to existing activity nodes etc. are all empirically substantiated.

The conditions for the emergence of crime hotspots are analysed with this model. Experiments are run analysing the influence of risk diffusion on the emergence of hotspots and of crime suppression strategies on their dissipation and displacement.

The most important findings are that there is no emergence of hotspots due to a lack of risk clusters if there is no overlap between the areas of influence of individual crimes. If the overlap is too large the diffusion of risk over space results in a homogenisation, also not leading to clustering of crimes. Only when the risk diffusion is relatively local, binding crimes together at a local level, do we have the emergence of hotspots.

Criminal hotspot policing strategies, when tested, have a positive result in this model, suggesting that suppression of risk may lead to effective wider neighbourhood effects.

A comprehensive collection of the use of computational methods in the analysis of crime can be found in Liu and Eck (2008). The collection encompasses state of the art crime modelling but is focusses heavily on the traditional environmental modelling paradigm. The integration of geographical information systems provides a new perspective on spatial modelling and improves the possibility of empirical validation of simulations.

3.5.2 *Poverty Ain't No Crime*

Economic conditions are often seen as *the* causes of crime. This is partly due to an intuitive linking of, for example, property crime with material deprivation and partly to a general notion of economic causes for social problems (see Grand et al. 1992). However, restricting the analysis of crime to economic variables is a mistake, as Ormerod (2005) points out. He focuses on the impossibility of explaining human behaviour with economic incentives alone. Essentially, the agents of microeconomic theory have fixed tastes or preferences and decisions are made by calculating the maximal utility of an action. But people's preferences and tastes are not fixed and stable over time, but changing and are influenced by their social environment. If we think about any fashion market, the preferences are by definition generated by the behaviour of others. Ormerod uses Christmas toys as an example: once it is clear what *the* Christmas toy of the year is, both price and demand can go up, thus fundamentally contradicting economic theory.

If a market like this does not behave according to perfect rationality, it seems likely that, when it comes to crime, social influence will play a major role.

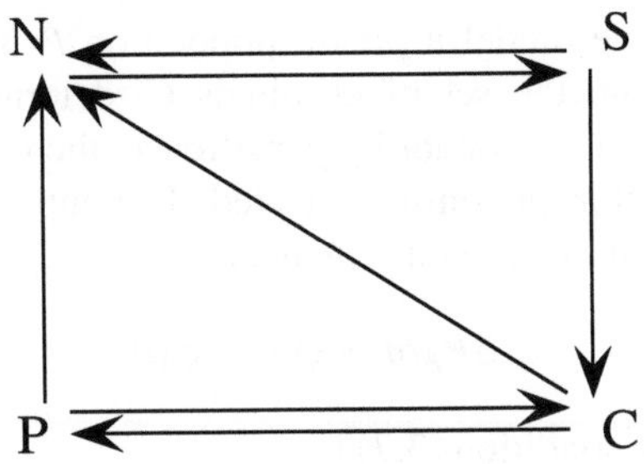

Fig. 3.3 Flow directions between population groups N, S and C (and P in *grey*)

Ormerod et al. (2001) and Ormerod (2005) develop a non-linear model of crime levels, based on epidemiological population dynamics. A population is divided into those non-susceptible to crime (N), those susceptible (S), criminals (C) (and those in prison (P) in the 2005 extension). These discrete population groups are connected by flows, see Fig. 3.3.

Ns never commit crimes, Ss commit some (one a year in the original model), Cs commit many crimes (ten a year) and Ps are in prison. Prisoners can become reformed (become Ns) or reoffend (go back to C). Criminals can become reformed (become Ns). A set of non-linear equations represents the flow rates of this interdependent closed system.

$$\delta N/\delta t = -\theta N + \mu S + \beta(N)C \tag{3.5}$$

The rate of change of N is determined by a continuous flow out of N, $-\theta N$. This flow occurs naturally, for example by the ageing of young boys into adolescents, increasing their propensity to commit crimes. Some S will always return to be N, here assumed to be a constant μ. The rate at which C return to N is determined by how much criminal action is disapproved in a population, calculated by the size of N and a parameter β representing the additional deterrence and social and economic conditions contributing to an agent committing a crime.

$$\delta S/\delta t = \theta N - \mu S - \alpha S - \lambda SC \tag{3.6}$$

In turn, the rate of change of S is given by the influx of θN into this category, μS agents leaving to become non-susceptible again, αS, a similarly fixed rate of agents going from S to C, and $\lambda(S)C$ a term expressing a social influence on an S becoming a C that depends on the size of C. Given that

$$N + S + C = 1, \tag{3.7}$$

the rate of change of C is fully determined by the above equations.

$$\delta C/\delta t = \alpha S + \lambda(S)C + \beta(N)C \tag{3.8}$$

In an extension to the model a prison population P is added (grey arrows in Fig. 3.3). In-flow is from the set of criminals C, determined by a variable φ_1, incorporating the conviction probability per offence, the rate of crime in C and the probability of being sent to prison if convicted. The outflow from P is determined by φ_2, the average length of a prison sentence.

$$\delta P/\delta t = \varphi_1 C - \varphi_2 P \tag{3.9}$$

We now have to replace condition (3.7) by

$$N+S+C+P=1. \tag{3.10}$$

The other three flow equations needs to be amended as the flow from P could go into any of the categories.

By analysing the flow rates, the consequences of different policies can be stipulated. For example, a higher flow from C to P will reduce the number of criminals. Traditional arguments for longer sentences and higher incarceration rates run along those lines. Another set of important flows is that from C and S back to N. Deterrence is the policy that tries to encourage these flows. The authors point out that the most important flow in the model, however, is that from N to S. If it is possible to curb the flow from non-susceptibles to susceptibles, criminal behaviour will be seriously undermined. The authors further argue that this flow is the most socially determined. There are two social influences on S. First, a higher rate of criminals (more agents in C) increases S assuming that susceptibility goes up in a culture where crime is rife. Second, a higher rate of non-susceptibles will naturally curb the rate of S as in such a population crime will be less accepted. We can clarify this with some simple examples: If paying cash to a tradesman is normal, people willingly participate in tax fraud. If downloading music is normal, people willingly participate in copyright theft. On the other hand, drink driving is no longer condoned in the UK and has become a relatively rare crime.

Although the model tries to implement social influences on criminal decision making, the conceptualisation of the strength of a social norm as proportional to the number of non-susceptibles or criminals is only a first approximation and does not lead to detailed policy recommendations.

3.6 Conclusion

This chapter gave an overview of theories of crime. We discussed four kinds of theories, individual based theories, deterrence theories, environmental theories and social based theories. We left out several others from our detailed discussion, such as anomie theories or strain theories. Our choice was informed by our conception of crime as a transgression of a norm, in this case a legal norm.

We only gave a very brief sketch of individual based models of crime as they are mainly irrelevant for the analysis of crime as the transgression of a norm. However, we mentioned Gottfredson and Hirschi's general theory of crime which, although basing the explanation of crime on the individual variable self-control, is based on the idea that self-control is internalised in the socialisation process, thus taking social factors into account.

Deterrence theories have their origin in rational choice theory focussing on punishment as a way of making crime 'not pay'. Rational choice is a formalism that captures some level of human decision making very well but, given empirical evidence of the insufficiency of deterrence, it is insufficient to explain criminal decision procedures. Nonetheless, this 'economic analysis' of crime was an important turning point in the development of theories of criminal behaviour. It dispensed with crime as pathological and the criminal as a passive 'victim' of external circumstances. Rather, it assumes that criminals are just like non-criminals in their decision making; it is only the incentive structures that are different.

The environmental theories of crime we discussed are routine activity theory, environmental criminology, situational crime prevention and broken window theory. They constitute another important innovation in criminology, away from an extreme focus on the offender. Environmental theories recognise that spatial and temporal variables are important parameters influencing social interaction (human ecology). One problem with the focus on spatial crime patterns is that it highlights certain kinds of crime like burglary, robbery and assault. It cannot provide explanations of 'white collar crimes' such as fraud, which are less dependent on physical aspects. However, environmental crime theories have been the backdrop of most models of crime to date, mainly due to the relative ease with which they can be implemented. We discussed one model in more detail.

We described two sociological theories of crime in particular differential association theory and social bond theory. Both kinds see the causes of crime in the social embedding of the agent. Differential association theory is a social learning theory of crime, social bond theory uses the bonds an agent has with society, to explain why people adhere to norms, with weak bonds being the explanation for criminal behaviour.

Finally we discussed two models of crime, the first explaining the emergence of crime hotspots from a distribution of risk, target vulnerability and offender routines, the second a model of the social dynamics of crime, showing the influence of population dynamics on crime rates.

We can see from this chapter and Chap. 2 that the analysis of norms and the analysis of crime have relatively few overlaps. This is surprising given the strong conceptual link between them we identified in the introduction. The only direct point of contact is rational choice theory and even there the focus is more on game theory in the case of social norms and deterrence in the case of crime. Other links are more subtle, as for example differential association theory's basis on social influence research discussed in Sect. 2.2.4 and the general theory of crime reliance on childhood socialisation and internalisation of self-control discussed in Sect. 2.2.1. Theories of social norms did not take any environmental variables into account whereas environmental explanations are aplenty in the explanation of crime.

References

Bandyopadhyay, S., Bhattacharya, S., & Sensarma, R. (2011). Determining crime in England and Wales: A quantile regression approach. Department of Economics Discussion Paper 11–12, University of Birmingham.

Becker, G. S. (1968). Crime and punishment: An economic approach. *Journal of Political Economy, 76*(2), 169–217.

Bosse, T., Gerritsen, C., Hoogendoorn, M., Jaffry, S. W., & Treur, J. (2008). Comparison of agent-based and population-based simulations of displacement of crime. In *International conference on web intelligence and intelligent agent technology*, Sydney.

Brantingham, P. L., & Brantingham, P. J. (1991). *Environmental criminology*. Prospect Heights: Waveland Press.

Carrabine, E., Iganski, P., Lee, M., Plummer, K., & South, N. (2004). *Criminology a sociological introduction*. London: Routledge.

Carrasco, M., Barker, E. D., Tremblay, R. E., & Vitaro, F. (2006). Eysenck's personality dimensions as predictors of male adolescent trajectories of physical aggression, theft and vandalism. *Personality and Individual Differences, 41*, 1309–1320.

Clarke, R. V. (Ed.). (1997). *Situational crime prevention*. Guilderland: Harrow and Heston.

Clarke, R. V., & Cornish, D. B. (1985). Modeling offenders' decisions: A framework for research and policy. *Crime and Justice, 6*, 147–185.

Cloninger, C. R., Svrakic, D. M., & Przybeck, T. R. (1993). A psychobiological model of temperament and character. *Archives of General Psychiatry, 50*, 975–990.

Cohen, L. E., & Felson, M. (1979). Social change and crime rate trends: A routine activities approach routine activities approach. *American Sociological Review, 44*, 588–608.

Cornish, D. B., & Clarke, R. V. (2002). Analyzing organized crime. In A. Piquero & S. G. Tibbetts (Eds.), *Rational choice and criminal behavior: Recent research and future challenges* (pp. 41–62). New York: Garland.

Cornish, D. B., & Clarke, R. V. (1986). *The reasoning criminal*. New York: Springer.

Cornish, D., & Clarke, R. V. (1987). Understanding crime displacement: An application of rational choice theory. *Criminology, 25*, 933–947.

Dahrendorf, R. (1959). *Class and class conflict in industrial society*. Stanford: Stanford University Press.

Durkheim, E. (1895). *The rules of sociological method*. New York: Free Press.

Eysenck, H. J. (1977). *Crime and personality*. London: Routledge and Kegan Paul.

Gibbs, J. P. (1989). *Control: Sociology's central notion*. Urbana: University of Illinoiis Press.

Gottfredson, M. R., & Hirschi, T. (1990). *A general theory of crime*. Stanford: Stanford University Press.

Grand, J. L., Propper, C., & Robinson, R. (1992). *The economics of social problems* (3rd ed.). Basingstoke: Palgrave Macmillan.

Groff, E. R., & Birks, D. (2008). Simulating crime prevention strategies: A look at the possibilities. *Policing: A Journal of Policy and Practice, 1*(0), 1–10.

Harcourt, B. E. (1998). Reflecting on the subject: A critique of the social influence conception of deterrence, the broken windows theory, and order-maintenance policing New York style. *Michigan Law Review, 97*, 291–389.

Harcourt, B. E. (2001). *Illusion of order: The false promise of broken windows policing*. Cambridge: Harvard University Press.

Harcourt, B. E., & Ludwig, J. (2006). Broken windows: New evidence from New York city and a five-city social experiment. *University of Chicago Law Review, 73*, 271–320.

Hawley, A. H. (1950). *Human ecology: A theory of community structures*. New York: Ronald Press.

Hirschi, T. (1969). *Causes of delinquency*. Berkely: University of California Press.

Kobrin, S. (1951). The conflict of values in denlinquency areas. *American Sociological Review, 16*, 653–661.

Liu, L., & Eck, J. (Eds.). (2008). *Artificial crime analysis systems: Using computer simulations and geographic information systems*. Hershey: Idea Group Publishing.

Matza, D. (1964). *Delinquency and drift*. New York: Wiley.

McCarthy, B. (2002). New economics of sociological criminology. *Annual Review of Sociology, 28*, 417–442.

McCrea, R. R., & Costa, P. T. (1990). *Personality in adulthood*. New York: The Guildford Press.

McKenzie, R. D. (1924). The ecological approach to the study of the human community. *American Journal of Sociology, 30*, 287–301.

Mehlkop, G., & Graeff, P. (2007). *How to model a rational choice theory of criminal action? Subjective expected utilities, norms, and interactions*. Paper presented at the annual meeting of the American Sociological Association, TBA, New York, New York City Online.

Merton, R. K. (1938). Social structure and anomie. *American Sociological Review, 12*, 99–107.

Miller, J. D., & Lynam, D. (2001). Structural models of personality and their relation to antisocial behaviour: A meta-analytic review. *Criminology, 39*(4), 765–769.

Ormerod, P. (2005). *Crime: Economic incentives and social networks*. London: IEA.

Ormerod, P., Mounfield, C., & Smith, L. (2001). Non-linear modelling of burglary and violent crime in the UK. Technical report, Volterra Consulting Ltd for the Home Office UK.

Pyle, D. (2000). Economists, crime and punishment. In N. G. Fielding, A. Clarke, & R. Witt (Eds.), *The economic dimensions of crime*. Palgrave.

Reckless, W. (1961). A new theory of delinquency and crime. *Federal Probation, 25*, 42–46.

Rimke, H. (2011). The pathological approach to crime: Individually based theories. In K. Kramar (Ed.), *Canadian criminology* (pp. 78–92). Toronto: Pearson Education Canada.

Shaw, C. R., & McKay, H. D. (1931). Social factors in juvenile delinquency: A study of the community, the family, and the gang in relation to delinquent behaviour. Report of the National Commission on Law Observance and Enforcement, Causes of crime, II(13). Washington, DC: GPO.

Short, M., & Dorsogna, M. (2008). A statistical model of criminal behavior. *Mathematical Models and Methods in Applied Sciences, 18*, 1249–1267.

Short, M. B., Brantingham, P. J., Bertozzi, A. L., & Tita, G. E. (2010). Dissipation and displacement of hotspots in reaction-diffusion models of crime. *Proceedings of the National Academy of Sciences USA, 107*(9), 3961–3965.

Sutherland, E. H. (1947). *Principles of criminology* (4th ed.). Philadelphia: J.B. Lippincott.

Szakas, J., Trefftz, C., Ramirez, R., & Jefferis, E. (2008). Development of an intelligent patrol routing system using gis and computer simulations. In L. Liu & J. Eck (Eds.), *Artificial crime analysis systems: Using computer simulations and geographic information systems*. Hershey: Idea Group Publishing.

Taqi-Eddin, K., & Macallair, D. (1999). *Shattering "broken windows": An analysis of San Francisco's alternative crime policies*. Center on Juvenile and Criminal Justice, www.cjcj.org

Tellegen, A. (1985). Structures of mood and personality and their relevance to assessing anxiety with an emphasis on self-report. In A. H. Tuma & J. D. Maser (Eds.), *Anxiety and the anxiety disorders*. Hillsdale: Lawrence Erlbaum Associates.

Toby, J. (1957). Social disorganization and stake in conformity: Complementary factors in the predatory behavior of hoodlums. *The Journal of Criminal Law, Criminology, and Police Science, 48*, 12–17.

Wikström, P.-O. H., Oberwittler, D., Treiber, K., & Hardie, B. (2012). *Breaking rules: The social and situational dynamics of young people's urban crime*. Oxford: Oxford University Press.

Wilson, J. Q., & Kelling, G. L. (1982). Broken windows. *The Atlantic Monthly*, pp. 29–38.

Witte, A. D. (1980). Estimating the economic model of crime with individual data. *Quarterly Journal of Economics, 94*, 57–84.

Zimbardo, P. (1969). The human choice: Individuation, reason, and order versus deindividuation, impulse, and chaos. *Nebraska Symposium on Motivation, 17*, 237–307.

Chapter 4
Agent-Based Modelling

If you have not grown it you have not explained it.

Joshua Epstein

In this chapter we introduce the main ingredients of agent-based modelling, outline how models are built, discuss how agent-based modelling is used in the study of social norms and relate it to simulation models of crime.

Over the past half century a new method has developed in the social sciences, the modelling of social phenomena. Previous research was empirical, based mainly on observations and theoretical analyses of social dynamics. Models, or what Merton calls 'midrange theories' were scarce. We saw in the introduction that agent-based models are somewhat related to thought experiments, another rare mode of investigation in the social sciences. The reason for the scarcity of both is that social phenomena are too complex to analyse in simple terms. However, complexity is becoming less and less of a problem and as a result of a paradigm shift in the social sciences, as we will see below.

One of the first and certainly the most famous 'agent-based models' of a social phenomenon is Schelling's (1971) model of Segregation, (discussed below). Schelling himself executed this model on a checkerboard, using dimes and pennies. Since then there have been many implementations and modifications of his idea (for example Wilensky 1997).[1]

In the last 20 years the modelling of social phenomena has taken on new momentum. Developments in computer technology, both in hardware and software,

[1] Schelling himself actually warned against the use of a computer in the execution of the model. The reasons for the insistence on the manual execution are mainly the impossibility of a visual output on computers at the time. For a full analysis of Schelling and the computer see Hegselmann (2012).

C. Elsenbroich and N. Gilbert, *Modelling Norms*, DOI 10.1007/978-94-007-7052-2_4,

mean that models incorporating huge amounts of data can be run with relative ease. Developments of object oriented programming languages allow the programming of single, 'independent objects' to interact with each other.

There are essentially three kinds of simulation methods used in the social sciences: Macro-simulation, micro-simulation and agent-based modelling.[2]

Macro-simulations investigate the dynamics of a system, at the system level, hence the alternative name 'system dynamics'. A system is described via a set of systems variables and dynamic equations, e.g. differential or integral equations. Although the dynamic equations do not have to be non-linear they often are, as linear equations are mostly solved analytically. The simulation shows the temporal unfolding of the dynamics represented by these equations step by step (or in differential terms, δt by δt). A causal connection between the variables is assumed and the causal influences of the system parts have to be explicitly programmed into the simulation. Macro-simulations are used for systems with interacting, interdependent variables and feedback loops. Weather forecasts are based on a kind of macro-simulation. In the social sciences they are used for example to model financial systems. Any system can be modelled using systems dynamics, *as long as the relevant causal connections and dynamic equations are known.* This is both the advantage and disadvantage of systems dynamics. If the connections are known, the simulation will be elegant and instructive but the causal connections need to be known in advance of the simulation and that poses a problem, in particular in the social sciences where knowledge of such causal connections is scarce. For a more comprehensive introduction to macro-simulation and their uses in the social sciences, see Gilbert and Troitzsch (2005), Chap. 3.

Micro-simulation is also based on change equations but this time the units they apply to are not system variables but individual parts of the system, such as persons, households and firms. Micro-simulation models the change of each individual separately by using a set of transition rules from one state or behaviour to another. The rules can be deterministic, for example when simulating a change in a specific policy, or probabilistic, for example when simulating an agent's likelihood of dying, giving birth or becoming unemployed. Taken together these separate transitions produce an aggregate system level analysis. Micro-simulation is used for example for population dynamics estimates and tax revenue estimations. It needs lots of input data to specify the individuals and the likely dynamics, and these are estimated from knowledge about the aggregate level, e.g. birth and death rates, income distributions etc. No causal interconnections between the constituent parts of the system are assumed. On the contrary, the parts are completely independently simulated. Because the specifications are made on the constituent parts, the individuals in the system, no causal connections need to be known, but there being no interaction between the

[2]Macro-simulation also runs under the name of *system dynamics* whilst agent-based modelling hides under many different guises such as *individual-based modelling, multi-agent modelling/simulation/systems, agent-based (social) simulation.* We will stick to the terminology of agent-based modelling as it seems to have somewhat stabilised as the common name.

individuals means that interconnections and feedback loops cannot be modelled. However, micro-simulation has been widely used as a tool for policy analysis.

Although macro- and micro-simulations are different in their level of specification, both are simulation techniques where the main concern is prediction and both are heavily reliant on large quantities of data. Agent-based modelling is an almost completely different approach. It does not rely on a set of differential equations to define the dynamics (although it may contain some), it does not rely on lots of data about a system or the individuals, and its main concern is not prediction but exploration and understanding.

Agent-based modelling was born as an offspring of the older, simpler simulation technique of cellular automata. A cellular automaton is a grid in of neighbouring cells, each of which has a set of properties and some interactions between the cells. Cellular automata have been used extensively in the natural sciences to model neighbourhood effects such as the Ising model of the ferromagnet. (For an implementation see Wilensky (2003).) Even with these very simple interaction possibilities many rudimentary social dynamics could be simulated (for an overview of cellular automata see Gilbert and Troitzsch (2005, Chap. 7)). Due to their simplicity cellular automata are fairly limited and the modelling ontology has been widened to that of agent-based models.

4.1 What Is Agent-Based Modelling?

Agent-based models have their origin in three different research camps; game theory, complexity science and distributed artificial intelligence. Models originating from game theory are studied to examine how cooperation can emerge from the interaction of selfish agents. The search is for payoff structures, incentives and disincentives that produce pro-social behaviour. The most famous examples of the integration of game theory into simulations is Axelrod's work on the emergence and evolution of norms (cf. Axelrod 1984, 1986).

The strand of modelling coming from complexity science uses work on ecology, population dynamics, or particle physics to model human behaviour. The fundamental idea is that there are many complex phenomena in the natural world and that we can use our understanding of these to guide the analysis of the social world. Cellular automata models such as the *Game of Life* (Berlekamp et al. 1982), zero intelligence models of economic markets (Mirowski 1999) and *Sugarscape* (Epstein and Axtell 1996) result from this approach.

The distributed artificial intelligence strand starts from a systems perspective. The aim of traditional AI is to find solutions for complex problems by the application of 'intelligence'. Some problems have been recognised as either unsolvable or as being less effectively solved by a single, monolithic system. Distributed artificial intelligence developed decentralised solutions for some of these problems. Rather than modelling a system as a whole, autonomous component parts are modelled, producing solutions via their interaction (Wooldridge 2002).

Table 4.1 Ingredients of ABMs

Concept	Explication
Agent	Agents are little computer programs, modules that together constitute a larger computer program
Autonomy	Agents are autonomous in the sense that there is no central decision maker orchestrating behaviour
Heterogeneity	Agents are heterogeneous in that they can have different attributes as well as different roles and behaviours
Environment	The environment can be a geography, the source of consumables (food, information, etc.) or a social environment in the form of a network

An agent-based model is a computer program that creates a world of autonomous, heterogeneous agents in which each agent interacts with other agents and with the environment (Gilbert 2008). There are some concepts in this definition of agent-based models that need explication, see Table 4.1.

As in micro-simulation, the specification level is the individual agent, such as people, households, firms or even nation states. It depends on whose interactions we want to simulate. For example, if we want to simulate how innovation affects the survival of companies in a competitive environment, we might model each company as an agent, whereas to model how structural changes to the labour force might affect the efficiency of a company we probably would model the employees as agents.

Simulations consist of two specifications, a static initialisation and a dynamic for transformation. In micro-simulation the static initialisation is the population of individuals with their particular attributes. The dynamics is a set of stochastic transformation equations. The initialisation in an agent-based model is similar with the addition that the individuals are situated in an environment, often represented as a 'grid'. The grid consists of individual 'patches' on which the agents are located. Each patch is surrounded by other patches, its 'neighbourhood'. The dynamics are determined by a set of interaction rules between the agents and their environment.

Agents have four general characteristics[3]:

1. Perception: Agents can perceive their environment, including other agents in their vicinity.
2. Performance: They have a set of behaviours that they are capable of performing, such as moving, communicating with other agents and interacting with the environment.
3. Memory: Agents have a memory in which they record their previous states and actions.
4. Policy: They have a set of rules, heuristics or strategies that determine, given their present situation and their history, what they should do next.

[3]The list is taken from Abdou et al. (2012).

The important elements of an agent in an agent-based model are its behaviour and its interactions with other agents and the environment. Although not data-independent, the kind of data used for the specification of an agent-based model is different from the data used for other simulation types. Agent-based models, for example, can use qualitative, ethnographic data to define these elements. It is a methodology that is often cited as a possibility for bridging the qualitative/quantitative divide in the social sciences, (Chattoe-Brown 2010; Yang and Gilbert 2008).

4.1.1 *Two Examples of Agent-Based Models*

Let us consider two agent based models, one for its simplicity, one for its wealth of applications.

The first example is the above mentioned model of racial segregation by Schelling (1971). The research question is to explain the persistent pattern of racial residential segregation in American cities. The environment is a grid of squares, each square representing a dwelling. Dwellings can be in one of three states: unoccupied, occupied by a red agent or occupied by a green agent. Agents are initially randomly distributed on the grid, with at most one agent occupying one dwelling. Agents can perceive their eight surrounding neighbours, know whether a dwelling is empty and can see the colour of the agents inhabiting occupied dwellings. Agents can be either happy or unhappy in their neighbourhood. Their happiness is determined by the 'neighbour-race-ratio', the ratio of same colour/different colour agents in their neighbourhood. An agent has a *tolerance-threshold* toward the other race, meaning it is happy with other coloured neighbours up to a certain ratio. Note that the ratio as well as the threshold is calculated taking unoccupied dwellings out of the equation. If an agent is unhappy, it moves to a different patch. There are different possibilities how an agent might choose it's new home. Let us first focus on a movement policy that is used most often in implementations of the Schelling model (see for example Wilensky 1997; Iozzi 2008).

In these implementations, if an agent is unhappy, it moves to a random, unoccupied patch. So, if a red agent has three unoccupied patches in its neighbourhood, two red ones and three green ones, its neighbour-race-ratio is $3/(2+3) = 60\,\%$. If this agent has a tolerance-threshold less than 60 % it will remain in its dwelling and if its tolerance-threshold is greater or equal to 60 % it moves. This simple interaction rule, when run in the simulation, leads to interesting clustering patterns. With this model we can explore the influence that tolerance-thresholds and population-density have on the segregation of agents.

For example, for a wide range of population densities, we get very strong segregation result even with a tolerance threshold of only 30 %. This is a surprising outcome as it seems that with only slight colour preference, segregation is a stable outcome. Very large thresholds result in a population that remains in flux as there are always some agents that have 'undesirable' neighbours making them move to a new place and potentially upsetting formerly stable neighbourhoods.

We cited the Schelling model above as an example of a cellular automaton and here as an agent-based model. The difference between the two can be demonstrated using this one model. If interpreted as a cellular automaton, the setup is simply a grid of squares or "patches" in three states, say red, green and grey. Grey patches can become red or green patches. Red and green patches can become grey patches. The transformation rules are as follows:

1. If a red patch has a red/green ratio $\geq$ a specified threshold it becomes grey and a random grey patch becomes red. Otherwise it remains red.
2. If a green patch has a green/red ratio $\geq$ a specified threshold it becomes grey and a random grey patch becomes green. Otherwise it remains green.

This specification does not have agents moving from dwelling to dwelling as in the description above. Why would we then start complicating things and talk about agents if we only need to describe a set of simple transformation rules?

The implementations of the Schelling model cited above are not faithful implementations. In Schelling (1971) agents do not move to a random unoccupied patch on the grid. Instead, they search their neighbourhood for the nearest patch that satisfies their tolerance threshold. This movement policy already exceeds what can be modelled in a cellular automaton as it needs the distinction between the agent and the environment.

Modelling agents separately from their environment also becomes important once we want to have more complicated interactions between the two, e.g. agents consuming resources in the environment.

The *Sugarscape* model is an example of such an agent-environment interaction going beyond what can be done in a cellular automaton. It was the first large scale model that combines agent-dynamics and environmental dynamics (Epstein and Axtell 1996). The setup of *Sugarscape* is a 51×51 grid with agents roaming around, consuming resources, interacting with each other by trading, reproducing and finally dying. Patches contain sugar with each patch having its own unique sugar level. Once consumed, sugar regrows at a uniform specified rate. Agents consume sugar in order to survive. Each agent has its own metabolic rate determining the amount of sugar it needs. If a patch contains more sugar than the agent requires, the agent can save the excess sugar and consume it later. Each agent has a range of vision determining how far it can see. Once an agent has harvested the sugar on one patch it moves towards the patch within its vision range that has the highest amount of sugar. If it runs out of sugar, the agent dies. Agents also die when they have reached their maximum lifespan, set according to a random uniform distribution. Dead agents are replaced with new agents with random characteristics. There is some survival of the fittest already in this model with 'unsuitable' agents dying quickly of starvation.

The purpose of the model is to investigate the dynamics of wealth distribution. Running the above specification shows that even an initial equal allocation of resources quickly develops into a strongly skewed distribution. Agents who have a larger range of vision do better than those with a smaller range.

This basic model is extended in Epstein and Axtell (1996) to investigate several different social dynamics. One amendment is to implement natural selection more strongly by allowing agents to mate and produce offspring. The offspring will inherit their parent's characteristics using a genetic algorithm (including some mutation), with more successful, i.e. more sugar-endowed parents, producing more offspring. Another interesting extension adds a second resource to the *Sugarscape*, Spice. Now agents have a preference for either sugar or spice and can trade the resources they have saved, creating market dynamics. A further extension implementing cultural dynamics is discussed in more detail in Sect. 5.1.1.

These two are good examples of agent-based models. They show the importance of an environment and how agents interact with it and with each other. The segregation model also shows the difference between a cellular automaton and an agent-based model. However, both models are relatively abstract and not based on very detailed empirically verified assumptions. More recently agent-based modelling has become more empirically minded and in particular the specification of agent behaviour is often based on rules extracted from qualitative research. The basic ideas of these more recent, less abstract, more empirical models, however, is the same.

4.1.2 Agent Architectures

In the above introduction to agent-based modelling we described agents as 'little computer programs'. We have seen that agents can have different attributes such as the tolerance threshold in the Segregation model or the metabolism rate in *Sugarscape*. Agent actions can be of varying levels of complexity. In the Segregation model, an agent simply moves if its neighbourhood no longer satisfies it. In *Sugarscape*, agents choose where to go and what to eat, store or trade. The range of perceptions and conceptualisations together with a procedure that leads to action choices that specify an agent is called an agent architecture. All agent specifications are based on an architecture but the term usually only becomes important when the agent specification includes some kind of cognition in addition to behavioural responses as in Segregation or *Sugarscape*. We discuss two basic architecture types in this section as we shall need them later in Chap. 9 when we discuss cognitive approaches to normative behaviour.

The standard agent architecture of agent-based modelling is the Belief-Desire-Intention (BDI) agent. Starting from the folk-psychological conception of actions being determined by beliefs, desires and intentions, the BDI agent has been the backbone of most multi-agent computation. In Fig. 4.1 the interactions of the components of the BDI agent are visualised.

For example in the segregation model the agents can perceive their direct neighbourhood and assess how many neighbours of each colour they have. The perceived ratio between same and other coloured neighbours can be called an agent's "belief" about its environment. The agent's "desire" is to live in a neighbourhood having a proportion of other coloured neighbours below its tolerance threshold. Its "intention" is to move if the ratio of other coloured neighbours is too high.

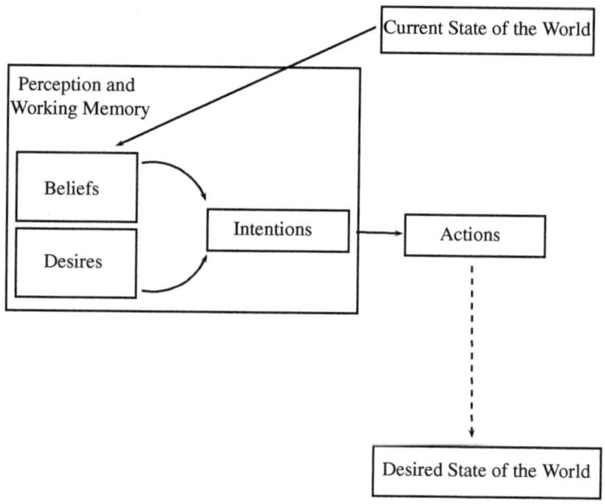

Fig. 4.1 The BDI agent architecture

The BDI agent can be a relatively simple behavioural agent as above but can also be highly cognitive. How the beliefs are acquired or organised and how the agent reasons from its beliefs and desires to intentions and future world states can be implemented very differently. Complex agent architectures are for example ACT-R (Anderson and Lebiere 1998), CLARION, (inter-agent) Neural Networks and SOAR (Newell 1990). All of these incorporate some findings from cognitive psychology.

One thing all these architectures have in common is that the agents are "social atoms", that is, they have no preset social interactions. They pursue their desires simply according to their own beliefs without initial consideration for other agents. This a-social specification might lead to conflicts between agents.

As a solution to the conflict-prone BDI agent type, the Belief-Obligation-Intention-Desire agent (BOID) was developed. The BOID agent also makes action decisions based on its beliefs and desires but has as an additional component, a set of obligations. Obligations are rules that constrain an agent's behaviour in case of social conflicts. The BOID was developed as the social equivalent to the BDI agent, Castelfranchi et al. (1999) and Dignum et al. (2000). Figure 4.2 provides a visualisation to compare with Fig. 4.1.

As a result of its obligations the BOID need not be a selfish agent. It now checks its actions against conflicts with other agents. A BOID agent interacts in the same way with the world as the BDI agent does but its decision space is limited by a set of obligations, essentially a defeasible set of rules. However, this simple addition of one more component leads to complications. Whereas the BDI agent simply assesses its desires and its knowledge of the world and makes a plan accordingly, the BOID agent has to resolve possible conflicts between desires and obligations.

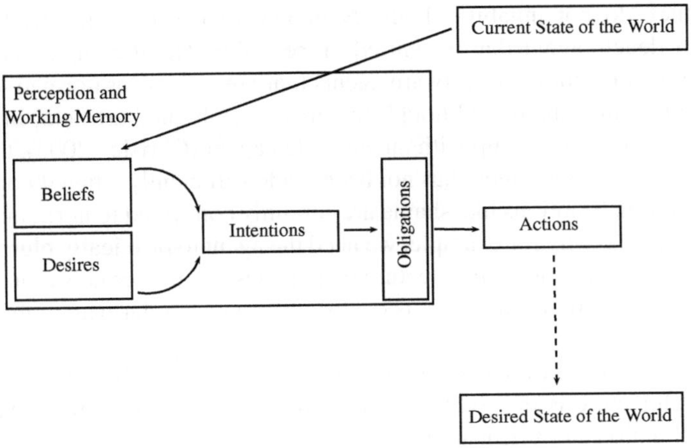

Fig. 4.2 The BOID architecture

So a BOID agent needs a resolution strategy for these conflicts. Although the BOID agent is an attempt to introduce normative behaviour into an agent framework, it falls short of capturing important features of the concept.

The main criticism of the BOID approach is that it is static. The set of norms or obligations in this architecture is fixed. The BOID is unable to change its existing or internalise new norms by learning from its environment. Some theories support a static set of internalised norms or obligations, e.g. social control theory (Hirschi 1969), but most theories see the social influence on norms and their internalisation as an essential part of normative behaviour.

As we noted in Chap. 2, one of the hallmarks of normative behaviour is the internalisation of norms. During childhood the child is socialised, meaning the norms prevalent in its social environment are instilled in the child, including self-punishment mechanisms such as shame and guilt for non-observance. Neumann (2009) criticises the BOID for this lack and points out that modellers seem not to pay enough attention to socialisation theory when it comes to constructing their agents. On comparing a host of different socialisation theories, from Durkheim through Freud to contemporary identity theories, he concludes that there are two obstacles in the way of modelling agents' norm internalisation. The first is that agents have no childhood. Once we have an agent architecture that can learn norms from its environment there does not seem to be a general problem in creating a childhood for agents. A decision has to be made how childhood should be modelled, i.e. whether it is simply a period in the agent's lifespan where a *tabula rasa* of norms is filled rapidly according to social interactions or whether we need to model power relations and coercion in order to capture the salient features of childhood. This kind of decision, i.e. abstracting to only the salient features, has to be made for all simulation tasks. The second major criticism of BOID, and to a large extent all virtual agents, is that they do not inhabit a body. Neumann relates this lack back to Freud's theory of development that is centred on sexuality. He also points at the lack of the emotional reactions in software agents that are salient for normative behaviour, such as pride and shame. Although the area of embodied artificial intelligence is thriving and might come up with an embodied agent (Chrisley 2003), the argument for the need for embodiment has not been made sufficiently when it comes to norm internalisation. Emotions like shame are certainly connected to norm internalisation but it is not clear why for example, we need the agent to physically blush. In Chap. 9 we will see the first agent architecture that tackles norm internalisation by allowing the agent to acquire norms from its environment in a similar way to the acquisition of beliefs.

This discussion shows up an important question in modelling: How do we decide which architecture is the right one? This question leads us to the next section on model validation and verification.

4.1.3 Verification and Validation

As Balci states: "model validation deals with building the right model ... [while] model verification deals with building the model right", (Balci 1994, pp. 121–123). Validation and verification are two important concepts in agent-based modelling and indeed in any computational methodology. We have seen in the introductory comparison of agent-based models to thought experiments that therein lies a big different between these two analytical methods. Thought experiment are easy to verify and validate. Their verification is whether they are consistent as arguments. Their validation is whether their assumptions are supported by our intuition. For computer models the processes of verification and validation are much more difficult.

The verification of a computer program is the check whether the program code makes the computer do what it is supposed to do. There can be two kinds of errors in a computer program. One is that the program is inconsistent. This is easily checked as the program will simply not run. The more difficult error is if the program generates behaviour but the behaviour is due to 'bugs' in the program. The program might display unexpected behaviour, making the bug easy to stop. It might, however, display just the desired behaviour but not as a result of the desired computation but of the mistake. These bugs are hard to spot. Verification is particularly difficult in social simulations as many parameters are implemented as random distributions, making no two runs identical. Only after averaging the results can we see whether the program behaves as it should.

After making sure the model was "built right", it now needs to be tested whether the model is the "right model". Right in this context means that it is a good model of the system it sets out to simulate, the target system. Usually validation is done by comparing simulation outcomes with empirical data from the target system. Often these data are of a statistical nature but for some, very abstract models, validation might only be possible by qualitative comparison or even just visual inspection. For example, the model discussed in Sect. 7.2.1 shows the expected dynamics of norm diffusion without there being any statistical data to compare it with. For more on program verification and validation see for example Gilbert and Troitzsch (2005), Chap. 2, and Ngo and See (2012).

4.2 Agent-Based Models of Normative Behaviour

Having introduced the general idea of agent-based modelling, we will now zoom in on models of normative behaviour.

As we noted in Sect. 4.1, agent-based modelling has three forebears: game theory, complexity science and distributed artificial intelligence. These three differ markedly in terms of their view, use and appreciation of norms. Agent-based models of norms also vary according to which strand they are closer to. We can distinguish three kinds of agent-based models of norms and roughly attribute them to the three forebears as in Table 4.2.

The meaning of 'norm' differs widely in the three fields. Compare three definitions using quotes from influential representatives of each field:

> A norm exists in a given social setting to the extent that individuals usually act in a certain way and are often punished when seen not to be acting in this way. (Axelrod 1986, p. 1097)

> First, [social norms] are self enforcing behavioural regularities. But second, once entrenched, we conform without thinking about it. (Epstein 2000, p. 1)

> A normative system is a social construction a society of agents uses to achieve a certain social order. (Boella and van der Torre 2004, p. 201)

The first definition focusses on punishment of deviance from a norm and assumes a norm is a regular behaviour. The second definition focusses on a norm being a behavioural regularity that coerces agents into behaving this way. There is no punishment aspect explicit in this definition. The third starts from a systems perspective where norms have the function of maintaining social order.

One could say that the three definitions simply focus on different aspects of norms, depending on their particular research question regarding normative behaviour (origin, diffusion or application). However, these definitions appear in the literature without caveats that a specific subdomain of norms is of interest. We next discuss three kinds of norm model in a little more detail.

Table 4.2 Models of norms, aims and origins

Kinds of models	Theoretical origin
Models of the emergence of norms	Game theory
Models of the diffusion of norms	Natural sciences
Models of the use/application of norms	Distributed artificial intelligence

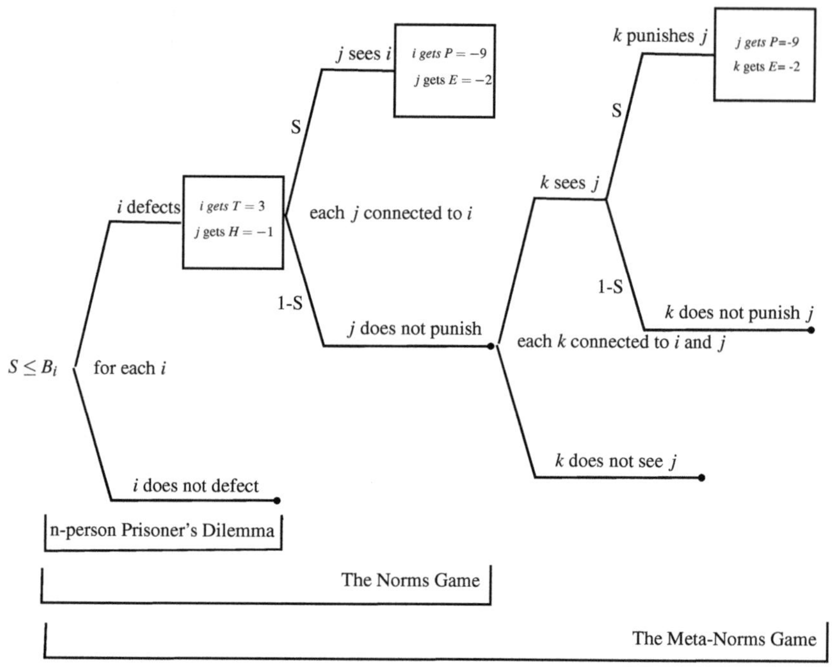

Fig. 4.3 Axelrod's norms and meta-norms game

4.2.1 *Emergence of Norms*

One of the most famous simulations of norm emergence is presented in Axelrod (1986). Letting the agents play intreated prisoner's dilemmas, agents have a choice between two kinds of actions: to cooperate/defect and to punish/not-punish if they observe a defection. Their strategy is determined by two parameters: boldness (acceptable risk of defection) and vengefulness (likelihood of punishing a defecting agent). By definition cooperation is more costly than defection and being punished is more costly than cooperation. There is also a cost associated with punishing a defector (rather than turning a blind eye; see Fig. 4.3).

Axelrod's original experiments define agents that play 1,000 rounds of prisoner's dilemma games. When the norm game is played, i.e. defectors are punished at the cost of the punisher, the outcome of the simulation experiments is that norms ultimately disappear. The vengefulness of the population initially reduces defection but after a period of norm adherence, vengefulness levels fall, leading to a rise in defection and irretrievable norm breakdown. Axelrod then added a meta-norm game, in which an agent that is observed not punishing a defector is punished. Axelrod reports that in this simulation, cooperation and thus a stable norm emerges, under a wide range of initial conditions.

The meta-norm simulation assumes: (a) a Hobbesian view of human nature as selfish and needing to be constrained, (b) that norms are necessarily costly for the individual, (c) that norms are sustained by punishment, and (d) the decision to cooperate or defect is a simple calculation and not dependent on the social setting (that is, there is no influence from other agents except for the possibility of punishment).

4.2.2 *Norm Adoption and Diffusion*

Models concerned with norm adoption and diffusion do not ask how general normative behaviour emerges but how a specific norm might be chosen and then diffuse through a population. There are several different kinds of diffusion model. Some are based on social learning (e.g. Lorscheid and Troitzsch 2009), some on memetics and imitation (e.g. Gatherer 2002; Flentge et al. 2001) and some on opinion dynamics (e.g. Hegselmann and Krause 2002; Deffuant et al. 2002). Both imitation and opinion dynamics models have their theoretical foundations in natural science dynamic models rather than the social sciences. Social learning models are a recent development relying on cognitively more complex agents than traditional agent-based models.

As an example of a model of diffusion, we focus on Epstein (2000). Epstein states two macro phenomena of normative behaviour: (a) norms are locally stable, i.e. a group of agents close to each other tend to adhere to the same norms and (b) norms are globally diverse. A micro assumption of the model is that agents adhere to norms "without thinking about them". The model starts by defining a binary norm and defining a norm change mechanism for agents. Norm change depends on two variables: the local environment and the amount of thinking about behaviour an agent does. At each step, an agent checks the norm of its neighbours within a personal vision radius. If the agent is in accord with its surrounding it keeps its norm and decreases its vision radius (less thinking). If it is not in accord it changes the norm and increases its vision radius (more thinking). The model results show the desired macro-behaviour, leading to local conformity and global diversity of norms. Agents at the heart of a norm no longer think about their behaviour whereas those at the borderline between norms have to choose between competing local norms. The model also captures the re-emergence of norm differentiation after a shock to the system. The model assumes: (a) the automatic adoption of the majority norm (b) habitual behaviour when agents are in a stable norm-environment, and (c) the non-enforcement of norms.

4.2.3 *Autonomous Agents Collaborating*

The distributed artificial intelligence origin of agent-based modelling is often referred to as the study of multi-agent systems. Multi-agent systems have a host of different applications such as disaster management, workflow scheduling, e-commerce, information retrieval and management, human-computer interfaces, virtual environments and games, Wooldridge (2002, Chap. 11). In multi-agent systems the starting point of formalisation is a distributed system of agents, each solving a component part of a larger task or problem.

The standard definition of multi-agent systems as a "system of autonomous, intelligent, interacting agents" sounds similar to our definition of an agent-based model in Sect. 4.1. Multi-agent systems were originally conceived as an application for problem solving in scenarios that were too hard or impossible to solve by a single system (e.g. disaster planning, e-commerce). The advantages of multi-agent systems over monolithic systems are that agents can execute actions in parallel, the systems are modular, making additions of new agents and hence new capacities relatively easy, and separate agents can represent different goals. Multiple agents are particularly important for the representation of conflicting goals because a single system would have to reason with inconsistency.

Multi-agent systems researchers are interested in exploiting the fact that different agents can work together to solve a problem, (Wooldridge 2002). The central problem of multi-agent systems is the coordination of autonomous agents trying to achieve their own goals. By design, multi-agent systems give up central control in favour of agents' autonomy but the overall system still needs to be controlled, just not necessarily by a central controller. For example, planning to complete a task in multi-agent systems can happen on different levels of agent autonomy. Following Durfee (1999), Wooldridge distinguishes the following three levels of autonomy Wooldridge (2002, p. 218).

1. *Centralised planning for distributed plans:* a centralized planning system develops a plan for a group of agents, in which the division and ordering of labour is defined. This 'master' agent then distributes the plan to the 'slaves', who then execute their part of the plan.
2. *Distributed planning:* a group of agents cooperate to form a centralized plan. Typically, the component agents will be 'specialists' in different aspects of the overall plan, and will contribute to a part of it. However, the agents that form the plan will not be the ones to execute it; their role is merely to generate the plan.
3. *Distributed planning for distributed plans:* a group of agents cooperate to form individual plans of action, dynamically coordinating their activities along the way. The agents may be selfinterested, and so, when potential coordination problems arise, they may need to be resolved by negotiation.

Agent-based modelling and multi-agent systems have an overlapping interest in the question of social control but they approach it from different vantage points. Whereas agent-based modellers ask how social control can come about given a set of autonomous agents (i.e. the emergence of social control), traditional multi-agent systems developers ask how a set of agents can be controlled (i.e. the constraint of the system). The problem for multi-agent systems is how to ensure the autonomy of agents within a smooth running, i.e. controlled system (Table 4.3).

The central aim of multi-agent systems is thus slightly different from the aim of agent-based models. The latter try to find explanations. By generating

Table 4.3 A comparison of agent-based modelling and multi-agent systems

Agent-based modelling	Multi-agent systems
Large number of simple agents	Small number of complex agents
Agents defined by their behaviour	Agents defined by their cognition
Social norms emerge from interactions	Social norms regulate interactions
Social norms change	Social norms are 'hard wired'
Simple communication	Complex communication

social phenomena from micro-behaviour, the goal is to uncover the underlying mechanisms. Multi-agent systems research is not interested in the explanation of norms but rather in how they can be used to coordinate agent behaviour, whether the norms emerge from interactions, are implemented into the agent directly (as in a BOID agent) or are built into the system (e.g. a centralised planner). Whilst explanatory agent-based models have to resemble in some way the dynamics of the target system, multi-agent systems often do not set out to model an external system. A normative multi-agent system might be judged on whether it implements agents autonomously, whether it runs smoothly, and whether it might be useful in a real world application but it matters less whether it simulates any actual social process.

4.3 Explanation, Application and Prediction

Why do we build simulation models at all? We are all familiar with simulations in every day life. We know flight or racing car simulations in seaside arcades, read about simulations of car crashes to test a car's safety, see a simulation of the weather every night on television and in the previous sections we described simulations of social norms. All these simulations have different motivations. A computer animated flight simulator might be built to train a pilot, in which case it is important that the simulation responds accurately to the pilot's manipulation of controls. If it is a flight or racing car simulator in an arcade, the purpose is fun and the most important feature is the visual animation. The car crash and weather simulations are used to predict the behaviour of the car in an accident and the weather. The car is a system governed by the laws of Newtonian mechanics and the simulation is executed mainly because testing real cars in crashes is costly. The weather is a complex system of which we know the general laws that govern the dynamics but slight changes in initial conditions might lead to big differences in the system's behaviour. Agent-based models deriving from game theory and complexity science use simulation to elucidate the mechanisms underlying the emergence and diffusion of social norms. Multi-agent systems, in contrast, use social norms as a way of constraining the action choices of autonomous agents. In this section we discuss some of the methodological and epistemological implications resulting from the different motivations for modelling and simulation. We will tackle one potential misunderstanding of agent-based modelling: the purpose of agent-based models is (usually) not prediction but the examination of mechanisms and dynamics that *explain* social phenomena. But what does it mean to explain a phenomenon? And what is the relationship between explanation and prediction?

In the first principled study of explanations in the philosophy of science, explanation and prediction were inextricably linked (Hempel and Oppenheim 1948). This link is a logical equivalence between prediction and explanation called the *symmetry thesis* stating that the logical structure of both explanation and prediction is the same and the only difference is the temporal orientation (prediction is future oriented whereas explanation is about the past). Essentially, if we can predict that a phenomenon will occur, we know what brings it about and thus have explained it. This equivalence resulted from a specific model of explanations, the *covering law model*. In the covering law model, an explanation is a deduction of the explanans from a (set of) general law(s) plus initial conditions.

The identification of prediction and explanation has long been debated, ever since the covering law model was proposed (see e.g. Rescher 1957) resulting in a proliferation of ideas about explanation divorced from prediction. Explanation learned to stand on its own as the goal of science with prediction relegated to the fringes.

For example, in a recent discussion on the epistemology of agent-based modelling, Epstein (2008) deliberately cuts the cord between prediction and explanation, saying that there are many other reasons for modelling. He is certainly right in arguing that prediction is not the sole justification of a model, in particular prediction as commonly defined in the natural sciences, i.e. predicting at a detailed level what will happen to a system or parts of a system in the future. Against this rather defensive position, Thompson and Derr (2009) argue that explanation and prediction must not and need not be divorced, but the notion of prediction needs to be widened to include more general predictions, such as "earthquakes happen" as a prediction of tectonic plate theory. Troitzsch (2009) makes an important distinction between three levels of specificity of predictions. He also distinguishes between stochastic and deterministic predictions. His solution to the debate on prediction and explanation is that any good explanation will yield at least a prediction of type one:

> Which kinds of behaviour can be expected [from a system like this] under arbitrarily given parameter combinations and initial conditions? (Troitzsch 2009, 1.1)

Sometimes it will even yield an explanation of type two:

> Which kind of behaviour will a given target system (whose parameters and previous states may or may not have been precisely measured) display in the near future? (Troitzsch 2009, 1.1)

It is, however, not necessary for an explanation to provide a prediction of type three:

> Which state will the target system reach in the near future, again given parameters and previous states which may or may not have been precisely measured? (Troitzsch 2009, 1.1)

Troitzsch's reply to Thompson and Derr's weakening of the notion of prediction to the prediction "earthquakes occur" from plate tectonics, is that humanity will know that fact after experiencing the first earthquake without needing any theory at all.

For Troitzsch the problem of prediction and explanation is a purely epistemic one of not knowing the initial conditions of a system well enough to warrant more detailed prediction. Troitzsch concludes that the symmetry thesis of explanation and prediction is alive and well "from a logic al point of view but not from a practical point of view" (Troitzsch 2009, 1.6).

Thus the interpretation of the symmetry thesis is that explanations and predictions are logically equivalent but due to a lack of knowledge of initial conditions we might have non-predictive explanations. It does not answer the problem of non-explanatory predictions.

The problem of non-explanatory predictions has been discussed widely in the philosophical literature. In Salmon (1978)'s "Why ask, 'Why?'?", he argues that if we had all the information in a deterministic world and are able to predict any future states exactly, we would still want more, an answer to Why-questions. The reason why we would still want such answers is that we would want knowledge of the underlying mechanisms bringing about the future states.

In a world where we *can not* predict everything perfectly, we need answers to Why-questions to provide knowledge of the underlying mechanisms because they help us make better predictions. Douglas (2009) argues along those lines that the symmetry thesis does not give an adequate account of explanation but neither does any account leaving out prediction altogether. For her, explanations are tools to help us generate predictions by providing conceptualisations of the world.

> Explanations help us to organize the complex world we encounter, making it cognitively manageable (which may be why they also give us a sense of understanding). (Douglas 2009, p. 454)

This cognitive account of explanation and prediction together with Troitzsch's different layers of system state prediction give us a handle on agent-based modelling.

For example, Gilbert et al. (2008) develop an agent based model of the English housing market. In this model there are agents acting as buyers, sellers and realtors (estate agents) according to different goals and intentions, leading to different roles in market interactions. The environment is a grid with houses of initially random values. The agents have different incomes and savings and are on different steps of the housing ladder (e.g. first time buyers). The model implements a host of economic variables, such as interest rates, inflation, income distribution etc. One of the most interesting outcomes of the model is that the level of interest rates has much less influence on house prices than the number of first time buyers entering the market. The model was published in 2008 and shortly afterwards the banking crisis was followed by the stagnation of the housing market. The banking crisis led to a lack of first time buyers as banks suddenly wanted a large deposit for mortgages, resulting in many people no longer being able to afford to enter the market as first time buyers.

This led to many properties staying on the market for a long time until the sellers reduced the price. The lack of first time buyers most likely contributed to the state of the market. The model of the housing market did not predict the housing market disruption but it did help to understand the influence of different parameters, such as interest rates, and model first time buyers' difficulty in securing mortgages, etc. on house prices.

This model of the English housing market is a prime example of how a simulation can help to explore mechanisms underlying phenomena, and can make predictions that can be tested empirically, e.g. the lack of first time buyers entering the markets will lead to a fall in house prices, but which is not predictive of the target system. In contrast to a *causal explanation* for which prediction and explanation are symmetric, this kind of explanation is called a *mechanism explanation* and does not have to satisfy the symmetry thesis (see Douglas 2009 for a discussion on mechanism explanations and prediction). A mechanisms explanation can be seen as a kind of causal explanation for complex systems (Machamer et al. 2000) and is the appropriate explanatory model to use in the context of agent-based modelling (Elsenbroich 2012).

4.4 Conclusion

There are some interesting and innovative features in agent-based modelling. First, social phenomena can be generated dynamically from some more or less simple agent specifications, (Epstein 2006). This dynamic approach is too rarely found in the social sciences where most studies are based on theories that are a-temporal, that is, have no time dimension and so no conception of social change. Generating the dynamics behind social phenomena also means there is some test of whether the agent specifications are right by comparing the simulation outcome to the real world.

Secondly, agent-based models can model heterogeneous agents. Whilst mathematical models need to make the assumption that agents are uniform, in agent-based models agents can vary in their preferences, behaviours, capabilities or any other attribute. This leads to the possibility of modelling human interactions more realistically.

Thirdly, agent-based models can model both the micro behaviour of agents and the macro influences on those micro behaviours. Agent-based modelling is particularly good at showing the emergence of macro phenomena from micro behaviours. In addition, agent-based modelling can show how these emergent phenomena can in turn affect micro behaviour. Agents can perceive other agents and the environment and as these change in the simulation, each agent can adapt its own behaviour to the new circumstances. There are different ways in which to implement this micro-macro link; a good example model is Lorscheid and Troitzsch's 2009 model of normative behaviour we discuss in more detail in Sect. 9.3.4.

Fourthly, agent-based modelling is a methodological tool that can be used to make the most of scarce and patchy data (Gilbert 2008). By using relatively little data (for example qualitative, ethnographic data) we can generate behaviour rules for agents, hypothesising that what we have found on the small scale is generalisable. In running the simulation we can test this hypothesis by comparing the simulation outcomes to data from the real world.

References

Abdou, M., Hamill, L., & Gilbert, N. (2012). Designing and building an agent-based model. In J. Heppenstal, A. Crooks, L. See, & M. Batty (Eds.), *Agent-based models of geographical systems* (pp. 141–165). Dordrecht/New York: Springer.

Anderson, J. R., & Lebiere, C. (1998). *The atomic components of thought*. Mahwah: Erlbaum.

Axelrod, R. (1984). *The evolution of cooperation*. New York: Basic Books.

Axelrod, R. (1986). An evolutionary approach to norms. *American Political Science Review, 80*(4), 1095–1111.

Balci, O. (1994). Validation, verification and testing techniques throughout the life cycle of a simulation study. *Annals of Operations Research, 53*, 121–173.

Berlekamp, E., Conway, J., & Guy, R. (1982). *Winning ways for your mathematical plays. Vol. 2: Games in particular*. London: Academic.

Boella, G., & van der Torre, L. (2004). An agent oriented ontology of social reality. In *Proceedings of FOIS'04*, Amsterdam (pp. 199–209). IOS Press.

Castelfranchi, C., Dignum, F., Jonker, C. M., & Treur, J. (1999). Deliberate normative agents: Principles and architecture. In N. Jennings & Y. Lesperance (Eds.), *Intelligent agents VI. Volume proceedings of the sixth international workshop on agent theories, architectures, and languages ATAL'99*, Orlando (pp. 364–378).

Chattoe-Brown, E. (2010). Gin and tonic or oil and water? Can we integrate research methods rather than just "mixing" them? A case study of social mobility research. http://www2.le.ac.uk/departments/sociology/people/echattoebrown/publications.

Chrisley, R. (2003). Embodied artificial intelligence. *Artificial Intelligence, 149*, 131–150.

Deffuant, G., Amblard, F., Weisbuch, G., & Faure, T. (2002). How can extremism prevail? A study based on the relative agreement interaction model. *Journal of Artificial Societies and Social Simulation*, 5(4), 1. http://jasss.soc.surrey.ac.uk/5/4/1.html.

Dignum, F., Morley, D., Sonnenberg, E., & Cavedon, L. (2000). Towards socially sophisticated BDI agents. In E. Dufree (Ed.), *Proceedings of the international conference on multi-agent systems, ICMAS'00*, Boston (pp. 111–118).

Douglas, H. E. (2009). Reintroducing prediciton to explanation. *Philosophy of Science, 76*, 444–463.

Durfee, E. H. (1999). Distributed problem solving and planning. In G. Weiss (Ed.), *Multiagent systems* (pp. 121–164). Cambridge: MIT.

Elsenbroich, C. (2012). Explanation in agent-based modelling: Functions, causality or mechanisms? *Journal of Artificial Societies and Social Simulation, 15*(3), 1.

Epstein, J. (2000). Learning to be thoughtless: Social norms and individual computing. Technical report, Center on Social and Economic Dynamics Working Paper, No. 6.

Epstein, J. M. (2006). *Generative social science studies in agent-based computational modeling*. Princeton: Princeton University Press.

Epstein, J. M. (2008). Why model? *Journal of Artificial Societies and Social Simulation, 11*(4), 12.

Epstein, J. M., & Axtell, R. (1996). *Growing artificial societies: Social science from the bottom up*. Washington, DC: Brookings Institution Press.

Flentge, F., Polani, D., & Uthmann, T. (2001). Modelling the emergence of possession norms using memes. *Journal of Artificial Societies and Social Simulation, 4*(4), 3. http://jasss.soc.surrey.ac.uk/4/4/3.html.

Gatherer, D. (2002). Identifying cases of social contagion using memetic isolation: Comparison of the dynamics of a multisociety simulation with an ethnographic data set. *Journal of Artificial Societies and Social Simulation, 5*(4), 5.

Gilbert, N. (2008). *Agent-based models* (Number 153 in quantitative applications in the social sciences). Los Angeles: Sage.

Gilbert, N., & Troitzsch, K. G. (2005). *Simulation for the social scientist* (2nd ed.). Maidenhead/New York: Open University Press.

Gilbert, N., Hawksworth, J. C., & Swinney, P. A. (2008). An agent-based model of the uk housing market. Technical report, CRESS University of Surrey, http://cress.soc.surrey.ac.uk/housingmarket/ukhm.html.

Hegselmann, R. (2012). Thomas C. Schelling and the computer some notes on Schelling's essay "On Letting a Computer Help With the Work". *Journal of Artificial Societies and Social Simulation, 15*(4), 9.

Hegselmann, R., & Krause, U. (2002). Opinion dynamics and bounded confidence: Models, analysis and simulation. *Journal of Artificial Societies and Social Simulation, 5*(3), 2. http://jasss.soc.surrey.ac.uk/5/3/2.html.

Hempel, C. G., & Oppenheim, P. (1948). Studies in the logic of explanation. *Philosophy of Science, 15*, 135–175.

Hirschi, T. (1969). *Causes of delinquency*. Berkely: University of California Press.

Iozzi, F. (2008). A simple implementation of Schelling's segregation model in netlogo. Working papers 015, Centre for Research on Social Dynamics (DONDENA), Università Commerciale Luigi Bocconi.

Lorscheid, I., & Troitzsch, K. G. (2009). How do agents learn to behave normatively? Machine learning concepts for norm learning in the emil project. In B. Edmonds & N. Gilbert (Eds.), *Proceedings of the sixth conference of ESSA*, Guilford.

Machamer, P., Darden, L., & Craver, C. F. (2000). Thinking about mechanisms. *Philosophy of Science, 67*, 1–25.

Mirowski, P. (1999). *More heat than light: Economics as social physics, physics as nature's economics*. Polity Press in association with Blackwell Publishers, Cambridge University Press.

Neumann, M. (2009). Dissecting the BOID perspective on norms. In B. Edmonds & N. Gilbert (Eds.), *Proceedings of the Sixth Conference of ESSA*, Guilford.

Newell, A. (1990). *Unified theories of cognition*. Cambridge: Harvard University Press.

Ngo, T. A., & See, L. M. (2012). Calibration and validation of agent-based models of land cover change. In J. Heppenstal, A. Crooks, L. See, & M. Batty (Eds.), *Agent-based models of geographical systems*. Dordrecht/New York: Springer.

Rescher, N. (1957). On prediction and explanation. *British Journal for the Philosophy of Science, 8*, 281–290.

Salmon, W. (1978). Why ask, 'Why?'? An inquiry concerning scientific explanation. *Proceedings and Addresses of the American Philosophical Association, 51*, 683–705.

Schelling, T. (1971). Dynamic models of segregation. *Journal of Mathematical Sociology, 1*, 143–186.

Thompson, N. S., & Derr, P. (2009). Contra Epstein, good explanations predict. *Journal of Artificial Societies and Social Simulation, 12*(1), 9.

Troitzsch, K. G. (2009). Not all explanations predict satisfactorily, and not all good predictions explain. *Journal of Artificial Societies and Social Simulation, 12*(1), 10.

Wilensky, U. (1997). NetLogo segregation model. Technical report, Center for Connected Learning and Computer-Based Modeling, Northwestern University, Evanston.

Wilensky, U. (2003). *NetLogo ising model*. Center for Connected Learning and Computer-Based Modeling, Northwestern University, Evanston.

Wooldridge, M. (2002). *An introduction to multi-agent systems*. Chichester: Wiley.

Yang, L., & Gilbert, N. (2008). Getting away from numbers: Using qualitative observation for agent-based modeling. *Advances in Complex Systems, 11*(2), 175–185.

Chapter 5
The Environment and Social Norms

> *The presentations and conceptions of the average man of the world are formed and dominated, not by the full and pure desire for knowledge as an end in itself, but by the struggle to adapt himself favourably to the conditions of life.*
>
> Ernst Mach

5.1 Social Norms Situated in Space and Time

This chapter discusses the simplest form of agent-based models of norms, environmental models. Chapter 3 concluded with a comparison of theories of normative behaviour and crime. We identified a surprising lack of similarity despite the conceptual closeness of the topics. In particular, we highlighted the prevalence of environmental explanations of crime but the lack of the environment in discussions of social norms. In contrast, agent-based models of social norms do take the environment as an important aspect of normative behaviour. We discuss *Sugarscape* as an example model of environmentally situated norm emergence and some models based on *Sugarscape* elucidating the function of norms for society. We also discuss an agent-based model of crime dispersion as an example of an agent-based model in criminology.

5.1.1 Sugarscape *and the Emergence of Norms*

This section discusses one of the classic models of social norms, based on the *Sugarscape* model in which Axtell and Epstein implement a host of social phenomena, from market mechanisms to war. The implementations are discussed in detail in Epstein and Axtell (1996). We have already briefly considered the version that examines wealth distribution in Sect. 4.1.1.

C. Elsenbroich and N. Gilbert, *Modelling Norms*, DOI 10.1007/978-94-007-7052-2_5,

The starting point of *Sugarscape* is an environment of resources, in this case, sugar. Patches are allocated different sugar levels forming a landscape with two sugar peaks descending into a surrounding low sugar valleys. Agents have several attributes. They have a *metabolism rate*, an *age*, a *sex*, a *fertility level*, a *sugar level*, a *vision range*, a *a cultural flag* and an unlimited sugar carrying capacity. The metabolism rate determines the amount of sugar an agent needs for its survival. The age determines whether the agent is still procreating or not and the time of death (agents have a maximum age). In order to procreate, two agents of the opposite sex and with sufficient fertility levels have to meet. The sugar level determines how rich an agent is, the vision range how far it can source food from and the cultural flag is a set of binary tags standing for the cultural attributes of an agent. Patches and agents have a set of behaviour rules:

1. M-agent: movement rule. Find maximum sugar cell in vision range. If more than one, choose the closest. Go to cell and collect all the sugar from the cell.
2. S-agent: sex rule. If (a) agent is fertile, (b) within age range and (c) has at least as much sugar as at its birth: select a neighbour from the Neumann neighbourhood. If the neighbour is fertile, of opposite sex, and there is at least one unoccupied cell neighbouring either agent, place a new agent on the empty patch. Characteristics are inherited from parents. The sugar level of an offspring is the sum of half the sugar levels that the parents had at their birth. If the initial agent still has sugar, reproduce again.
3. K-agent: cultural transmission rule. Choose one tag of a neighbour. If that tag is different from that of the choosing agent, set the tag to the value of the choosing agent's tag. Do nothing otherwise.
4. $G\alpha$-patch: sugar grow-back rule. Sugar regrows by α units until the cell maximum is reached. The overall landscape is a torus with two sugar peaks.

Migration, wealth distribution and similar mechanisms can be seen quickly with this setup. By adding a second resource, spice, an agent's preference for either spice or sugar, and an exchange mechanism for sugar and spice between agents, market mechanisms are generated. The cultural tags do not influence behaviour directly but can encode attributes such as whether an agent is a sugar or spice lover or which group or tribe it belongs to an implementation of tribal conflict.

We will encounter *Sugarscape* at various points in the book as it is the basis for many models of social norms.

5.1.2 Function of Norms for Society

Conte and Castelfranchi (1995) examine the effects of normative behaviour on a society of agents. The parameters investigated are aggression levels in society, the average strength of agents and the variability of strength. The setup is a 10×10 *Sugarscape* grid with food and agents in random locations. Agents have six actions they can execute: *eat, move-to-food-seen, move-to-food-smelled, aggress,*

	Str	st. dev.	Var	st. dev.	Agg	st. dev.
Blind	4287	204	1443	58	9235	661
Strategic	4727	135	1775	59	4634	248
Normative	5585	27	604	41	3018	76

Fig. 5.1 The effect of the three strategies, blind aggression, strategic aggression and normative behaviour on the society. Overall it seems that normative behaviour has the most positive effects. Strength is higher, society is more equal and aggression is much lower

move-random and *pause*. All actions last one tick except for eat, which lasts two. Agents' ability to see is restricted to the four surrounding patches; their ability to smell goes two patches further in each direction. If an agent moves towards smelled food it does not know whether another agent might already be eating it. If an agent finds another agent eating it can consider attacking the agent. All actions, except 'pause', have a cost. A move to an adjacent patch costs 1 unit of resources. Attacking another agent has an associated cost of 4 units.

An experiment consist of 2,000 ticks. Fifty agents with initial strength of 40 and 25 food items with a nutritional value of 20 are randomly allocated on the grid. The experiments compare three strategies:

1. *Blind Aggression:* In this strategy an agent attacks another agent that is eating food unless there is free food available on one of the other three patches the agent can perceive.
2. *Strategic Aggression:* An agent attacks another agent that is eating food, unless that agent is stronger or there is free food available on one of the other three patches the agent can perceive.
3. *Normative:* The 'finders keeper' norm is implemented as follows: Agents become owners of the food that is in their initial von Neumann neighbourhood. Food is flagged so that all agents know to whom it belongs. Agents cannot attack an agent eating its own food.

Homogenous societies, i.e. societies in which all agents are the same, are compared for the parameters *average strength* (Str), *variability of strength* (Var) and *aggression* (Agg) (this is the number of attacks over the whole experiment). The results can be seen in Fig. 5.1. Normative behaviour comes out as overall the most beneficial for society. The average strength of agents is significantly higher than for the other strategies, the number of aggressive interactions is much lower and the society is more equitable (the variability is lowest).

The above simulation analyses homogenous societies, i.e. all agents employ the same strategy. In Castelfranchi et al. (1998) the question of heterogenous societies is addressed. The general experimental setup is the same, but with the population split so that each half follows a different strategy. Comparisons are made between Blind/Strategic, Blind/Normative and Strategic/Normative. This simple amendment makes the normative strategy exploitable by other agents, in particular the strategic ones. The experiment is expanded by a redistribution of the cost of normative behaviour using a reputation mechanism.

	Str	st. dev.	Var	st. dev.	Agg	st. dev.
Blind	4142	335	1855	156	4686	451
Strategic	4890	256	1287	102	2437	210
Blind	5221	126	1393	86	4911	229
Normative	4124	187	590	80	1856	74
Strategic	5897	85	1219	72	3168	122
Normative	3634	134	651	108	2034	71

Fig. 5.2 Comparative data for mixed (50%/50%) populations. Normativity is detrimental for individual agents

	Str	st. dev.	Var	st. dev.	Agg	st. dev.
Cheaters	4968	309	2130	108	2417	227
Respectfuls	4734	301	737	136	2031	253

Fig. 5.3 Respectfuls perform nearly as well as Cheaters and achieve a much more equitable society when they communicate their social knowledge

Agents now hold information about the behaviour of other agents. An agent can either be a "Respectful" or a "Cheater". All agents are assumed to be Respectfuls at the start. In this setup, a normative agent behaves normatively towards a Respectful agent, but if it learns that an agent is a Cheater the norm is lifted and the agent can be attacked (strategically). Two experiments were conducted using this setup. In the first, agents only gain knowledge from their own experience and in the second, communication between normative agents is added. This means that normative agents can attack Cheaters without having had previous experience with them.

First, the results from the experiments with mixed populations. The normative agents are outperformed by both the strategic and the blindly aggressive agents in terms of strength. The aggression of normative agents is much lower as is the variance between agents. Although normative agents are beneficial for society by reducing aggression and inequality, the normative strategy is detrimental for the individual agent, as can be seen in Fig. 5.2.

The results from the experiment without communication are even worse for normative agents, with the Cheaters, i.e. the strategic agents, increasing their strength slightly. It thus seems that individual knowledge about reputation does not help agents to make informed choices about whom to trust. This situation changes in the last experiment in which Respectfuls can exchange information about other agents' reputation. When two Respectfuls meet they exchange information about which agents are Cheaters. This way, agents can make an informed choice about whether to interact with a Cheater. Figure 5.3 shows the results for this communication experiment. These results suggest that social knowledge, i.e. knowledge of the reputation of other agents, is only useful if it is obtained not only by personal experience but also from other agents. The reason is that encountering a Cheater is costly for a Respectful whereas obtaining knowledge of cheating from others is free and enables the Respectful to avoid Cheaters.

	Str	st. dev.	Var	st. dev.	Agg	st. dev.
Blind	4832	37	202	31	14153	125
Strategic	5935	29	244	32	5844	76
Normative	7387	27	77	10	1835	67

Fig. 5.4 Equal inheritance, $\alpha_i = \alpha_j = 0.5$

	Str	st. dev.	Var	st. dev.	Agg	st. dev.
Blind	4852	34	7662	836	14059	130
Strategic	5958	32	9304	1074	5790	67
Normative	7404	29	11392	1227	1808	67

Fig. 5.5 Unequal inheritance, $\alpha_i = 0.9.\alpha_j = 0.1$

In Saam and Harrer (1999) the authors expand on the work by Conte and Castelfranchi (1995) and Castelfranchi et al. (1998). We have seen that normative behaviour results in favourable outcomes for society by lowering aggression, and increasing strength and overall equality. Saam and Harrer contend that this positive effect of normative behaviour is reserved for egalitarian societies. They replicate the model and build two extensions. The first investigates the effect of inheritance on measurements of strength, aggression and equality. Strength is passed on from parents to children with two agents producing two offspring, giving each a proportion α_i of their combined strength. Experiments are conducted with equal inheritance, $\alpha_i = \alpha_j = 0.5$, and with very unequal inheritance, $\alpha_i = 0.9$ and $\alpha_j = 0.1$. The parent agents die after reproduction.

The second extension investigates the effect of unequal renewal of resources (also known as the "Matthew Effect", see Merton 1968). Whereas before, food was replenished at random patches with a constant nutritional value of 20, now, if the patch has an agent on it, the nutritional value of the food is dependent on the strength of that agent. The higher the agent's strength, the higher the nutritional value (v) of the food.

$$v_t = 20 + \beta(s_{t-1} - 40) \tag{5.1}$$

Their version gives qualitatively similar results to the original model, suggesting that the replication was successful. However, when the model is extended with inequality measures, the unequal inheritance of strength from parents to children and the unequal regrowth of food causes the normative behaviour's advantage for society to break down. Figures 5.4 and 5.5 show the values for the equal inheritance of strength by offspring (0.5 each) and a severely unequal inheritance (0.9, 0.1 respectively). Overall agent strength stays about the same as does the aggression level for all three strategies. However, there is an explosion of inequality with the normative strategy leading to the worst, i.e. most unequal, outcome and blind aggression leading to the most equal outcome.

The unequal renewal of resources also results in the normative strategy losing its equalising function. Three experiments are conducted using the regrowth formula (5.1) with β-values 0.2, 10 and 0.037. For the values 0.2 and 10 there is a time restriction for the consumption of resources. An agent needs two rounds to eat a portion of 20 nutrition units. A food item is split into n nutrition units of 20; an agent thus needs $n \times 2$ time steps to consume it. For the β-value 0.0375 the authors removed the time restriction. A comparison between $\beta = 0.2$ and $\beta = 10$ shows that a higher Matthew effect leads to much higher inequality with values rising by 50–60 % for blind and strategic aggression, and for the normative strategy almost tripling, going from 2,275 to 7,879. However, aggression is significantly lower for all three strategies. When the time restriction is lifted, even the low Matthew effect of 0.0375 leads to extremely high values of strength, inequality and aggression. This model shows that the benefit of normative behaviour is interdependent with other societal variables such as how egalitarian a society is.

Environmental models of norms use the environment to represent resources. Norms are equated with property norms. One major research question is the function of social norms on society. Although they examine the functional aspect of social norms for society, these models are not teleological. Normative behaviour does not come about *because* it is beneficial for society. The benefits of social norms are generated from independently defined micro behaviours of agents.

5.2 An Agent-Based Model of Routine Activity Theory

Although simulation methodology has been taken up in criminology better than in other social sciences, agent-based modelling has been relatively slow in making an impact. This has changed rapidly in the recent past with pioneering models such as van Baal (2004) modelling deterrence (see Sect. 6.2.1) and more recently Groff (2007) modelling street robbery, Brantingham and Tita (2008) modelling offender mobility, Dray et al. (2008) modelling crime prevention interventions and Bosse et al. (2010) modelling police deployment. Malleson (2012) gives an overview how to use agent-based modelling in crime research.

In Chap. 3 we discussed routine activity theory as a theoretical approach based on human ecology, locating the causes of crime in the environment. Its origin in human ecology makes routine activity theory a perfect theory for simulation. A very simple implementation of routine activity theory in an agent-based model is the Cops & Robbers simulation discussed in Birks et al. (2008). The model reports crime and detection rates from the interactions of three kinds of agents: offenders, targets and guardians. A *crime* occurs when an offender and target happen to be on the same patch, unless there is a guardian present. If a guardian is present a *detection* of crime occurs. This simple model can give some idea of the interaction between the density of agents of different kinds, for instance by how much does the number of detections increase if the number of cops is doubled.

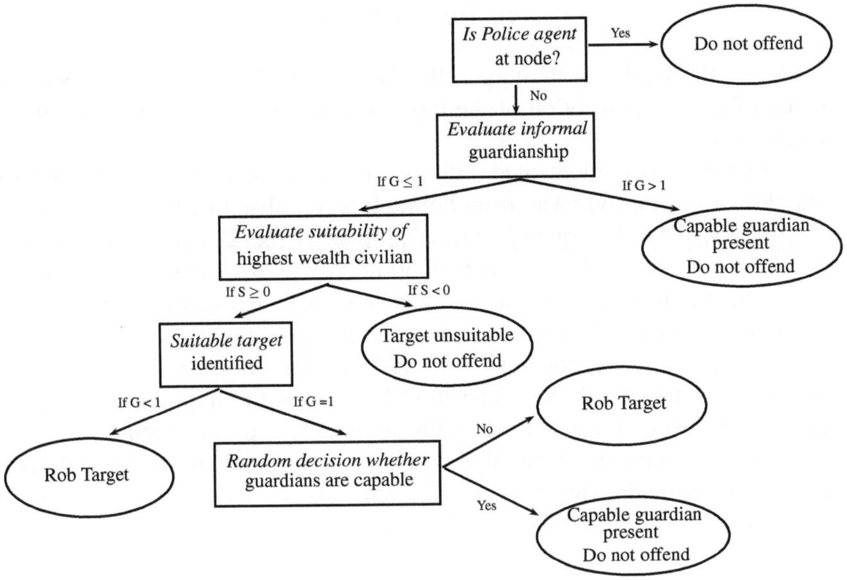

Fig. 5.6 Decision tree of potential offender (Groff 2007, p. 89, Fig. 2)

A more involved implementation of routine activity theory into an agent-based model is developed in Groff (2007). The paper sets two research hypotheses:

1. Does the shift of routine activities away from home increase the incidence of street robberies?
2. What is the impact of increasing time spent away from home on the spatial pattern of street robberies?

In order to facilitate interpretation, the initial model is made as simple as possible, implementing only the core concepts of routine activity (Groff 2007, p. 80). There are two types of agents in the population, civilians and police officers. Civilians can be offenders, victims and guardians. Police officers are only guardians but whereas civilians present at a potential crime scene *might* deter crime, a police officer *always* deters crime. The environment is an actual cityscape, in this case Seattle, Washington.

The decision tree in Fig. 5.6 is based on two equations. The first determines whether a guardian is capable or not.

$$G = (N_A - 2) + P_G \tag{5.2}$$

where N_A is the number of agents at the location and P_G is the perception of capability of guardians who are present (a uniform random number between -2 and 2). The second determines whether a target is suitable for robbery, i.e. whether its wealth is great enough.

$$S = (W_T - W_A) + P_S \tag{5.3}$$

where W_T is the wealth of the target, W_A the wealth of the potential offender and P_S is the offender's perception of the target's suitability (a uniform random value between -1 and 1).

The simulation is implemented with five different values between 30 and 70 % for the time agents spend away from home. It is initialised with 1,000 agents, 200 police officers, and a 20 % rate of criminal propensity (i.e. 200 agents might commit a crime). The initial wealth of agents is 50 units with a standard deviation of 20. After a certain number of ticks there is a payday and each agent receives 5 wealth units. During a robbery, 1 unit of wealth is forfeit by the target.

Groff's first hypothesis concerns the interdependency of time spent at home with the number of street robberies. The model confirms the hypothesis, with street robberies increasing almost linearly with the increase in time agents spend away from home. The number of possible incidents, i.e. situations where a motivated offender and a potential victim meet, rise even faster as does the number of crimes deterred by police (Groff 2007, p. 93, Table 4).

The second hypothesis was about the spatial pattern of robbery. The model is implemented on a map of Seattle. Locations are implemented as road intersections, which Groff calls nodes. As time away from home increases, the concentration of robberies at particular nodes increases, as does the spread of crime. Spread increases most between the 30 and 40 % away from home conditions. Thus both hypotheses are corroborated by the model.

5.3 Achievements and Shortcomings

In this chapter we discussed agent-based models of normative and criminal behaviour that use the environment as the factor influencing dynamics. In *Sugarscape*, the environment represents resources and puts a bound on the social interactions agents can have. In the crime simulation, the environment is an actual space, Seattle. The environment also puts a bound on the activities and is used to situate routines and deterrence factors. As to be expected, this implementation of routine activity theory is a purely spatial analysis of crime without touching on social influences on a criminal's decision process. It is nonetheless interesting because it shows the emergence of patterns such as the concentration and spread of crime depending on agent routines. This is rather similar to the spatial patterns resulting from simulations such as *Sugarscape* . Importantly, although agents interact in these models, none of the models have agents influencing each other, and all normative dynamics are transmitted through the environment.

References

Birks, D. J., Donkin, S., & Wellsmith, M. (2008). Synthesis over analysis: Towards an ontology for volume crime simulation. In L. Liu & J. Eck (Eds.), *Artificial crime analysis systems: Using computer simulations and geographic information systems*. Hershey: Idea Group Publishing.

Bosse, T., Elffers, H., & Gerritsen, C. (2010). Simulating the dynamical interaction of offenders, targets and guardians. *Crime Patterns and Analysis, 3*, 51–66.

Brantingham, P. J., & Tita, G. E. (2008). Offender mobility and crime pattern formation from first principles. In L. Liu & J. E. Eck (Eds.), *Artificial crime analysis systems: Using computer simulations and geographic information systems*. Hershey: Idea Group Publishing.

Castelfranchi, C., Conte, R., & Paolucci, M. (1998). Normative reputation and the cost of compliance. *Journal of Artificial Societies and Social Simulation, 1*(3), 3.

Conte, R., & Castelfranchi, C. (1995). Understanding the functions of norms in social groups through simulation. In N. Gilbert & R. Conte (Eds.), *Artificial societies. The computer simulation of social life*. London: UCL Press.

Dray, A., Mazerolle, L. G., Perez, P., & Ritter, A. (2008). Drug law enforcement in an agent-based model: Simulating the disruption. In L. Liu & J. E. Eck (Eds.), *Artificial crime analysis systems: Using computer Simulations and geographic information systems*. Hershey: Idea Group Publishing.

Epstein, J. M., & Axtell, R. (1996). *Growing artificial societies: Social science from the bottom up*. Washington, DC: Brookings Institution Press.

Groff, E. R. (2007). Simulation for theory testing and experimentation: An example using routine activity theory and street robbery. *Journal of Quantitative Criminology, 23*, 75–103.

Malleson, N. (2012). Using agent-based models to simulate crime. In A. J. Heppenstall, A. T. Crooks, L. M. See, & M. Batty (Eds.), *Agent-based models of geographical systems*. Dordrecht/New York: Springer.

Merton, R. K. (1968). The matthew effect in science. *Science, 159*, 56–63.

Saam, N. J., & Harrer, A. (1999). Simulating norms, social inequality, and functional change in artificial societies. *Journal of Artificial Societies and Social Simulation, 2*(1), 2.

van Baal, P. H. M. (2004 dissertation). *Computer simulations of criminal deterrence: From public policy to local interaction to individual behaviour*. Rotterdam: Boom Juridische Uitgevers.

Chapter 6
Punishment and Social Norms

The measure of a man's character is what he would do if he knew he never would be found out.

Thomas Babington Macaulay

6.1 Rational Choice and Game Theory Simulations

This chapter discusses simulation models of normative behaviour starting from rational choice and game theory. We have already discussed rational choice both in the context of theorising norms in the form of individualism in Sect. 2.1.4 and as a criminological theory in Sect. 3.2. We have also discussed social norms as solutions to coordination and strategic interaction games. It became clear that both rational choice theory and game theory were excellent raw material for agent-based models. Both propose an individual decision mechanism in the form of a utility calculation, thus providing the micro-level for an agent-based model. Iterations of many agents executing their rational or strategic decisions lead to macro-phenomena such as conventions or norms. As these iterations are too complicated or complex to execute on paper, agent-based models can provide a 'laboratory' in which to conduct experiments. This chapter describes some examples of this kind of model. We start with game theory simulations by Axelrod that have influenced a huge body of work and continue to influence current research. We then discuss two models that implement deterrence explicitly, first a model of criminal deterrence formulated by van Baal (2004) that is based on Becker's rational choice theory of crime and secondly a model of ostracism as deterrent from de Pinninck et al. (2008).

C. Elsenbroich and N. Gilbert, *Modelling Norms*, DOI 10.1007/978-94-007-7052-2_6,

6.1.1 The Evolution of Cooperation

We have discussed the prisoner's dilemma as a paradigm dilemma of game theory in Sect. 2.1.5. The only rational choice to be made by each agent was to defect as the minimal payoff of defection is greater than the minimal payoff of cooperation. What happens if the prisoner's dilemma is iterated and what are the most successful strategies in repeated interactions? This is the question Axelrod asked himself and in turn others. He asked game theory experts to submit agent strategies for a repeated prisoner's dilemma.

Axelrod (1984) describes the outcomes and how cooperation can evolve in a society of selfish individuals. The submitted strategies were played against each other in computer simulations to see which one got the highest payoff in the long run. The winner was a simple strategy, labelled Tit-for-Tat: cooperate in the first instance and then do whatever the other player did in the previous interaction. Axelrod published these findings and started another round of submissions. Many more strategies were submitted by experts and laymen alike. Tit-for-Tat prevailed as the most successful strategy. Tit-for-Tat is what is called a *nice strategy*, never being the first to defect. It is also provokable, i.e. it retaliates for defection. It is important that retaliation for defection occurs quickly to undermine immediately the idea that defection can pay. Strategies that were 'slower to anger' performed worse than the simple Tit-for-Tat. It is also important to forgive immediately and resume cooperating. The Tit-for-Tat strategy does not set out to do better than the partner. It might thus seem surprising that it leads to high payoffs in the long run. By not trying to outdo one's partner, the strategy scores the medium payoff and rarely ends up empty handed. More complex strategies often perform worse as they try to be too clever guessing the behaviour of the other agent and often get it wrong.

Successful strategies can be summarised as follows:

1. *Be nice:* never be the first to defect.
2. *Be provokable:* retaliate immediately for defection.
3. *Be forgiving:* resume cooperation as soon as possible.
4. *Don't be envious:* do not try to do better than your partner.
5. *Don't try to be too clever:* do not try to scheme your way through games.

What does this have to do with social norms? As we have seen in Chap. 4, one origin of agent-based models of social norms is game theory. Social norms are operationalised as the establishment of cooperation in a population. The possibility of cooperation evolving in a society of selfish agents is a foundation for the possibility of a social norm emerging. The next section will look at the emergence of social norms in a game theoretic framework in more detail.

6.1.2 An Evolutionary Approach to Norms

Following the work on the evolution of cooperation, Axelrod turned to apply game theory to the emergence of social norms as the prevalence of cooperation in a population.

The main ingredients of a social norm, according to Axelrod, are that agents 'usually' adhere to it in a social setting and that defectors are 'often' punished. These rather abstract requirements lead to the conceptualisation of social norms as cooperative behaviour by agents. We have already discussed the setup of this model in Sect. 4.2.1. Let us recap the main points in this section and have a closer look at the results. In the model, agents have a choice between two strategic actions: to cooperate/defect in prisoner's dilemma game and to punish/not-punish if they observe a defection. Each agent's strategy is determined by two parameters: the agent's *boldness* (risk accepted for defection) and the agent's *vengefulness* (likelihood of punishing a defecting agent). In each round agents decide whether to cooperate or defect and if they observe a defection, whether to punish or not. At the end of each round, the payoffs of the agents are calculated. The next generation of agents is initiated as offspring of the current population with differing reproduction rates for different agents. Agents with a payoff exceeding the population average by at least one standard deviation are replicated twice (i.e. they produce two offspring with the same strategy as the parent, subject to mutation) and agents with a payoff at least one standard deviation below the population average are eliminated without being replicated. All other agents are replicated once. The number of players is kept constant in each generation (Axelrod 1986).

This model has quite a number of assumptions. Cooperation, and in turn adherence to social norms, is defined as being costly for the individual. No distinction is made for example between the long term and short term costs of norm adherence. Punishment is carried out by individuals and is also costly; there is no social cost sharing or ostracism option.

Axelrod's original simulation experiments go through 100 generations of agents. When defectors are punished at the cost of the punisher, the 'norm game', norms ultimately collapse. The vengefulness of the population initially reduces defection but after a period of norm adherence, vengefulness levels fall, leading to a rise in defection and irretrievable norm breakdown. Axelrod adds a further twist, the 'meta-norm game', in which an agent that is observed not punishing a defector is punished in addition to the punishment of defectors. In this simulation a wide range of initial conditions result in high levels of cooperation and thus the establishment of a norm.

However, later work shows that the meta-norm game also breaks down eventually and that a much larger number of runs produce relevantly different results (Mahmoud et al. 2010). The authors replicate Axelrod's model and do 10 runs with a duration of 1,000,000 generations each, as opposed to 100 generations in the original. The authors show that rather than a norm emerging due to the establishment of a society with high vengefulness and low boldness, norms break down in those longer run simulations. The reason for the norm breakdown is exactly the same as for the norm game: the society initially eradicates high boldness leading to a decline in vengefulness. If, through mutation, a high boldness agent enters a very low vengefulness society, it will dominate the society as it will not be punished. A longer simulation run increases the chance of such a mutation happening, hence increasing the chance of a norm-breakdown.

Still, the 'norm' and 'meta-norm' games give us an interesting take on the problem of social norms. First, the breakdown of cooperation without punishment shows the difficulty of establishing a social norm if it is costly for individuals. Secondly, the dynamics of decreasing boldness, followed by decreasing vengeance and the possibility of exploitation by a single defecting agent, shows the establishment of cooperation to be volatile.

6.2 Deterrence Simulations

Although punishment plays a role in Axelrod's models of the emergence of cooperation it is only used to diminish the payoff of defection rather than prevent defection directly in the form of deterrence. In this section we discuss models that use deterrence explicitly to define agent behaviour. The first model we discuss is of criminal decision making from van Baal (2004). The second is a model where the sanction is ostracism rather than direct payoff reduction (de Pinninck et al. 2008).

6.2.1 Criminal Deterrence

In van Baal (2004) a simulation model of criminal decision making is described. Agents are boundedly rational agents, i.e. their decision is based purely on the expected utility of the action and they have bounded knowledge regarding the outcome space. The model is a cellular automaton, with each location on the grid representing one agent. Agents situated next to each other are neighbours, i.e. are in each others' social network. At each step, agents decide whether to commit a crime or not. Committing a crime without getting caught has a positive payoff, while norm compliance has a payoff of zero and being audited on committing a crime is sanctioned by a negative payoff (a cost). A law enforcement agency checks agents at random, representing the probability of getting caught. The agent bases its decision on whether the expected payoff of crime is greater than the expected payoff for compliance. The expected payoff is calculated, following Becker, by weighing the potential payoff of transgression against the probability and cost of getting caught. The payoff and cost of transgression is known to the agent. The probability of getting caught (of being audited) is estimated by the agent from its social network. Agents commit a crime if they perceive crime as profitable.

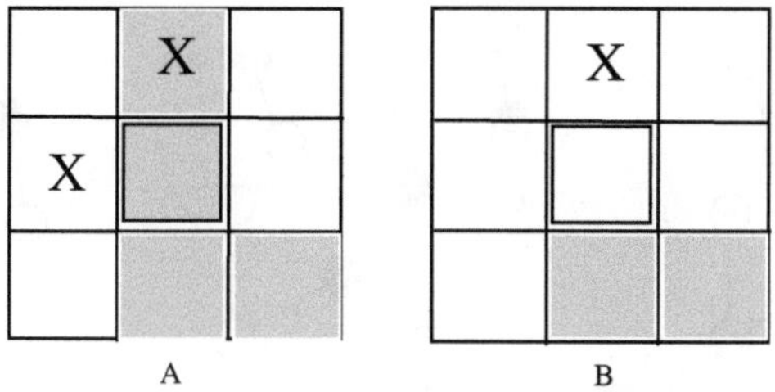

Fig. 6.1 Transgressions (*shaded*) and audits (*X*) is two social networks (van Baal 2004, p. 25, Fig. 2.4)

Figure 6.1 shows the social networks of two agents, A and B. In A's social network, four agents, including A itself, commit a crime, one gets caught and one agent is audited without having committed a crime. In B's social network, two agents commit a crime and one agent is audited without having committed a crime. An agent knows how many agents in its social network commit a crime and it knows if an agent is caught. It does not, however, know about audits of norm compliant agents including itself. This means that agent A will increase its probability of getting caught in the next round, whilst agent B will decrease it.

In the first model only legal sanctions are implemented, meaning the agents use their social network only to estimate the probability of being audited. As expected, higher sanctions and higher audit probabilities lead to higher levels of compliance. Other variables investigated are the size of the assessment gap, i.e. the difference between the estimated and actual audition probability, and the clustering of crime. The assessment gap is particularly large for agents in social networks with little crime committed and for smaller social networks. The reason for this is that agents with little crime in their social networks have less information about assessments as auditing of complying agents is not disclosed. Clustering is higher if agents are homogeneous in their assessment of the audition probability, because agents adjust their assessment probability on almost the same information as their surrounding agents. Heterogeneity of agents undermines this similarity.

A second model adds informal sanctions, implemented as disapproval from an agent's social network. Only complying agents can disapprove. A transgression becomes more costly for an agent the more compliant its social network. Whereas before the social network was only used to calculate the auditing probability, now it has an influence on both the probability and the cost of transgression. This means that the formerly fixed cost of transgression now varies during the simulation.

Social sanctions have a marginal deterrent effect but they do support law enforcement. Their deterrent effect increases as local conformity increases, through the clustering of compliance, which in turn increases the deterrence of social sanctions. There is no influence of social sanctions on the assessment probability.

This model implements a bounded rational choice approach to crime and helps to explore how the restriction of information about the assessment probability to an agent's social network and the severity of legal sanctions influence deterrence.

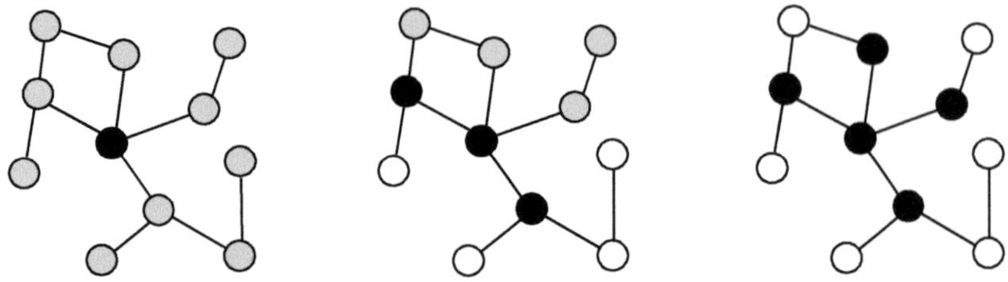

Fig. 6.2 Ostracism in a social network (de Pinninck et al. 2008, p. 303, Fig. 2)

The social sanction extension to the model is influenced by Differential Association Theory (see Sect. 3.4.1) and shows how compliance and transgression within a social network can influence an agent's decision to commit crime. The social dimension of the second model makes it a model of normative behaviour in which a social norm is established within a social network through the deterrent of social sanctions.

6.2.2 Distributed Norm Enforcement via Ostracism

The previous model demonstrated the influence of a social network on an agent's decision to commit a crime. Agents were deterred from crime by expecting disapproval from their neighbours. The cost was implemented as a reduction in payoff. The model we discuss in this section takes the idea of social pressure to conform one step further by implementing ostracism as the sanction for defection. Ostracism is a common sanction for norm transgression (Opp and Hechter 2001, pp. 35–37). The advantage of ostracism is that it is cheap for the punisher, an important parameter for deterrent simulations as we have seen in Sect. 6.1.2.

In de Pinninck et al. (2008), the authors model ostracism in social networks; Fig. 6.2 shows the progression of ostracism of a defector in a social network.

The setting for the model is a prisoner's dilemma game. An agent A (the initiator agent) chooses another agent B along the paths of its social network. Agents at nodes along this path are 'mediator agents'. A asks one of its neighbours, say C, to return a list of its neighbours. A picks one of those neighbours and asks it again to return a list of neighbours and so on until A has found a partner agent B. There are three agent types in a network, meek agents, violator agents, and enforcer agents. Meek agents always cooperate and do not stop interacting with defectors. Violator agents always defect. Enforcer agents are cooperators but they stop interacting with violator agents. Once they have played a violator agent, they store the information in a list (the block list). They also communicate the information to other mediating agents, that is they 'gossip'. A violator agent can only play an enforcer agent once. There are two strategies for information communication:

1. (UDB) unidirectional blockage in which an enforcer agent, when asked for the list of its neighbours, returns the full list or
2. (BDB) bidirectional blockage in which an enforcer agent reduces the list by those agents it knows to be violators.

If a querying agent is in an enforcer's block list it returns an empty list. UDB benefits enforcer agents as they can still use violator agents as mediators, leaving communication channels open without danger of interacting with them again. Meek agents however, benefit from BDB as it is the only way to shield themselves from interactions with violators.

The number of violations suffered by norm abiding agents goes down rapidly when ostracism is applied to violator agents. The higher the enforcer to meek agent ratio, the higher the reduction. Different social structures influence the number of violations with tree structures reducing violation very efficiently whilst small-world and random networks are much less effective. This is not surprising as in a tree structure there is only one path between any two agents making blocking very efficient. The other network structures leave gaming opportunities open to violators as there are many paths to other agents, retaining access even if one route is blocked. The most interesting finding is that ostracism makes cooperation the rational strategy in a society as the payoffs for norm-abiding agents (meek and enforcers) increase dramatically whilst defection payoffs drop to zero.

This simulation model suggests that ostracism is indeed an efficient norm enforcement mechanism. It is cheap to implement, i.e. the enforcer agent has no cost associated with sanction. Secondly, ostracism shields other agents from interacting with violators. Thirdly, by ensuring that cooperators mainly play with cooperators, their payoffs increase. Fourthly, by restricting violators to interact only with other violators, violation no longer pays.

6.3 Achievements and Shortcomings

Rational choice and game theory are fruitful starting points for the simulations of social norms. Both theories are a formalisation of agents' decisions thus providing the micro-behaviour to start the modelling process. We discussed Axelrod's work on game theory strategies and how strategies that are nice, provokable and forgiving are the most successful. This is in line with a view of social norms as adhered to voluntarily with transgressions punished but not too severely. Axelrod's work on norm emergence shows that without enforcement, cooperation is not a stable outcome in a society of selfish agents. Punishment has to be two layered for stable cooperation to emerge, because the norm transgression needs to be punished as well as the non-enforcement of a norm. However, recent research shows that this additional layer only delays norm collapse.

In van Baal's model of criminal behaviour rational choice theory is implemented as the micro-mechanism underlying criminal decision making. The output shows the expected sensitivity of decisions to the probability of being caught and severity of punishment. In an extension to the model social sanctions are implemented on top of legal sanctions. Social sanctions serve to establish a local norm of either law transgression or conformity. The final model we discussed makes the sanctioning of transgression fully distributed, so that no single agent bears the cost of punishment. By ostracising defectors from the social network, agents can shield themselves and others from being taken advantage of. Ostracism is a well known sanctioning mechanism for the enforcement of social norms.

The models have a rather narrow view of social norms, however. Using the conceptualisation of norms as cooperation achieved by direct enforcement, these models do not take into account other features of normative behaviour such as habitual and wider social influences.

References

Axelrod, R. (1984). *The evolution of cooperation*. New York: Basic Books.

Axelrod, R. (1986). An evolutionary approach to norms. *American Political Science Review, 80*(4), 1095–1111.

de Pinninck, A., Sierra, C., & Schorlemmer, M. (2008). Distributed norm enforcement via ostracism. In *Coordination, organizations, institutions, and norms in agent systems III* (Number 4870 in Lecture notes in computer science, pp. 301–315). Berlin/Heidelberg: Springer.

Mahmoud, S., Griffiths, N., Keppens, J., & Luck, M. (2010). An analysis of norm emergence in Axelrod's model. In *8th European workshop on multi-agent systems*, Paris.

Opp, K.-D., & Hechter, M. (2001). *Social norms*. New York: Russell Sage Foundation.

van Baal, P. H. M. (2004 dissertation). *Computer simulations of criminal deterrence: From public policy to local interaction to individual behaviour*. Rotterdam: Boom Juridische Uitgevers.

Chapter 7
Imitation and Social Norms

> *Most people are other people. Their thoughts are someone else's opinions, their lives a mimicry, their passions a quotation.*
>
> Oscar Wilde

7.1 Norm Diffusion and Imitation

In this chapter we discuss agent-based models of norm diffusion. These models rely on diffusion mechanisms such as imitation and the direct transmission of cultural units such as 'memes'. Whilst in Chap. 6 the assumptions of the rational agent and strategic social interactions used for models of normative behaviour originated in economics, in this chapter they come from the natural sciences. This strand of modelling uses work on ecology, population dynamics and particle physics to model human behaviour. The fundamental idea is that there are many complex phenomena in the natural world and that we can use the same methods used to study them to analyse the social world.

Imitation dynamics models have their theoretical foundations in the natural sciences. Models using memes are based on work on an evolutionary theory of culture. The specific term 'meme' was coined by Dawkins (1976) and is the unit of selection of cultural evolution parallel to the gene in natural selection. We start by discussing very simple imitation models, followed by more involved imitation models based on memes.

7.2 Adoption and Diffusion

Diffusion is a particularly fruitful area for agent-based modelling. Much work has been done on the spread of disease and on information diffusion and technology uptake. A simple example is the Rumour Mill model, Wilensky (1997), which shows

C. Elsenbroich and N. Gilbert, *Modelling Norms*, DOI 10.1007/978-94-007-7052-2_7,

the spread of a rumour through a population. Agents pass a rumour on to a random one of their neighbours. The rumour spreads throughout the population, but not always along exactly the same path. The rumour spread is thus not predictable in detail but the macro phenomenon of spread and acceleration of spread. (For a fuller discussion of information diffusion models, see Gilbert and Troitzsch 2005, pp. 140–142). Like fashion, social norms get established by spreading through a population. As examples of models of norm diffusion, we discuss two models, diffusion by majority counting (Epstein 2000), and the diffusion of a standing ovation through an audience (Muldoon et al. 2012).

7.2.1 *Diffusion and Non-Thinking*

Epstein (2000) describes one of the most well known models of norm diffusion in the literature. A social norm is defined by Epstein as follows.

> First, [social norms] are self enforcing behavioural regularities. But second, once entrenched, we conform without thinking about it. (Epstein 2000, p. 1)

Norms are self-enforcing regularities, not the incentivised behaviours they were in the previous chapter. Whereas the agents in Chap. 6 calculated at every step whether adhering to a norm is beneficial for them, here normative behaviours are exactly those behaviours without that kind, or any other kind, of thought. And whereas in Chap. 6 the goal was to obtain cooperation from the assumption of selfishness, here the goal is to obtain patterns of norm clustering from a set of simple assumptions; some adherence to social norms is assumed.

Epstein assumes two macro phenomena of normative behaviour: (a) norms are locally stable, i.e. a group of agents close to each other adhere to the same norms and (b) norms are globally diverse. A micro assumption of the model is that agents can adhere to norms "without thinking about them". The model starts by assigning a binary norm and a norm change mechanism to agents. Norm change depends on two variables: the local environment and the amount of thinking about behaviour an agent does. At each step, every agent checks the norm of its neighbours within a personal vision radius. If the agent is in accord with its surrounding agents, it keeps its norm and decreases its vision radius (less thinking). If the agent is not in accord it changes the norm and increases its vision radius (more thinking). The model shows the desired macro-behaviour, leading to local conformity and global diversity of norms. Agents at the heart of a region conforming to a norm no longer think about their behaviour whereas those at the borderline between norms have to choose between competing local norms. The model also captures the re-emergence of norm differentiation after a 'revolution', a shock to the system.

The model assumes: (a) the automatic adoption of the majority norm (b) habitual behaviour when agents are in a stable norm-environment (c) the absence of enforcement of norms.

The computational model is set up as follows. Agents have fixed positions in a circle. Each agent thus has two direct neighbours. A norm is binary, like driving on the left (*L*) or driving on the right (*R*) hand side of the road. Initially *L* and *R* are distributed randomly over the agents. Each agent checks their neighbourhood at each step of the simulation for the prevalent norm. The size of the neighbourhood is updated according to the following rules: Let us assume agent *A* follows norms *R* with initial radius *r*.

1. *A* computes relative frequency of norm *R* at radius *r*: $F(R)^r$.
2. *A* computes relative frequency of norm *R* at radius $r+1$, $F(R)^{r+1}$. If $F(R)^{r+1} \neq F(R)^r$, update *r* to $r+1$.
   If equal proceed to Step 3.
3. *A* computes relative frequency of norm *R* at radius $r-1$: $F(R)^{r-1}$. If $F(R)^{r-1} = F(R)^r$, update *r* to $r-1$.
   If unequal keep *r*.

The norm adopted is simply the majority norm in an agent's radius. Some noise can be added to the system such that agents have a certain probability to adopt a norm randomly.

Without noise the simulation very quickly results in a monolithic block of one norm. If some noise is added, the simulation leads to the establishment of local conformity to specific norms as well as global diversity. Norms stabilise up to a threshold of noise. Agents deeply entrenched in a norm have short search radii whilst agents at norm-borders have varying radii. Shocks, i.e. random redistributions of norms over agents, quickly re-stabilise into entrenched norms.

This is a particularly simple model of the diffusion or adoption of social norms. It relies on the idea of the adoption of a majority norm, assuming therefore that agents want to "fit in" with their social environment. The transmission of a norm is there achieved by means of the majority calculation.

7.2.2 Standing Ovations

A recent analysis of the emergence of normative behaviour (Muldoon et al. 2012) makes an important terminological distinction between descriptive, social and moral norms. Descriptive norms are considered to have less normative weight than social and moral norms and are norms such as table manners, fashions and, the case discussed in detail, standing ovations after live performances.

In this model of the standing ovation personal preferences and social factors interact to different extents in different variations of a baseline model. Agents are situated on a grid, all facing the same way (towards the 'stage'). Agents have an *intrinsic preference* q_i to stand up. Different ways of implementing the social influence factors are tested. In the baseline model, the social influence is calculated from the number of agents standing up in the previous round. Agents have full information, i.e. they have knowledge of how many agents sit and how many stand. The overall or *effective propensity* $P_i^{(n)}$ of an agent to stand up is calculated in round n as

$$P_i^{(n)} = \sigma_i \left(\frac{S^{n-1}}{M} \right) + (1 - \sigma_i) q_i \tag{7.1}$$

where M is the overall number of agents, S the number of agents standing up in round $n-1$, and σ_i is the social sensitivity of agent i, i.e. how much influence the standing population has on its decision to stand or remain seated. The baseline model investigates the interaction between personal propensity and social sensitivity. Convergence is accelerated for lower values of σ as well as q. This is to be expected from the mathematics of the model. Both q and σ influence the speed of convergence with social sensitivity accelerating convergence more than personal propensity.

In the baseline model agents have full information about what other agents are doing. This is not the case in an audience as one normally only sees those agents in front and possibly to each side, but rarely those behind. The model is therefore extended to have agents only influenced by agents within a vision cone. The above equation is amended by replacing $S^{(n-1)}/M$ by

$$\frac{1}{|M_i|} \sum_{j \in M_i} s_j^{n-1} \tag{7.2}$$

Such incomplete information slows down the convergence process, but otherwise does not change the behaviour of the baseline model. Although these models show how a reaction can travel through a population, they fall short of implementing important features of social norms. For example, a social norm does not have to be adopted by everyone in the population; there is likely to be what Epstein called 'local conformity and global diversity'.

To implement this characteristic of social norms the baseline model (with complete and incomplete information) is extended to the *inertia model*. Two changes are made to the baseline model. A scaling factor $e^{-\alpha n}$ is introduced, so that the decision to stand up becomes less likely the more time has passed (the larger n), and the size of the group is taken as a parameter of its influence. The contagion factor β is introduced, $0 < \beta < 1$. The smaller β is, the more likely it is that a small number of agents influences the rest of the population. The baseline equation becomes

$$P_i^{(n)} = e^{-\alpha n} \left(\sigma_i \left(\frac{S^{n-1}}{M} \right)^{\beta} + (1 - \sigma_i) q_i \right) \tag{7.3}$$

Increases in either α or β reduce ovation size with α having twice the influence of β. Increasing α increases the stubbornness of agents to join in the ovation and undermines the forming of larger groups, which in turn hinders the influence

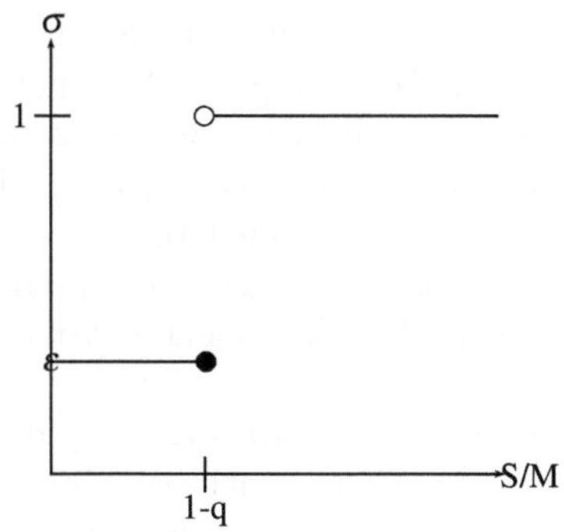

Fig. 7.1 Discontinuous social influence (Muldoon et al. 2012, p. 13, Fig. 13)

of group behaviour on the individual as a critical mass is not formed. Whether the model uses complete or incomplete information makes little difference to the outcome.

The third extension is called the *Endogenous Social Sensitivity Model.* Whereas in the baseline model, social sensitivity has been implemented exogenously as a static threshold, in this model social sensitivity is implemented as an endogenous agent variable meaning that its value changes depending on the proportion of the group that has adopted the norm. The social sensitivity term is defined as:

$$\sigma\left(\frac{S}{M}\right) = \begin{cases} 1, \text{ if } S/M = 1 - q, \\ \varepsilon \text{ otherwise.} \end{cases} \tag{7.4}$$

As the intrinsic propensity q of an individual i to stand up increases, the lower the number of people standing up that are necessary to "activate" an individual's social sensitivity. The relationship can be seen in Fig. 7.1.

The discontinuous function for σ is implemented in the baseline model with complete information. As in the original baseline model, convergence speeds up as values for q increase.

The final extension is the *Symmetry* model. The idea is that norms are not quite as binary as they were so far portrayed. To make the point, the authors provide the example of the different use of a fork in Europe and the US. Whilst in Europe the fork is held in the left hand throughout a meal, in the US it is held in the left hand while cutting food but then transferred to the right hand for raising the food to the mouth.

Four changes are made to the baseline model. First, agents are divided into two types, each having a preference for one norm. Second, personal preference q is reinterpreted as a variable $0 \leq q \leq 1$ with a midpoint at 0.5 meaning an agent with $q = 0$ or 1 has a strong preference for either norm and $q = 0.5$, meaning ambivalence. Third, agents can change their mind and switch from one norm to the other, rather than as before when they could only change from sitting to standing.

Fourth, the preference for one norm or the other is randomly allocated to agents in the initialisation of the model. This setup has three potential outcomes. First, the emergence of one norm, i.e. the whole population subscribing to one behaviour. For this, half the population must change behaviour from its initial preference. Second, agents stay true to their initial preferences without any social influence, with the two norms leading a parallel existence. Third, a mix of initial behaviours and influences where some agents are influenced by their social surroundings whilst others stick to their initial preferences.

Outcome one, the emergence of a norm shared by the whole population is rare in the symmetric model. Only when social sensitivity σ is much stronger than individual preference q does such a norm emerge. Agents staying true to their initial preferences occurs for a wider range of values, provided that the individual preferences are high enough. The most likely outcome is a mix of initial behaviours and influences, leading to a distribution of behaviours similar to the initial conditions but with some agents having changed their allegiance.

The authors conclude that,

> ... though descriptive norms are quite common and are found in a very wide variety of social situations, there are many more possible descriptive norms than there are actual descriptive norms. Most of our day to day behaviours are not norm-governed, even though many are. (Muldoon et al. 2012, p. 19)

This set of models demonstrates the interactions of personal preferences and social factors on the behavioural choices of agents and the resulting emergence of a norm within a population. It is an interesting investigation into the difference between the diffusion of, say, a virus and a norm, which shows clearly that the baseline model, which is essentially an epidemiologic al model, is insufficient for the modelling of social norms. Whereas a virus is transmitted without a person's consent, norm adoption is more complex, as implemented here in the inertia, the endogenous and the symmetry models.

7.3 Imitation and Memetics

Imitation has long been seen as one of the major transmitters of culture, and thus of social norms (e.g. Boyd and Richerson 2005; Hurley and Chater 2005; Buchanan 2007). It is the simplest mechanism underlying social learning. Imitation here is usually treated as a purely behavioural issue, of the 'monkey see, monkey do' variety. In economic settings, agents imitate successful strategies, i.e. behaviours with the highest payoffs. Thus, rather than a calculation of cost and benefit, behaviour is determined by who imitates who's behaviour. Simple imitation can be equated to models of disease or information transmission. As well as just asking "who imitates whom", a further question is, what exactly is imitated. One answer is that the cultural units of transmission are 'memes'. The term 'meme' was coined in Dawkins (1976) as the cultural equivalent of the biological unit of gene.

The existence of memes is highly controversial (Aunger 2006). Some scientists see the existence of mirror neurons as the neurologic al equivalent of memes (for a discussion see Borg 2007). Mirror neurons are neurons that fire on imitation behaviour. It is, however, very unclear whether we can identify actual cultural units as memes that correspond to the imitation (Edmonds 2005). Despite their undecided ontological status, memes have been used for modelling the diffusion of social norms. Often the term "meme" is just used as an analogy.

7.3.1 Possession Memes

For example, Flentge et al. (2001) describe the transmission of possession norms in a population via memes on top of the Sugarscape simulation discussed in Sect. 5.1.1. The authors implement memes represented by tags, as in Sugarscape, the agents are characterised by flags with 11 tags in each flag. Different from Sugarscape, two of the tags have an influence on the agent's behaviour. The first special tag is the possession meme, roughly meaning that the agent acknowledges private property. If an agent has the possession meme, it can take possession of a patch and will not acquire any patch that is already in the possession of another agent. The second special tag is the sanction meme. If an agent has the sanction meme it can sanction agents that transgress the possession norm. Only agents with the possession meme can have the sanction meme.

The model is a model of evolutionary norm emergence. The rules of Sugarscape are amended slightly to fit the new memetic framework:

1. *MS*-agent: if an agent is not fertile, perform rule *M*. Otherwise, search all unoccupied cells in vision range neighbouring a fertile agent of the opposite sex. Find the cell with the maximum quantity of sugar. If number of maximal cells >1 choose the closest, if the number of cells $= 0$ perform *M*. Collect all the sugar from the cell.
2. *S*-agent: the sex rule is performed as described in Sect. 5.1.1.
3. K^{+}-agent: select one meme from each of neighbouring agents. If the meme is not equal to the current agent's meme, change the meme value to that of the agent with more sugar. If the sugar levels are equal, adopt the meme value of the newly arrived agent. If the memes are equal do nothing.

The initial conditions of the model are similar to the original Sugarscape, with the same landscape being used (i.e. a torus world with two sugar peaks) and a growback rule of $\alpha = 1$, meaning that at each step all patches have one unit of sugar added. The initial number of agents is 400. Using the rules *MS*, *S*, and *K*, K^{+}, culture is only passed on from parents to offspring. Metabolism and vision range are systematically varied as are the penalties for norm transgression and the cost for the punishing agent. The authors evaluate the impact of the possession meme on the survival of the society as a whole.

Without the possession meme, societies with a metabolism rate higher than 2 become extinct. The vision range has no influence on the outcome. If all agents have the possession meme, society survival becomes a stable outcome for any vision range and metabolism rates lower than four. However, the number of agents surviving is higher in possession meme societies than no-possession meme ones and decreases consistently with rising metabolism rates.

Setting the possession meme at 50 % of the population and the sanction meme at 0 % yields findings similar to the experiment without the possession meme, the reason being that the meme does not establish itself overall and as soon as it disappears, the society becomes extinct. The proportion of about 50 % of agents having the possession meme remains although the overall population shrinks dramatically (see Flentge et al. 2001, p. 16, Fig. 9). The population then grows again, the proportion of the possession meme staying low, between 10 and 20 %. Not having a possession meme results in a short term reproductive and cultural transmission advantage for agents.

The introduction of a costless sanction meme helps to establish the possession meme. Initially all agents having the possession meme also have the sanctioning meme. Survival rates increase dramatically, in particular for higher vision ranges as more agents can observe and sanction a norm transgression. At low vision ranges the possession meme does not get established, whereas for the surviving societies with high vision ranges, the whole of the population has the possession meme after a number of generations. Also, the higher the sanction, the higher the survival rate of the society.

Adding a cost for sanctioning changes the picture. Non-sanctioning agents now have the short term advantage, leading to the sanction meme and then the possession meme dying out. The situation is slightly better if there is no cultural transmission, or transmission occurs with rule K^+ rather than with rule K.

The authors conclude that a possession meme is desirable as it ensures a society's survival but that its implementation can only be achieved with sanctioning with the cost is either shared between agents (through institutions for example) or by the introduction of a metanorm as in Axelrod (1986). The authors' own criticism of their model is that it does not contain any learning over the lifetime of an agent, a point to which we will return in Sect. 8.3.

7.3.2 *The Emergence of Culture*

In Sect. 7.2.1 we saw that one feature of social norms is local conformity combined with global diversity. A similar pattern can be observed with cultures. We shall treat social norms and cultures as related by

Definition 7.3.1. A culture is a set of social norms.

For example, the culture of being a goth is traditionally associated with the fashion norm of black clothing and dark hair, behaviour norms such as non-violence,

56829	98374	98374	94058	...
34908	04194	**29038**	05723	...
49878	34908	**39204**	30498	...
⋮	⋮	⋮	⋮	⋱

Fig. 7.2 An example of agent tags in Axelrod's model

and a liking for a certain kind of music, as well as symbols of death (e.g. graveyards, coffins and skulls) (Hodkinson 2002). The culture of being middle class is associated with norms such as a posh accent, property ownership, upward social striving, in particular for one's children, a certain kind of taste (from balsamic vinegar to the *Boden* catalogue) and lifestyle choices such as skiing, golfing and sailing. Clearly, not all members of such cultures will keep to all the norms, but by adhering to a majority or some salient ones, they can be classified as members of the group. For example, someone with a rough accent, not owning property and never having skied, golfed or sailed in her life but coaching her child to get into the local grammar school could be described as "having middle class aspirations". A simulation using the idea of cultural similarity can be found in Axelrod (1997).

Axelrod's model consists of a 10×10 grid of patches, each of which has a cultural tag consisting of five cultural features that can take one of ten different states (0–9). Each patch is a culture, in Axelrod's interpretation, "a homogenous village". We shall just call each patch an agent. Each agent can interact with its four neighbours (von Neumann neighbourhood). When interacting, agents assimilate if they have at least one cultural feature in common. If they are altogether different, no assimilation occurs. Cultural similarity is defined as the number of cultural features that two agents have in common. The model dynamics consist of only two steps in a loop:

1. Pick an agent at random and pick one of its neighbours.
2. The two agents assimilate with probability equal to their cultural similarity. Assimilation means choosing one of the features the agents differ on and setting the active agent's feature to the value of the neighbour's.
3. Loop.

In Fig. 7.2 agent 29038 is marked by black print. It can only interact with its neighbour to the south (bold print) as it does not have any feature in common with its other three neighbours. An interaction takes place with a probability of 20 % as they have one feature in common. If an interaction takes place, say 29038 changes to 39038, the next time an interaction happens, the probability will be 40 % and so on.

Results from this model are that under a wide range of circumstances, cultural variation is maintained at the global level, at a mean of around 3.5 cultures, while maintaining clustering or local conformity. Axelrod investigates the influence of a number of parameters on the cultural variation.

1. *Size of grid:* the initial simulation contains 10 × 10 patches. Axelrod varies the grid from 20 × 20 to 100 × 100. Up to a size of 15 × 15, the number of surviving cultural regions increases, but for larger grid sizes, cultural variation decreases sharply; a novel and surprising result.
2. *Number of cultural features:* in the initial simulation, the number of cultural features is set at five. What happens if the number is increased? Axelrod tests 5, 10 and 15 cultural features resulting consistently in a reduction of cultural variation; another surprising result.
3. *Number of traits:* rather than varying the number of cultural features, the number of traits per feature is increased. An increase in the number of features leads consistently to an increase in cultural variation although the effect is reduced somewhat the more cultural features there are (see Axelrod 1997, p. 212, Table 2).

Whereas Axelrod's initial work on social norms focussed on cooperation (see Sects. 6.1.1 and 6.1.2), his work on culture focusses on diffusion, maintenance and variability of specific traits (which can be interpreted as norms) within populations. Results suggest that for larger regions conformity increases (i.e. cultural variation decreases) and that large numbers of competing norms can be maintained within a population.

7.3.3 Memetic Isolation

In a similar vein to Axelrod's culture model, Gatherer (2002) investigates cultural influence and the geographic isolation of traits. His model is less focussed on the parameters of size and number of traits than on the transmission mechanisms of culture. This model is again based on a grid. This time, however, the patches on the grid are not homogeneous "villages" but locations containing heterogeneous agents. Agents are specified by their location, their *gene* and their *meme*. Both genes and memes are binary concepts. Genes can take the values A or B, memes 1 or 2 (or yellow and grey in the visualisation in the original paper). Thus there are two binary cultural features, but they have different transmission mechanisms. A gene is transmitted vertically, i.e. from one generation to the next. A meme is transmitted horizontally, within one's own society (within the same patch) or to a neighbouring society (across one border). The culture of a society is determined by majority counting. For example, for a patch with three agents, two of which are yellow, the culture will be yellow.

Agents have a range of actions. They can reproduce (r) (i.e. produce a copy of themselves), teach a member of their own society (o) (this is transmission of a meme within a society), teach a member of a neighbouring society (n) (transmission of a meme across a border), migrate (m) into a neighbouring patch, and die (d).

The model is used to study cultural (memetic) isolation, in particular how the different transmission mechanisms (horizontal meme and vertical gene) influence cultural isolation. A cultural isolate is a patch in the grid with a majority culture different from all its surrounding neighbours. Simulation runs are executed with and without cultural and natural selection advantages for one meme/gene.

The first result is that horizontal transmission, that is meme transmission, leads to much less cultural isolation than vertical (gene) transmission. This effect is slightly lessened if there is selection on the vertical transmission (and this is strongest if selection is both natural and cultural). No selection leads to some remaining cultural isolation of horizontal traits that is almost completely eliminated if cultural selection is at play.

Like Axelrod's, this model explores the transmission of culture. Rather than using imitation, it uses genes and memes to encode vertical and horizontal transmission respectively. Using selection pressures on both genes and memes (natural and cultural selection), the simulations show that minority cultures can survive within majority culture regions. It also shows that cultural (meme) transmission leads to less isolated minorities.

7.4 Achievements and Shortcomings

In this chapter we discussed some models of norm diffusion using relatively simple assumptions about imitation mechanisms and the direct horizontal transmission of culture via memes. The two simple diffusion models relying on imitation are based on different calculations of who influences an agent and whether there is some threshold delaying behaviour change. In the Epstein model behaviour change is instantaneous. In the standing ovation model there are two values, a propensity to stand up and a social sensitivity. The examples given in the literature suggest different extents to which these mechanisms influence behaviour. For example driving on the right or on the left hand side of the road is easily perpetuated by simple imitation. However, as we will see in the following chapters, for the norm of right of way to emerge, simple imitation is insufficient as a mechanism but a social learning game can bring about the effect (Sect. 8.3.1) and the establishment of a zebra crossing for pedestrians needs yet more complex learning of the agents (Sect. 9.3.3).

In the simulations discussed above, operationalising culture as meme units is used to measure the similarity or cultural closeness of agents. It is clear that simple imitation is insufficient to model the complicated social world human beings inhabit. How could sharing the abstract meanings of institutions such as money or weddings come about purely behaviourally? However, what these models show is that micro-behaviours *like* imitation lead to one macro-phenomenon of social norms: local conformity while retaining global diversity.

The simulations of culture using discrete entities for cultural transmission, such as memes are harder to defend as they make an ontological assumption about how culture transmits. It is hard to see how culture can be discretised in this way and not surprisingly, there is no independent evidence for the existence of memes.

References

Aunger, R. (2006). What's the matter with memes? In A. Grafen & M. Ridley (Eds.), *Richard Dawkins: How a scientist changed the way we think*. Oxford: Oxford University Press.

Axelrod, R. (1986). An evolutionary approach to norms. *American Political Science Review, 80*(4), 1095–1111.

Axelrod, R. (1997). The dissemination of culture: A model with local convergence and global polarization. *Journal of Conflict Resolution, 41*, 203–226.

Borg, E. (2007). If mirror neurons are the answer, what is the question. *Journal of Consciousness Studies, 14*(8), 5–19.

Boyd, R., & Richerson, P. J. (2005). *Not by genes alone: How culture transformed human evolution*. Chicago: University of Chicago Press.

Buchanan, M. (2007). *The social atom*. New York: Bloomsbury.

Dawkins, R. (1976). *The selfish gene*. New York: Oxford University Press.

Edmonds, B. (2005). The revealed poverty of the gene-meme analogy – why memetics per se has failed to produce substantive results. *Journal of Memetics – Evolutionary Models of Information Transmission, 9*. http://jom-emit.cfpm.org/2005/vol9/edmonds_b.html.

Epstein, J. (2000). Learning to be thoughtless: Social norms and individual computing. Technical report, Center on Social and Economic Dynamics Working Paper, No. 6.

Flentge, F., Polani, D., & Uthmann, T. (2001). Modelling the emergence of possession norms using memes. *Journal of Artificial Societies and Social Simulation, 4*(4), 3.

Gatherer, D. (2002). Identifying cases of social contagion using memetic isolation: Comparison of the dynamics of a multisociety simulation with an ethnographic data set. *Journal of Artificial Societies and Social Simulation, 5*(4), 5.

Gilbert, N., & Troitzsch, K. G. (2005). *Simulation for the social scientist* (2nd ed.). Maidenhead: Open University Press.

Hodkinson, P. (2002). *Goth: Identity, style and subculture*. Oxford: Berg.

Hurley, S., & Chater, N. (2005). *Perspectives on imitation: From neuroscience to social science: Vol. 1: Mechanisms of imitation and imitation in animals*. Cambridge: MIT.

Muldoon, R., Lisciandra, C., Bicchieri, C., Hartmann, S., & Sprenger, J. (2012). On the emergence of descriptive norms. *Politics, Philosophy and Economics*. doi:10.1177/1470594X12447791.

Wilensky, U. (1997). NetLogo Rumor Mill model. Technical report, Center for Connected Learning and Computer-Based Modeling, Northwestern University, Evanston.

Chapter 8
Socially Situated Social Norms

Days, weeks, months go by in which I engage in no real deliberation about what to do.

Alan Goldman

8.1 Norms in a Social Setting

This chapter discusses models of more complex socially informed behaviours. Rather than modelling relatively simple imitation behaviour as in the previous chapter, the following models rely on concepts of social influence and social learning. The models are still concerned with the diffusion of behaviours but, rather than agents being passive receivers and adopters of behaviours or memes, agents become more actively involved in their social environment, deciding whether to join or adopt. The models we discuss are based on the interactions of personal and social preferences, opinion dynamics, social learning mechanisms and social impact theory.

8.2 Social Influence

First we discuss models of social influence. Social influence here means that an agent has a set of preferences determining its behaviour which is altered depending on its social surrounding, i.e. different social surroundings produce different behaviour outcomes.

C. Elsenbroich and N. Gilbert, *Modelling Norms*, DOI 10.1007/978-94-007-7052-2_8,

Table 8.1 Attitude matrix for different groups

	Toward own group	Other group
Attitude of squares	+1, 0, −1	+1, 0, −1
Attitude of crosses	+1, 0, −1	+1, 0, −1

8.2.1 Sakoda's Model of Social Interaction

Possibly the single most cited agent-based model is the Schelling model of residential segregation (for a citation analysis see Hegselmann and Kurz forthcoming). It is used as a paradigm example of how simple local interactions of agents, according to a set of preferences, can lead to surprising macro outcomes. It is also used as one of the standard examples to introduce agent-based modelling, just as we have done in the introduction. Schelling's model was published in the first issuc of thc *Journal for Mathematical Sociology* in 1971. The same issue of the journal contains another modelling paper called *The Checkerboard Model of Social Interaction* (Sakoda 1971). Rather than trying to generate a specific social phenomenon, like the segregation Schelling set out to understand, Sakoda produces what he calls a "general model of social interaction", which can be adapted to model different particular social dynamics.

Sakoda starts off with an 8×8 checkerboard representing what he calls the "social field". There are two groups, represented by two sets of six pieces each, one group by squares, the other by crosses. Each piece has a tuple of attitudes (see Table 8.1):

The choice whether and where to move is calculated taking into account the attributes of all other pieces in the social field. The importance of pieces diminishes by distance. The distance is calculated as the Euclidian distance between pieces i and j (see Eq. 8.1).

$$D = (X_i - X_j)^2 + (Y_i - Y_j)^2 \tag{8.1}$$

Depending on the value V of the attitude, the distance is either evaluated as positive or negative. Additionally, the distance is weighted by taking the nth root, expressed by the value w in Eq. 8.2. The higher the value for w, the more far away pieces matter relative to nearer pieces. The weighted attitude is calculated for every piece on the board.

$$f = \sum\left(\frac{V}{D^{1/w}}\right) \tag{8.2}$$

Pieces evaluate all possible positions in their range according to Eq. 8.2 and move to the best one, i.e. the one satisfying their preferences most. Usually pieces move one step within their Moore neighbourhood but in case they are closed in by other pieces they are allowed to 'jump' to a square in the larger 5×5 neighbourhood. One cycle in the simulation is each piece making one move.

The initial output of this simulation was the position of each piece after each cycle, the number of cycles, the centroids of either group, the distance between the groups' centroids and the index of dispersion, calculated as

$$Dis = \sqrt{\frac{\Sigma(X_i - \overline{X})^2 + \Sigma(Y_i - \overline{Y})^2}{N}}, \tag{8.3}$$

where $\overline{X}$ and $\overline{Y}$ are the group's centroid coordinates and N the number of members of group i.

Sakoda runs a set of simulations varying the attitudes of agents towards the in- and out-group respectively obtaining interesting final configurations, such as segregation, group formations in the different areas of the checkerboard, group mingling, coupling and ingroup-outgroup configurations (see Sakoda 1971, pp. 125–131).

Looking at this model it seems rather surprising that Schelling's model is one of the most cited models in history whereas Sakoda's model is more or less forgotten. The two models have so much in common: Agents are located on a grid, they evaluate their neighbourhoods and decide on whether they want to stay or move and they evaluate their neighbourhood for a better place to be.[1] For a full discussion of the relationship between Sakoda and Schelling see Hegselmann and Kurz (forthcoming). The paper shows that both Schelling and Sakoda can be reconstructed as instances of what the authors call "configuration games". A configuration game is a game consisting of the following four components: A group structure G, a social space S, an evaluation of neighbourhoods E, and a migration regime M (Hegselmann and Kurz forthcoming, p. 27).

The Schelling model of segregation shows that the macro-phenomenon of segregation can result from simple local interactions, without for example a social norm of strong racism. Instead, a 'norm' in which agents simply do not want to be in the minority is sufficient to obtain strong segregation. Schelling's is almost a model that shows that social norms are not necessary for the explanation of social phenomena, in particular in the implementations where agents move randomly to a free patch when unhappy. Sakoda explicitly models some social interactions based on norms. The game with the attitude matrix below, is explicitly interpreted as the norm of social climbing. One group admires the other group and despises its own whilst the other one likes to be left alone, expressed by liking itself but not the others. The easiest interpretation is possibly a class one in which the middle classes are in awe of the upper classes which in turn despise the middle classes (Table 8.2).

[1] In our description of the Schelling model in the introduction, agents moved to a random free patch on the grid if their neighbourhood was not satisfactory. In the model described in Schelling (1971) the movement is not random but agents move to the nearest patch that satisfies their neighbourhood constraints, thus optimising their position similar to the Sakoda model.

Table 8.2 Attitude matrix for social climbers

	Toward own group	Other group
Attitude of squares	−1	1
Attitude of crosses	1	−1

Table 8.3 Attitude matrix for husband-wives

	Toward own group	Other group
Attitude of squares	−4	1
Attitude of crosses	2	2

This configuration does not usually produce a stable result as one group needs to move away, the other group steady in pursuit. But sometimes, the social climbers 'trap' the others in a corner of the board from where they cannot escape.

Another game configuration explicitly modelling a social norm is the Husband and Wife configuration (Table 8.3).

Sakoda's explanation of the above attitude matrix is worth quoting

> In American society females probably have greater negative attitudes towards other females than to males, and they represent the force toward keeping the couples apart. The males, on the other hand, frequently desire male companionship, fishing and hunting, golfing, playing poker or attending the Playboy Club. (Sakoda 1971, p. 131)

Sakoda's model of social interaction, together with Schelling, are among the first explicit simulations of social processes based on an agent-based model. Whereas The Schelling model explores the possibility of segregation resulting from simple local interactions rather than an overarching norm of racism, Sakoda stipulates different attitude matrices as representing particular social phenomena.

8.2.2 *Opinion Dynamics*

Opinion dynamic models are one of the earliest implementations of social dynamics in an agent-based model. Some prominent examples are Deffuant et al. (2002) and Hegselmann and Krause (2002). We discuss the former simulation in a little more detail as it is one of the models we use later in Chap. 11 as the basis for a model of juvenile delinquency.

8.2.2.1 How Can Extremism Prevail?

In Deffuant et al. (2002) agents have an opinion (a rational number from the interval $[0, 1]$) and a confidence level (a number between 0 and ∞). Initially the opinion and the confidence levels have a random normal distribution. Agents are located on a line, representing the opinion interval. At each step, every agent picks another agent at random to interact with.

Agents change their opinions given the assumption of bounded confidence. Bounded confidence means that influence only takes place between agents that are either close enough in their opinions or far enough apart in confidence. For instance, a Labour voter might not be influenced by a right wing Conservative unless the Labour voter is really not sure at all (i.e. not confident) in his or her opinion. Bounded confidence is calculated as an intersection between the opinion-confidence segments of two agents. If this overlap is sufficiently large, the agents will influence each other and their opinions will meet in the middle. (see Deffuant et al. 2002, 2.3–2.4 for details.)

Examining under what conditions extremism can prevail in a model of opinion dynamics, the simulation results point to the most important variable being the level of uncertainty. Whilst only agents that were initially close to extreme opinions in the first place became extreme when general uncertainty was small, high uncertainty led to a bifurcation of opinions or even convergence to a single extreme. (See Deffuant et al. 2002, 3.8–3.11 for details.) Some interesting and surprising results are that the movement to a single extreme is led by initially moderate agents rather than by already more extreme ones and that a shift to radicalisation often happens after a moderate period. This model is similar to the symmetric model of norm emergence discussed in Sect. 7.2.2. Whereas in the symmetric model that the establishment of a complete norm was a rare event using just social influence, the establishment of extreme opinions is common when a level of uncertainty is added.

8.2.2.2 The Norm of Truth

People have opinions about music, films, plays, books, food, politics and even religion. As we have seen in the previous section, we can analyse the radicalisation of political opinions. The same results can also be interpreted as the dynamics with which fashions come about although the opinion space has to be reinterpreted slightly. Many issues are simply social constructs, and some philosophers would argue that everything is (see von Glaserfeld 1997). But what about issues where there might be a right and wrong, a true and false?

In Hegselmann and Krause (2006) an opinion dynamics model is developed in which the existence of an actual truth and the possibility of finding it are explored. The truth is simply one value in the opinion space. Agents differ in their desire to find the truth. The equation governing opinion change is

$$x_i(t+1) = \alpha_i T + (1-\alpha_i) f_i(x(t)), \tag{8.4}$$

with $1 \leq i \leq n$. The equation contains as an objective part T, and an opinion dynamic part in which f_i is a bounded confidence update (see Hegselmann and Krause 2002) such that agent i updates its opinion by averaging over the opinions of all agents j for which $|x_i(t) - x_j(t)| \leq \varepsilon$. The value of ε gives a symmetric confidence interval to the left and right of an agent's opinion i and generates an *opinion profile* over the whole opinion space. How much an agent's opinion is influenced either by the objective truth or the social opinion space is modulated by the value α. If $\alpha = 0$ the function collapses to the normal bounded confidence opinion dynamics discussed for example in Hegselmann and Krause (2002).

In Hegselmann and Krause (2006) convergence to the truth of the overall population is explored for a variety of value combinations of α and ε and the position of T within the opinion space. Some results are that societies with a limited number of truth seekers (agents with $\alpha \geq 0$) can result in a consensus at the truth. There are some conditions under which this is not the case though:

1. The truth is at an extreme point in the opinion space: Although society might still reach consensus leaning towards the truth, the extremity of the position might mean that consensus is reached before truth.
2. The truth seekers are too efficient in getting to the truth: A high value of α can lead to truth seekers getting to the truth too fast, leaving behind some non-truth seekers at the fringes. This can be remedied to some extent by increasing the value of ε.
3. Too few truth seekers: A low percentage of truth seekers might lead to not enough pull to reach the truth.

For a large class of cases convergence to the truth is, however, proven in Hegselmann and Krause (2006) by the 'Funnel Theorem'. The specific class of cases is defined as those where the social process is 'range preserving', meaning that the updated opinion of each agent in $t+1$ remains in the range of opinions of t, formally expressed as

$$min\{x_j | j \in I\} \leq f_i(x) \leq max\{x_j | j \in I\}, \tag{8.5}$$

for the set of all agents, $I = \{1, 2, \ldots, n\}$ and of all opinion profiles $x = (x_1, x_2, \ldots, x_n)$.

This model is relevant to the understanding of social dynamics as not only does allow for the investigation of dynamics of social influence but also conditions of convergence to specific values. Here the value is truth and, at first glance, truth and social norms do not seem natural allies, with one seeming arbitrary, the other eternal and fixed. However, it can help to understand how a group of agents, behaving according to a particular norm can influence society to converge to that norm. This dynamic, in turn, will help to understand the role power relationships in the emergence of norms.

8.2.3 *Diffusion and the Theory of Reasoned Action*

In Sect. 2.3.1 we discussed the theory of reasoned action as a theoretical model of social influence. There have been surprisingly few agent-based simulations using the theory of reasoned action and none related to the uptake of social norms. Sogani et al. (2005a,b) implement the theory of reasoned action to simulate the acceptance of new computer technology. The diffusion of a technology can be seen as similar

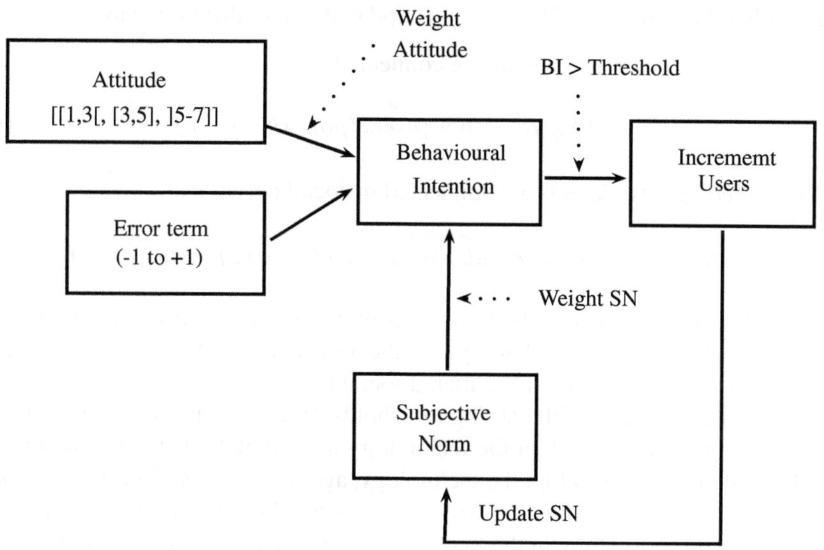

Fig. 8.1 Implementation of the theory of reasoned action for technology uptake (Sogani et al. 2005a, p. 472, Fig. 2)

to the diffusion of a social norm. Five kinds of agents are identified with different 'speeds of' or 'thresholds for' the adoption of a new technology, from 'innovators', i.e. early adopters, to 'laggards'. The model showed a rising S-curve for the uptake of new technologies. A division of the population into heterogeneous agents with different thresholds can also be found in Rogers (1995) in relation to innovations and in Elster (1989) in relation to social norms. Elster considers this heterogeneity as one of the major features of norm adoption that distinguishes it from simple imitation.

As seen in Eqs. 2.1 and 2.2, the behavioural intention (*BI*) of an agent α in this adoption model is defined from two parameters; α's attitude towards o, ($A_\alpha(o)$) and α's subjective norms ($SN_\alpha(o)$), each weighted to represent their relative influence using w_1, w_2. The authors add an error term to the classic theory of reasoned action framework, e_α, ranging from -1 to 1.

$$BI_\alpha(o) = w_1 \times A_\alpha(o) + w_2 \times SN_\alpha(o) + e_\alpha \tag{8.6}$$

In addition agents have a threshold value ranging from 1 to 7 describing the point at which they become a user of new technology. The population of 100 agents is divided into three categories, laggards, undecided and innovators, based on their attitudes. Laggards' attitudes range from 1 to 3, undecideds 3–5 and innovators 5–7 (see Fig. 8.1). In the model, the behavioural intention (*BI*), composed from the attitude, the social norm *SN*, and the error term, determines the rate of adoption. A low *BI* thus means a reluctance and a high *BI* an eagerness to adopt. The technology is adopted by an agent if the BI is greater than the adoption threshold.

Initially all agents have $SN = 1$. SN is updated in two different ways:

1. *Independent agents:* All agents are connected.

$$SN_\alpha(o) = (6 \times (users/pop\_size)) + 1 \tag{8.7}$$

2. *Networked agents:* Agents are connected in social networks.

$$SN_\alpha(o) = (6 \times (friend\_users_\alpha/number\_of\_friends_\alpha)) + 1 \tag{8.8}$$

According to the first equation, the overall number in the population who have already adopted the new technology is the relevant variable, while the second equation takes into account differentiated social ties.

Thc simulation is run with varying thresholds. If the threshold is set to 1, i.e. the lowest setting, all agents adopt the technology immediately. If the threshold is set to 5, only the innovators adopt the technology, again in the first time step. No other agents adopt. If the threshold is set to 3, adoption develops over time. The innovators take up the new technology in the first instance and then adoption slowly rises until there is a sharp increase up to saturation. The uptake curve becomes the signature S-curve of diffusion. Uptake might not reach 100 %. The two different ways of calculating the social influence (SN), either by using the whole population (Eq. 8.7) or a personal social network (Eq. 8.8), lead to slightly different uptake curves. Although still following an S-curve embedding the agents in a social network leads to slower uptake because agents are exposed to fewer social influences, i.e. only those of their network rather than the whole population.

The authors point out that the slow start of a technology uptake is commercially interesting as other companies could come in at this stage of the uptake, piggybacking on a technologic al innovation. It is thus particularly important to keep in mind that embedding into social networks slows down uptake.

8.2.4 Social Impact Theory

In this section we discuss a computer implementation of the Dynamic Social Impact Theory discussed in Sect. 2.3.2. The model is taken from Nowak et al. (1990). Agents are situated on a 40×40 grid with each patch representing one individual. Attitudes are initially randomly distributed. The agents are defined by four parameters. The first is their individual attitude where an attitude is binary, partitioning the population into two opposing subgroups. The second parameter is their ability to persuade people from the opposing group. Persuasiveness is a number between 0 and 100 randomly assigned. It is not a fixed parameter but changes during the simulation whenever an agent changes its attitude. On every attitude change persuasiveness is reassigned randomly, representing that an attitude change might lead to more fervour in persuasion (e.g. Born Again Christians) or to a less convincing, wishy-washy character. The third is the agent's ability to give support to people in their own group. Supportiveness is again a number between 0 and 100 randomly assigned and reassigned on attitude change. Both persuasiveness and supportiveness are uniformly distributed. The fourth parameter is the social impact notion of 'immediacy', how close an influence is to an agent. It is calculated as the Euclidian distance (d_i) between agents using the positions of agents on the grid to structure the social interactions.

The simulation is based on two change equations using the above parameters, the impact of persuasion (I_p) and the impact of support (I_s).

$$I_p = N_o^{1/2}[\sum(p_i/d_i^2)/N_o], \tag{8.9}$$

where N_o is the number of opposing agents, and p_i and d_i the persuasiveness and distance of agent i respectively.

$$I_s = N_s^{1/2}[\sum(s_i/d_i^2)/N_s]' \tag{8.10}$$

where N_s is the number of supporting agents, and s_i and d_i the persuasiveness and distance of agent i respectively. Note that the influenced agent is an element of N_s.

Both I_p and I_s are calculated for each agent at each step. An agent changes its attitude if $I_p > I_s$.

For experimentation, attitudes are randomly distributed with different majorities. An initial 70 % majority opinion leads to a very high (85–95 %) majority equilibrium after around 30 simulation steps. However, minorities always persist, often at the fringes of the grid. Initial minorities of 10 % were erased in some simulation runs but already at 20 % the minority persisted, even if smaller at the end. Equal initial groups lead to completely unpredictable results. The supportiveness of minority members was higher at the end of the simulation than at the beginning and if minority members survived the first few steps they often converted surrounding majority members.

In Sect. 7.3 we discussed models of cultural transmission investigating variation of cultures and the persistence of minorities. Similarly Dynamic Social Impact Theory investigates the emergence of a majority opinion and the persistence of minorities. The major difference is that the mechanisms of Dynamic Social Impact Theory are supported empirically as mechanisms underlying human opinion (and in turn norm) adoption. It shows that minority norms can survive in societies at relatively low minority thresholds but that unification and hence adherence to one majority norm happens rapidly.

8.2.5 Drugtalk

The next model of social influence is a model of drug uptake, developed and discussed in Agar (2005). This model is based on Agar's ethnographic study of drug use (Agar 2006). Agar makes a distinction between the first experience of drugs and the continuation of drug use. A similar distinction is made in Situational Crime Prevention Theory (Cornish and Clarke 1986) where different models are used for the initial involvement in criminal behaviour and the continuation of a life of crime.

Drugtalk consists of an environment in which agents meet each other, exchange experiences, observe each others' behaviours and take drugs. Agents have two kinds of social interaction, meeting with members of their social network and random encounters. In general, the more drugs there are available and the more drug users there are, the more new agents try drugs. A drug comes in different qualities, formalised as "Goodstuff" and "Badstuff". There are four influences on drug use: (1) availability, (2) personal experience, (3) the experiences of those in an agent's social network and (4) the experiences arising from random encounters. Continuing to take drugs is determined by whether agents get positive or negative reports of drugs from others and how many addicts there are in an agent's surroundings with addicts deterring agents from further drug use.

The analysis of *Drugtalk* in Agar (2005) is preliminary and qualitative. Nonetheless, it shows interesting patterns of drug uptake and addiction rates as well interesting variations between runs. The setup for analysis is 500 agents, Goodstuff set at 70 % and Badstuff at 30 %. The attitude is set to 50, the median value, reflecting a relative openness of agents to drug experiences.

The number of addicts is consistently around the 10 % mark, which corresponds to empirical findings of 10–15 % for drug epidemics in communities with relatively easy access to drugs and relative openness to them. Although in all runs the number of users is significantly higher than the number of agents at risk, the development might be rapid, taking less than 40 steps until the number of users overtakes the number at risk or steps can be much slower with the crossover point at around 150.

The results suggest that epidemics can have different trajectories even with the same initial conditions. Agar points out that these differences lead to different policy responses. For example, for extremely rapid epidemics, education efforts will most likely be too late. It might be better to monitor the supply of new drugs before an epidemic kicks off.

This simulation also shows the influence of an agent's social circle on its behaviour. The prevalence of drug use in an agent's circle, and the resulting increase in the likelihood of the agent trying drugs if the general mood is supportive, is a set of norms to which the agent adheres or not. The model also shows how the availability of artefacts (here drugs, but it could also be revolutionary pamphlets or iPads) might influence the spread of norms.

8.2.6 Misbehaving in the Classroom

The final social influence model we discuss is of social network effects on juvenile delinquency (Bosse et al. 2009). Several social influences on the agents are taken into account, including the ethos of their school, their parents and their peers. The

Table 8.4 Relevant parameters

	Pupils	Parents	School
Delinquency	✓	✓	✓
Dominance	✓	✓	✓
Age	✓		
Influenceability	✓		

agents in the model change their delinquency depending on these influences. The authors describe the model as a model of ‘social learning’ but we have categorised it as a model of social influence because the cognitive capacities of the agents are too simple to represent social learning in any useful definition of that term.

The model is based on a school class of ten adolescent pupils. There are three kinds of agents: pupils, school and parents. Only pupils are modelled in the simulation with parents and school being groups to which the agents are related via attachment relations. The model is formalised in a predicate logic called Temporal Trace Language (TTL), devised by the authors. TTL is a language that combines the use of qualitative/logic al aspects of a scenario with quantitative numerical aspects, thus enabling the analysis of delinquency both in its qualitative guise of peer/parent/school influence through relationships and making a numerical analysis of the actual change of delinquency possible. Furthermore, the language is dynamic, enabling the analysis of delinquency over time. For a more formal discussion of TTL see Bosse et al. (2006) (Table 8.4).

The variables in the model are *delinquency, age, influenceability* and *dominance*, all of which are real numbers from the interval $[0, 1]$. For schools and parents, the delinquency parameter is static, i.e. does not change during the simulation. The meaning of delinquency in the context of these two types of agent is whether it is a ‘bad school’ or a ‘bad family’. For the pupils it is a measure of how many crimes they committed in the past. Dominance is a character trait for pupils and in the context of schools the authors interpret it so that a stricter school is more dominant. We assume that the interpretation is the same for parents, i.e. a strict family background more dominant. Age and influenceability are pupil variables only. All pupils are connected to each other and to their school and each pupil is connected to one set of parents. Each link has a different weight, thus modelling differentiated attachment between agents. The simulation models the delinquency of the overall group, given initial group compositions, e.g. nine ‘good kids’ and one ‘bad one’ and parameter values, e.g. a high difference between ‘good’ and ‘bad’.

The authors investigate four scenarios. The first is to have one pupil with high delinquency (0.8) and criminal parents (0.8) in a class with the other pupils having delinquency of 0.3, parental influence of 0.7 and parental delinquency of 0.2. The question is whether the criminal pupil will influence the class more. The outcome is that the criminality of the delinquent agent goes down to that of the other pupils.

The second scenario looks at the influence of the school on a pupil’s delinquency. The other variables are kept the same as in the previous scenario. The outcome is that a more delinquent school raises the delinquency of pupils substantially more than a single delinquent peer. The third and fourth scenarios look at interactions between groups of peers. In the third scenario, half the pupils have a high delinquency and half have the same settings as in Scenario 1. The pupils converge towards a median level of delinquency. The fourth scenario has three groups, three delinquent pupils in a high attachment group, three non-delinquents in a high attachment group and four pupils with high influenceability, one of which is attached to a delinquent and one to a non-delinquent. The result is again a convergence of delinquencies (Bosse et al. 2006).

This model shows the influence of factors such as delinquent peers on the overall delinquency of pupils in a class. It implements many theoretical features of norms, for example that individuals are influenced by a variety of sources (peers, parents and the school ethos) and their family background.

8.3 Social Learning

In the previous section we discussed models of social influence. In this section we turn to social learning. Although the boundary is difficult to draw precisely, the two mechanisms are different in some important ways. First, social learning is cumulative. In the previous simulations, agents' attributes or attitudes were calculated taking into account the strength and importance of different external influences. In the following simulations, agents learn cumulatively from their surrounding, either by experience as in the first simulation, or successively by updating their initial attitude depending on their experiences of specific other agents.

8.3.1 Learning the Highway Code: Part I

Sen and Airiau (2007) investigate the emergence of a norm in the setting of a social dilemma: Given two cars arriving at a crossroads, one from the east and one from the south, who has right of way? If both proceed there will be an accident, if both yield the traffic will halt. Hence, some rule has to emerge, one of two possible norms, either the one on the right has right of way or the one on the left. If the scenario is played out in the strict two player (i.e. car) setting, a third option can emerge in which one car becomes the dominant player that always has right of way. However, as soon as there are more than two players, this norm can no longer emerge as agents do not know which other player they are facing.

In each round of the 'road intersection game' all players play against one other. In each interaction one player takes the part of the column player (P_{col}) the other the row player (P_{row}). Each player can evolve one of two policies, yield to the right (Y_R) or yield to the left (Y_L), meaning that P_{row} or P_{col} respectively goes first. The payoff matrix for the game (Table 8.5) shows the negative outcome if the norms are not aligned.

Table 8.5 Payoff matrix for the road intersection game

	Go	Y_L
Go	$-1, -1$	$3, 2$
Y_R	$2, 3$	$1, 1$

The authors then test the emergence of a norm using three different learning algorithms: Q-Learning (Watkins and Dayan 1992) with ε-greedy exploration, WoLF-PHC (Bowling and Veloso 2002) and Fictitious Play (FP) (Fudenberg and Levine 1998). In order to optimise their payoffs, agents have to conform to a common single norm.

As expected, each norm emerges roughly 50 % of the time. Initially agents prefer to yield a lot as the payoff is higher than being involved in an accident. Which norm wins in the end depends on which player first understands the situation and starts exploiting the higher payoff of *Go*. The larger the population, the longer it takes for a norm to emerge. The authors adapt the game to the n-action scenario by giving agents a payoff of 4 if they choose the same action and -1 if they choose different actions. A higher number of actions also delays the emergence of the norm. Finally they examine the influence of the different learning algorithms. With a population of 200 agents. Q-learning is by far the fastest with a norm emerging very quickly after only around 100 iterations. WoLF takes ten times as long and Fictitious Play is even slower with 40,000 iterations needed for a stable norm. When part of the population uses one algorithm and part another, the time until the emergence of a norm is between the times for the pure algorithms.

In the case that the population contains agents with a fixed predetermined strategy, either Y_L or Y_R, the population always ends up with the respective norm, even for a very small bias towards one strategy. Local sub-norm emergence is investigated by letting subgroups of agents interact infrequently. For low interaction probabilities (0.2), sub-groups of norms emerge whilst with an interaction probability above about 0.3 the whole population adopts the same norm.

The above is a very simple example of social learning in an agent-based model of norms. It relies mainly on a game theoretic matrix and the potential of agents to adopt winning strategies. Note the difference between this game theory model and those discussed in Chap. 6: here agents learn to adapt their strategies over their lifetime whereas in the other models successful strategies were selected by natural (or cultural) selection over generations. In the next chapter, in Sect. 9.3.3, we will discuss a much more involved case of social learning via norm invocation in a traffic environment. But first, we discuss another model of social learning where an agent's learning is triggered by the wish to understand its social group.

8.3.2 Group Norms and Learning

Verhagen (2000) developed a model of social learning in which an individual's behaviour is informed by its perception of the prevalent group values. Agents are set in a two-dimensional world with two resources, A and B. Patches of the world can contain one, both or neither of the resources. Agents can decide to consume one of the resources, move to another patch or do nothing. They base their decisions on two decision trees, a personal one and a group one. The personal decision tree determined by the utility the agent gets from the action. The group decision tree represents the agent's interpretation of the group norms. The group model can be more or less 'objective'. For example it could be the same for all agents (fully objective), different for different agents in a random way or identical to each agent's self model (subjective). To make a decision, the agent's personal decision tree and its representation of the group decision tree are combined and the action having the highest utility is chosen. Subsequently the agent receives feedback from the group on its decision resulting in an update of the group decision tree.

Agents can be more or less autonomous. More autonomous agents choose to act according to the group action tree less often. For example an autonomy value of 0.4 means that the agents choose to act according to the public tree in 40 % of cases. The research hypotheses for the model are that a higher degree of autonomy will lead to higher variance of behaviour, and that the agents will adopt the group-model more slowly if each agent's group-model equals its self-model. The rationale behind the second hypothesis is that the similarity of the group model to the self model will lead to less effective feedback, resulting in slower updating and hence slower assimilation. In Verhagen (2000, Chap. 11), the model is run with autonomy values 0, 0.4 and 0.8. The first hypothesis is supported because agents take longer to adopt a common norm as autonomy increases. The second hypothesis is, however, not supported (Verhagen 2000, p. 85, Figs. 11.1 and 11.2).

This model shows how new norms can be learned by agents. In this model, agents establish a set of social norms together. By feedback on its behaviour, an agent realises whether its representation of the group norms is adequate and adapts this representation accordingly. Rather than having norms emerge from a society without any norms, here all agents are aware of the existence of norms from the start. The agents do not know initially what behaviour the group norms prescribe. Agents learn the content of their society's norms together in a process of trial and error.

8.3.3 The Evolution of Symbolic Communication

An agent-based model of the emergence of a shared lexicon is developed in Salgado (2012). Rather than having social norms as a starting point, the model explores the origins and conditions for the emergence of language. Salgado argues for language resulting from three roots: a social system, individual cognition and biological evolution (see Fig. 8.2). Language is one form of symbolic communication. Social norms can also be seen as a form of symbolic communication with adherence to norms signalling intentions and trustworthiness (Falk et al. 2003; Bicchieri 2006).

Following Tomasello (2000), Salgado argues that *cognition* is needed for the development of a theory of mind in order to recognise others as intentional and

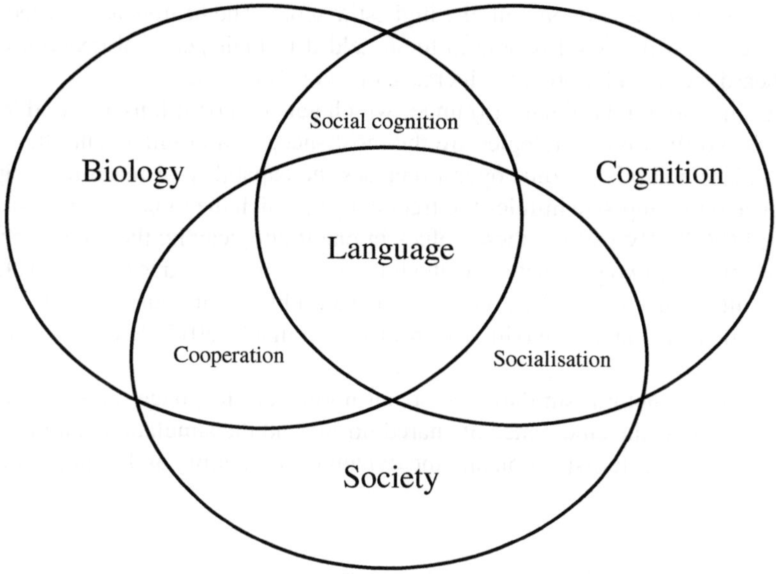

Fig. 8.2 The triple root of language (From Salgado 2012, Fig. 3.1, p. 57)

mental beings similar to oneself. *Society* is a result of communication resulting from this cognitive capacity. Complex social structures, cultural artefacts and social norms can emerge and evolve based on symbolic interchanges between people. *Biology* brought about physical changes making symbolic communication and language possible and making more complex forms of cooperation necessary (e.g. long infant dependency coupled with fast female reproduction).

The model is based on a, 80×80 grid with four regions, green, yellow, purple and blue. Each region contains the same four objects, a flower, a leaf, a tree and a plant. Groups of ten agents are allocated to each region at the start of a run, defining them as a group. Agents move around randomly, interacting with agents from other groups. Agents can see objects, utter a word w and hear an utterance (u_n) from another agent n. Agents have different loudnesses leading to different *audibility radii* (r_a) of each agent's utterances and different step lengths s_a with which they traverse the grid, depending on their group membership. All objects have the same visibility area and visibility areas do not overlap. A word consists of a four letter string drawn from a shared alphabet. The first letter signifies the group membership of the speaker. The following letters follow the rule Consonant-Vowel-Consonant. Words have a score (κ) signifying their prevalence.

The communicative interaction involves one object (the topic of communication), one agent acting as a speaker and at least one agent acting as a hearer. Each time step one agent in each region is selected as the speaker. It utters a word creating an association between the word and the objects in range. Initially random words are created by agents. Once words have been associated with objects, speakers choose the word from their lexicon with the highest κ score. The hearers acknowledge the utterance and if the word is new to them, add it to their personal lexicon, if they have heard the word before, they increase the word's κ score.

The simulation investigates (a) under which general conditions a shared lexicon emerges and (b) which strategies are the most successful in influencing the shared lexicon. The audibility radius operationalises the capability of reaching recipients (CRR), and the step-size mimics the frequency at which the topic of conversation is changed (FCT). By varying these values in one group, leaving the others constant, the impact of the two parameters on the influence on the shared lexicon is evaluated. The result is that high CRR, i.e. a large audibility radius and low FCT, i.e. a low speed, result in the maximal impact (see Salgado 2012, Sect. 4.4, for more details).

Given the structural similarity of social norms and language, these results can be interpreted as the emergence of shared norms and the simulation can be used to investigate norm internalisation and the dynamics of majority and minority norms.

8.4 Achievements and Shortcomings

Whereas the last chapter used simple imitation or the transmission of memes as mechanisms of norm diffusion, this chapter looked at more involved mechanisms of social influence and social learning. As stated above, the dividing line between imitation and social influence is not very clear but the models we called social influence models all rely on a psychological notion of influence and usually some form of social structure (e.g. network), whereas the imitation models do not.

Opinion dynamics models represent one of the earliest uses of agent-based modelling in the social sciences. They show the importance of the range of influence, determined by the interaction policy between agents. They also introduce the concept of bounded confidence, meaning that only similar agents can influence each other. The theory of reasoned action is a theoretical model of social influence used in a variety of settings. The model shows how very simple influence and interaction mechanisms can lead to very different outcomes. Simulation makes a dynamic implementation of the initially static social impact theory possible. Drugtalk is based on rich qualitative data on how people describe their journey of drug consumption. It takes into account many parameters such as personal propensity, availability of drugs and, crucially for social learning, the experiences of a drug by other, surrounding agents. Finally, the model of peer influence of delinquency models the combination of school, home and peers as an influence on an agent.

The social learning models we discussed implement very different mechanisms to represent social learning. The traffic example is based on a game theory matrix and reinforcement learning to solve the coordination game of right of way at a junction. The model of the learning of group norms uses group feedback on an agent's decision for the interaction between personal and group norms for the agent to learn. Finally, the model of the development of a shared lexicon shows how symbolic communication, of which social norms can be seen as one kind, can emerge.

Social influence and social learning models of norms are models of the diffusion of specific norms, an opinion, the uptake of a drug or the emergence of a right of way rule. They implement a variety of inter-social mechanisms underlying diffusion and allow some testing of proposed models, such as the theory of reasoned action and social impact theory. Most importantly, they highlight the importance of a social embedding of the agents with, for example, the opinion dynamics model and the theory of reasoned action model clearly showing the difference in diffusion between different interaction policies. They implement in a rudimentary way the influence of the majority on an individual's behaviour but fall short of modelling the feedback between the macro and micro level. We turn to this feedback mechanism in the next chapter, where we discuss cognitive models of normative behaviour.

References

Agar, M. (2005). Agents in living color: Towards Emic agent-based models. *Journal of Artificial Societies and Social Simulation, 8*(1), 4. http://jasss.soc.surrey.ac.uk/8/1/4.html.

Agar, M. (2006). *Dope double agent: The naked emperor on drugs*. Morrisvilee: Lulubooks.

Bicchieri, C. (2006). *The grammar of society: The nature and dynamics of social norms*. New York: Cambridge University Press.

Bosse, T., Jonker, C. M., van der Meij, L., Sharpanskykh, A., & Treur J. (2006). *Specification and verification of dynamics in cognitive agent models* (pp. 247–254). Los Alamitos: IEEE Computer Society Press.

Bosse, T., Gerritsen, C., & Klein, M. C. (2009). Agent-based simulation of social learning in criminology. In *International conference on agents and artificial intelligence*, Porto.

Bowling, M., & Veloso M. (2002). Multiagent learning using a variable learning rate. *Artificial Intelligence, 136*, 215–250.

Cornish, D. B., & Clarke, R. V. (1986). *The reasoning criminal*. New York: Springer.

Deffuant, G., Amblard, F., Weisbuch, G., & Faure, T. (2002). How can extremism prevail? A study based on the relative agreement interaction model. *Journal of Artificial Societies and Social Simulation, 5*(4), 1. http://jasss.soc.surrey.ac.uk/5/4/1.html.

Elster, J. (1989). *The cement of society*. Cambridge: Cambridge University Press.

Falk, A., Fehr, E., & Fischbacher, U. (2003). On the nature of fair behaviour. *Economic Inquiry, 41*(1), 20–26.

Fudenberg, D., & Levine, K. (1998). *The theory of learning in games*. Cambridge: MIT.

Hegselmann, R., & Krause, U. (2002). Opinion dynamics and bounded confidence: Models, analysis and simulation. *Journal of Artificial Societies and Social Simulation, 5*(3), 2. http://jasss.soc.surrey.ac.uk/5/3/2.html.

Hegselmann, R., & Krause, U. (2006). Truth and cognitive division of labour: first steps towards a computer aided social epistemology. *Journal of Artificial Societies and Social Simulation, 9*(3), 10. http://jasss.soc.surrey.ac.uk/9/3/10.html.

Hegselmann, R., & Kurz, S. (forthcoming). Checkerboards, networks and neighbourhoods – history and analysis of configuration games.

Nowak, A., Szamreja, J., & Latané, B. (1990). From private attitude to public opinion: A dynamic theory of social impact. *Psychological Review, 97*(3), 362–376.

Rogers, E. M. (1995). *Diffusion of innovations*. New York: Simon and Schuster.

Sakoda, J. M. (1971). The checkerboard model of social interaction. *Journal of Mathematical Sociology, 1*(1), 119–132.
Salgado, M. (2012). *More than words: Computational models of emergence and evolution of symbolic communication*. Ph.D. thesis, Department of Sociology, University of Surrey.
Schelling, T. (1971). Dynamic models of segregation. *Journal of Mathematical Sociology, 1*, 143–186.
Sen, S., & Airiau, S. (2007). Emergence of norms through social learning. In *IJCAI-07*, Hyderabad.
Sogani, S., Muduganti, R., & Hexmoor, H. (2005a). Comparison of information technology adoption rates across laggards, innovators and others. In *Proceedings of IEEE international conference on information technology innovators and others (ITCC 2005)*, Las Vegas.
Sogani, S., Muduganti, R., Hexmoor, H., & F. Davis (2005b). Introducing agent based implementation of the theory of reasoned action: A case study in user acceptance of computer technology. In *Knowledge intensive multi-agent systems (KIMAS)*, Waltham.
Tomasello, M. (2000). *The cultural origins of human cognition*. Cambridge: Harvard University Press.
Verhagen, H. (2000). *Norm autonomous agents*. Ph.D. thesis, Royal Institute of Technology and Stockholm University, Sweden.
von Glaserfeld, E. (1997). *Wege des Wissens: Konstruktivistische Erkundungen durch unser Denken* (2nd ed.). Heidelberg: Carl-Auer-Systeme Verlag.
Watkins, C., & Dayan, P. (1992). Q-learning. *Machine Learning, 3*, 279–292.

Chapter 9
Internalisation and Social Norms

Tradition is a guide and not a jailer.

W. Somerset Maugham

9.1 Cognitive Models of Norm Internalisation

This chapter discusses models of social norms that go beyond the mainly behavioural models of the last two chapters. Rather than taking their origin in game theory or the natural sciences, these models originate from research in multi-agent systems (cf. Sect. 4.2.3). We briefly discuss the outline of a model for the involvement of emotions in the internalisation of norms. Unfortunately, although it seems promising, the model remains at the outline stage of development. We then discuss an agent architecture and modelling platform for normative behaviour originating in multi-agent systems research that has been fully developed and applied to a range of scenarios.

We have discussed the BOID agent architecture earlier in Sect. 4.1.2 and criticised it for a static implementation of a set of obligations representing social norms. We argued that the idea of 'hard wired' static norms does not gel with modelling social phenomena; it is just not how social agents operate. Agents must be able to learn new norms and modify their old norms. Neumann (2009) criticises existing models of norms for not touching on important features of normative behaviour derived from psychological research. One is that normative behaviour is related to emotions such as guilt and shame that none of the existing models capture. Social norms only work because humans are socialised over the course of their lives, internalising social norms as behavioural blueprints. If we model social norms without emotions and internalisation, we might be modelling behavioural regularities but we do not model genuine normative behaviour, Neumann argues.

To see how one might respond to this criticism, we start by examining a model of the influence of emotions on normative behaviour before turning to norm internalisation.

C. Elsenbroich and N. Gilbert, *Modelling Norms*, DOI 10.1007/978-94-007-7052-2_9,

9.2 Agents That Love to Conform

In von Scheve et al. (2006) a cognitive approach is taken to the implementation of social norms. Although norms are adhered to by an individual because transgression is costly, Scheve et al. do not model the cost directly via payoff reduction but indirectly via an emotional response to the disapproval by another individual (see Fig. 9.1).

This model takes several ideas from the models of normative behaviour we discussed earlier. For example, agents have a representation of social norms that is updated according to social feedback, similar to Verhagen's model of group norms discussed in Sect. 8.3.2. A norm violation is punished if it is observed by another agent, similar to Axelrod's norm game, discussed in Sect. 6.1.2. It has however two new and interesting features: (a) instead of a reduction in payoff for the goal state, the norm violating agent is exposed to a disapproving emotion such as contempt, disgust and disdain by the observer. This exposure leads to an emotional response from the violator agent, such as shame, guilt or embarrassment. These emotions in turn lead to an updating of the agent's representation of social norms, and their internalisation.

9.3 EMIL: Emergence in the Loop

In Chap. 6 we looked at the emergence of cooperation from purely selfish individuals. In Chap. 7 we looked at the diffusion of social behaviour using different mechanisms of transfer. In both chapters there were models of the emergence of social phenomena ('cooperation' or 'cultures'), but no feedback from these emerged phenomena back to the individuals' behaviour. In terms of the ontological discussion in Chap. 2, there is the emergence of social facts but they do not have any causal or coercive powers. The models have thus not gone beyond individualism.

There is however growing interest in going further than this and using agent-based modelling as a method to do so. If we can specify agents and generate models of social phenomena, it should also be possible to have the agents be influenced by those phenomena. This mechanism is called *immergence*, *second-order emergence*, the *micro-macro link* or simply the *feedback loop* between the social and the individual.

EMergence In the Loop (EMIL) is a project concerned with this feedback between the micro and macro level (Conte et al. 2013). EMIL is a comprehensive account of the computational requirements needed to implement normative feedback or normative learning. EMIL comprises both an architecture for normative learning and implementations in several simulation environments. The first implementation is a traffic simulation in which pedestrians cross a stream of traffic (see Sect. 9.3.3). The second demonstration example is an implementation of a Wikipedia-like environment in which communication is regulated by discussion

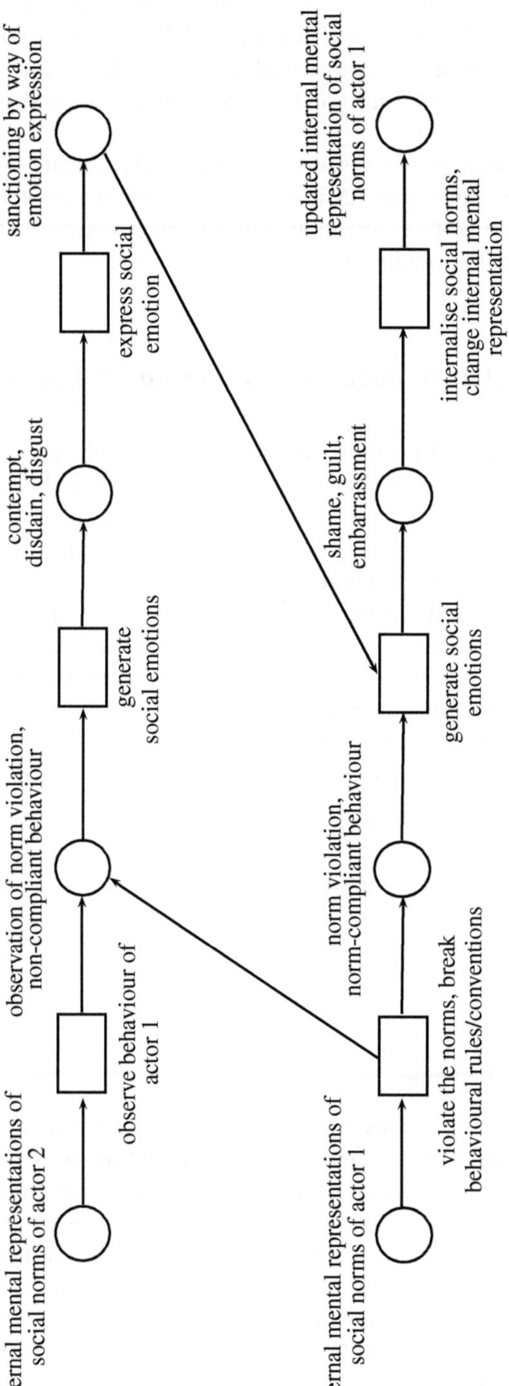

Fig. 9.1 Internalisation of social norms via emotions (Fix et al. 2006, p. 106, Fig. 1)

norms (Lotzmann 2010). The third is a micro finance simulation (Lucas et al. 2010). The fourth implementation uses both normative (EMIL-S) and conforming agents (social imitators) in a multi-scenario world of an airport in which agents need to make decisions such as declaring goods, waiting in queues and picking up their luggage (Campenní et al. 2010).

In the following sections we discuss the main achievements of EMIL starting with the theoretical architecture, EMIL-A, followed by two implementations, one using normative (i.e. EMIL-S) agents in a traffic environment and one analysing different algorithms for normative learning.

9.3.1 *EMIL-A: An Architecture for Normative Feedback*

One of the first agent architectures to be concerned with norm adaptation and innovation is the EMIL-A architecture first developed in Andrighetto and Campenni (2007). Its starting point is a division of agent knowledge into factual (event) and normative (rule) knowledge. The agent has a normative interface with the world as well as the factual one of the BDI and BOID agents.

The EMIL-A architecture has two kinds of memory, an *event board*, which stores facts and events and a *normative frame* to infer and store rules from the event board. In addition agents are informed of norms that have emerged communally by the *normative board* where this common information is stored. The focus is on how agents understand, learn and change norms by adaptation and invocation.

The EMIL-A architecture consists of three types of representations:

1. Normative Beliefs (N-Beliefs)
2. Normative Goals (N-Goals)
3. Normative Intentions (N-Intentions)

and four procedures:

1. Norm Recognition
2. Norm Adoption
3. Decision Making
4. Normative Action Planning.

The normative representations correspond to the ingredients of the BDI agent. Instead of factual beliefs, desires and intentions, the EMIL-A agent has normative beliefs, normative goals (instead of desires) and normative intentions. Corresponding to these representations, the agent can recognise a norm as a norm, adopt it, and use it in its decision making and its action planning using the normative procedures. The normative level of the agent is thus implemented in parallel to the factual level with a close correspondence between the two (Fig. 9.2).

The most important part of the EMIL-A architecture is that it is endowed with two interactions with the world. As it is based on the BDI architecture (4.1), it can

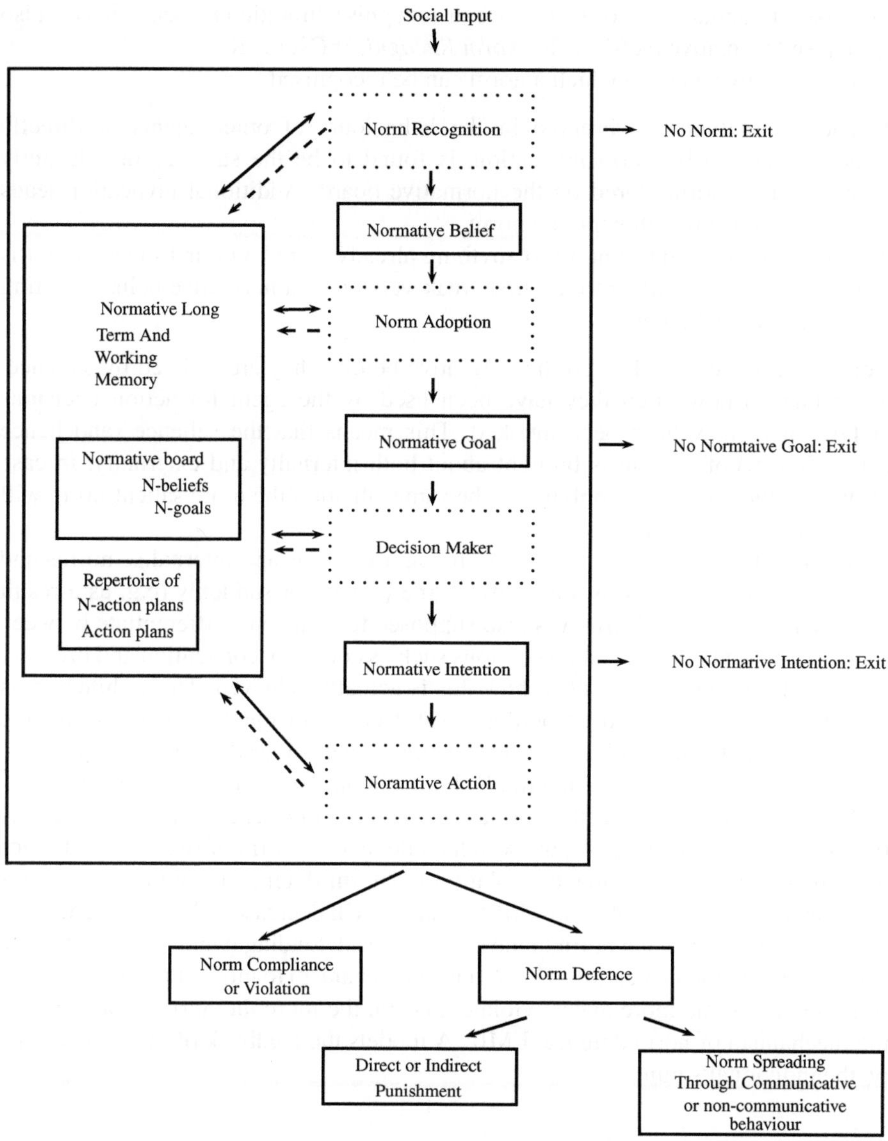

Fig. 9.2 The EMIL-A architecture: the representations are in *thick boxes*, *dotted boxes* indicate procedures. *One directional arrows* indicate information flow, *bidirectional arrows* indicate storing and *dotted arrows* indicate activation-search (The figure is reproduced from Andrighetto et al. 2010, p. 78)

form beliefs about the world, i.e. it can recognise 'traditional facts'. It can also recognise 'normative facts' via its *Norm Recognizer* (Norm-R).

There are two ways in which a norm can be recognised:

1. The external norm, observed in the behaviours of other agents or directly communicated by norm invocation, is found to be the same as or relevantly similar to a norm stored on the normative board. Additional invocation leads to increased entrenchment of a norm.
2. The external norm has no fit to anything already stored. On first invocation it is stored as a *candidate norm*, a first weak version of a normative belief awaiting further entrenchment.

Norms become entrenched on the normative board. They are ordered by salience, depending on how often they have been used by the agent for action decisions or how often they have been invoked. This means that the salience (and hence entrenchment) of a norm is brought about both internally and externally. In case of two conflicting norms applying to the same situation the more salient norm will be used for the decision.

The EMIL-A architecture is able to recognise norms and internalise norms and is also able to forget norms, either over time (decay) or suddenly (e.g. as a result of a traumatic event). EMIL-A is also supposed to be able to differentiate between social norms and other social invocations such as coercion, convention and ordinary requests. However, it is not clear how this is actually achieved. The architecture is sensitive to the fact that not all actions result from deliberated decisions. Using the idea of shortcuts, internalised norms can trigger behaviour directly in response to external stimulus (e.g. we do not think about stopping our car at a red light).

Non-shortcut actions use the normative board to motivate actions. This deliberation results in behavioural outputs which could take the form of two different kinds of normative actions, compliance/violation and norm-defence. Compliance to norms will increase their entrenchment whilst violation will decrease it. Norm-defence will decrease the salience of a norm in the agent that is defending it and increase it in the agent receiving the invocation. This is a neat mechanism to model the empirical fact of norm decay: the more agents violate a norm, the more the norm decays. Using the mechanism of norm defence, EMIL-A models the feedback of the societal fact on the individual's mind.

9.3.2 EMIL-S: The Norm-Feedback Simulation Environment

The EMIL-A architecture is a theoretical framework for an agent able to negotiate the normative world. The architecture is implemented in a simulation environment as the EMIL-S agent. EMIL-S is an almost one-to-one implementation of EMIL-A (Troitzsch 2010, p. 202). The only difference is that in the initial conception of EMIL-A, different deliberation and decision mechanisms were envisaged for normative and other kinds of reasoning whilst the final implementation uses the same mechanisms for both.

9.3.3 Learning the Highway Code: Part II

EMIL-S has been applied to a number of scenarios. In one, the agents are set in a traffic scenario, although this time it is not a crossroad as in Sect. 8.3.1 but pedestrians crossing a road along which cars drive. The purpose of the simulation is to see whether agents learn the norm of using a pedestrian crossing rather than crossing at arbitrary spots, even if it means they have to make a detour on their way to their goal.

The scenario in this simulation is a road with a meadow either side. Car-agents are driving on the road and pedestrian-agents walk about on the meadows. One area of the road has a pedestrian crossing. Sometimes pedestrians want to cross the road. They can either cross wherever they are or use the pedestrian crossing. Depending on where they are, using the pedestrian crossing might mean a detour (i.e. a longer route), but is the safe (normative) thing to do. Similarly car drivers have to make the decision to stop at the crossing, which means a time delay although stopping is the safe (normative) thing to do.

The EMIL-S agents are implemented with event-action trees containing the probabilities of selecting certain actions. For example, the environmental input that there is a pedestrian on the road has possible actions to accelerate, stop or slow-down. The probabilities of each action depend on the successes of that action in the past. The updating of action probabilities in the event-action tree are how agents learn.

In a similar way to the traffic simulation in Sect. 8.3.1, agents have a payoff matrix for getting to their target quickly. In contrast to that simulation, agents learn about norms, not simply from the payoff of past behaviour, but also from their surrounding agents. With both cars and pedestrian users of the road, collisions can happen easily. A collision is an undesirable outcome and will delay both the pedestrian and the car driver. But an actual collision is not the only cause of delays. Sanctions are introduced for causing *near-accidents*. The sanctions are executed as a temporary stop to an agent's movement. Whether an agent is sanctioned for a near accident depends on whether it receives norm invocations from other surrounding agents witnessing the accident. Both actual accidents and near accidents are counted as norm invocations and sanctioned, albeit with different strengths. Their sources are different actions, one being an 'admonition' ("You should not ...") the other being 'blame' ("You must not ..."). Blame carries more delay than admonition.

The pedestrian crossing emerges as an institution where car-agents are expected to slow down and stop when they see pedestrians approaching and pedestrians learn to use the crossing even if it means a detour from their direct route.

Although agents with simple payoff matrices could have learnt to use a pedestrian crossing, the benefit of the crossing would have had to be programmed into the matrix. In the case of the EMIL-S agents, the crossing emerges as the 'right' place to cross the road and, by adding mutated copies of existing event-actions-trees, thus making connections between different event-action trees, agents learn about and follow the emerging norm.

Table 9.1 Implementing reinforcement and normative learning with brave and anxious agents

	Reinforcement learning	Normative learning
Anxious	Red and blue agents segregate into large red and blue areas	Red and blue agents segregate into large blue and red areas
Brave	Red and blue agents segregate into small red and blue areas. Some patches are coloured purple	Most patches are coloured purple with some small areas remaining blue or red

9.3.4 Painting the Town Red

The previous model was an implementation of the EMIL-S architecture. Agents learned about norms by other agents blaming or admonishing them for actions leading to accidents or near accidents. Learning in that model was executed by reinforcement learning. The event-action trees were updated according to the results of their actions (e.g. reaching the goal faster by crossing outside the pedestrian crossing).

But is reinforcement learning sufficient? Lorscheid and Troitzsch (2009) identify reinforcement learning as one underlying mechanism but argue that it is insufficient to model norms. They add *normative learning* that is, learning from normative invocation messages sent between agents. The mechanism of norm invocation messages incorporates a penitence level, a threshold for individual agents at which they change their behaviour, and a social hierarchy, by having the authority levels of agents matter for norm adherence. The decision of whether to adhere to a norm or not is made according to the penitence level and the relative authority of the invocating agent. This way a kind of deliberation is operationalised.

In their model the agents colour in the world. There are red and blue colouring agents, colouring the patches they stand on. The agents have a personal colour value and are confronted with public values in the form of norm invocations. Agents send norm invocation messages to surrounding agents, telling them to adopt their colour. These messages can be read as 'use more blue/red' depending on the colour of the invocating agent. There are three kinds of agents defined by their penitence levels. *Impervious agents, guilty agents* and *embarrassed agents* change their values at different rates, after ten invocations, five invocations and one invocation respectively. The penitence level represents that agents do not just conform blindly to public demands but use some time to 'deliberate' on them. Agents can also be *brave* or *anxious*. Depending on which they are, they move towards an area maximally or minimally different from themselves.

Two kinds of learning are implemented and compared. The first is reinforcement learning (RL) in which the probability values in the event-action-trees are updated according to observations of the environment. The second is normative learning in which the probabilities in the event-action-trees are updated according to norm invocations from other agents. Both learning mechanisms are implemented with both anxious and brave agents. Table 9.1 presents the outcomes.

For anxious agents the choice of learning mechanism makes little difference. With both learning mechanisms agents cluster with other similar agents without a new colour (norm) emerging. Agents move away from agents of the other colour thus minimising norm invocations that will change their colouring behaviour. Once an area of similar agents is established there is no reason to change. For brave agents the learning mechanisms do make a difference. Whilst reinforcement learning establishes some purple areas, i.e. a new norm emerging, normative learning makes the newly emerged norm the prevalent norm with most areas coloured purple.

Given the action possibilities of either adopting a new norm or moving to join agents similar to oneself, the comparison between reinforcement and normative learning shows that the former leads to segregation for all agent types whereas the latter establishes norm adaptation for brave agents. This result hints at how the societal dynamics of segregation and norm adoption might interact.

9.4 Achievements and Shortcomings

EMIL has been a valuable contribution to the application of multi-agent systems to the investigation of normative behaviour. By defining a cognitive agent that is able to learn norms from its environment, EMIL shows how one might model norm internalisation and norm change.

The EMIL-S agent is implemented with event-action trees containing the probabilities of selecting certain actions. For example the environmental input that there is a pedestrian on the road has possible actions to accelerate, stop or slow-down. The probabilities of each action depend on the successes of that action in the past as well as on norm invocations of the agents around them. Updating the action probabilities in the event-action tree is the mechanism of norm internalisation. Mutations of the event-action trees allow agents to learn new norms, and make connections between different trees.

The implementation of penitence levels reproduces the mechanism of deliberation (rather than simple stimulus response). Social hierarchies (in the form of agent authority levels) represent some aspects of social structure. The EMIL architecture has been implemented in interesting case studies. The traffic simulation discussed above shows the emergence of a 'real life' social norm, i.e. the institutionalisation of a pedestrian crossing. In addition there have been implementations of a Wiki-like environment that reproduces both group and norm dynamics and a micro-finance implementation that corroborates this emergence of norms via agent learning. Of particular interest are two implementations comparing normative and simple conforming agents in the multi-scenario simulation of an airport (Campenní et al. 2010) and rule and normative learning in a norm emergence simulation (Lorscheid et al. 2010). The first clearly shows the advantage of normative behaviour over simple imitation that leads to arbitrary regular behaviours that depend on the choice of a few initial agents. The second simulation shows the importance of normative learning for the emergence of norms rather than a segregation of society into groups of different norms.

EMIL achieved its goal of designing a normative agent that does not rely on a static set of norms but can learn normative behaviour from its environment. Moreover, EMIL demonstrated that the agent is simple enough to be implemented in an agent-based model. EMIL-A is thus a major advance over the static BOID agent in that it can learn new norms and can internalise norms learned from the environment. It goes a long way beyond the behavioural simulations of norms discussed in the previous chapters.

In the next chapter we reflect on the simulations seen so far and compare them to features of normative behaviour considered to be important in other disciplines, in particular social psychology. We will see that, although major progress has been made, there are still important features of normative behaviour that cannot be captured by an EMIL-A agent.

References

Andrighetto, G., & Campenni, M. (2007). On the immergence of norms: A normative agent architecture. In *AAAI symposium, social and organizational aspects of intelligence*, Washington, DC.

Andrighetto, G., Campenni, M., & Conte, R. (2010). Making the theory explicit: The EMIL-A architecture. In *EMergence In the Loop: Simulating the two way dynamics of norm innovation* (chap. 9, pp. 77–88). EMIL Deliverable 5.1 EMIL-T. http://cfpm.org/EMIL-D5.1.pdf.

Campenní, M., Henn, S., Jazayeri, P., Lotzmann, U., Möhring, M., Oberhausen, M., Tohum, M.-H., & Weyrich, J. (2010). Demonstrating the theory 4: Multi-scenario world – the sequel. In *EMergence In the Loop: Simulating the two way dynamics of norm innovation* (chap. 17, pp. 191–199).

Conte, R., Andrighetto. G., & Campenní, M. (2013). *Minding norms – Mechanisms and dynamics of social order in agent societies* (Oxford series on cognitive models and architectures). Oxford: Oxford University Press.

Fix, J., von Scheve, C., & Moldt, D. (2006). Emotion-based norm enforcement and maintenance in multi-agent systems: Foundations and petri net modeling. In *AAMAS'06* (pp. 105–107), Hakodate, Hokkaido.

Lorscheid, I., & Troitzsch, K. G. (2009). How do agents learn to behave normatively? Machine learning concepts for norm learning in the emil project. In B. Edmonds & N. Gilbert (Eds.), *Proceedings of the sixth conference of ESSA*, Guildford, UK: University of Surrey.

Lorscheid, I., Lotzmann, U., Möhring, M., & Troitzsch, K. G. (2010). Summary of major advances in EMIL-A and EMIL-S. In *EMergence In the Loop: Simulating the two way dynamics of norm innovation* (chap. 19, pp. 203–211).

Lotzmann, U. (2010). Demonstrating the theory 1: Traffic. In *EMergence In the Loop: Simulating the two way dynamics of norm innovation* (chap. 14, pp. 139–147).

Lucas, P., Lotzmann, U., & Pauli, M. (2010). Demonstrating the theory 3: Micro finance. In *EMergence In the Loop: Simulating the two way dynamics of norm innovation* (chap. 16, pp. 169–189).

Neumann, M. (2009). Dissecting the BOID perspective on norms. In B. Edmonds & N. Gilbert (Eds.), *Proceedings of the sixth conference of ESSA*, Guildford.

Troitzsch, K. G. (2010). Demonstrating the theory: Conclusion of scenario results. In *EMergence In the Loop: Simulating the two way dynamics of norm innovation* (chap. 12, pp. 201–202).

von Scheve, C., Moldt, D., Fix, J., & von Luede, R. (2006). My agents love to conform: Norms and emotion in the micro-macro link. *Computational and Mathematical Organization Theory, 12*, 81–100.

Chapter 10
Modelling Norms

The most beautiful as well as the most ugly inclinations of man are not part of a fixed biologically given human nature, but result from the social process which creates man.

Erich Fromm

After introducing a range of models of normative behaviour in the past five chapters, this chapter reflects on what is missing from those models. We show that some concepts salient for normative behaviour have not been implemented. This chapter is the foundation for the remainder of the book in which we introduce models of normative behaviour that implement the main missing features.[1]

We are now at a point where we can dig deeper into the agent-based modelling of normative behaviour. In previous chapters we discussed environmental models of norms (Chap. 3), behavioural models based on game theory (Chap. 6), imitation and social influence (Chap. 7) and some more cognitive models of norm learning and internalisation (Chap. 9).

The models discussed so far still leave much to be desired and so the rest of the book will discuss models addressing some of the missing attributes of normative behaviour. This chapter considers what is missing in current models of normative behaviour, setting the scene for the three models described in the remainder of the book. However, first there is a note on levels of abstraction and simplicity in modelling.

[1]This chapter is partly based on collaborative work with Maria Xenitidou and uses parts of our publications Xenitidou and Elsenbroich (2010) and Elsenbroich and Xenitidou (2012).

C. Elsenbroich and N. Gilbert, *Modelling Norms*, DOI 10.1007/978-94-007-7052-2_10,

10.1 KISS vs KIDS

Occam's Razor states: "From a set of competing hypotheses select the one that makes the fewest assumptions". It is a law of parsimony, called a razor as unneccessary assumptions are 'shaved off' a theory. A perfect instantiation of this kind of minimalist approach is the K.I.S.S. principle (Keep-It-Simple-Stupid) advocating that simpler models are (intrinsically) better models (Axelrod 1997, p. 5). Edmonds and Moss (2005) argue against this in favour of descriptive and truthful models. They suggest that the K.I.S.S. principle is founded on a false premise, that simpler models are more likely to be true (for a rebuttal of this premise see Edmonds 2004) and that it is unlikely that a simple model will adequately represent a complex real world phenomenon. The authors advocate the K.I.D.S. principle instead: Keep-It-Descriptive-Stupid. Rather than starting from the simplest model (and then adding features if the simple model is inadequate) the starting point should be a model that is as descriptive of given data and evidence as possible. Once this model is understood, it can be simplified if parts are found to be superfluous to the modelling of a specific phenomenon.

There are many reasons to advocate simplicity in modelling. Computer models are difficult to validate and the more complicated the setup, the harder the validation (see Sect. 4.1.3). It becomes more difficult to know whether the model is circular (whether the outcome was programmed into the model) and what the influence of particular parameters is on the outcome. This implies that if we can reconstruct a phenomenon with less assumptions we should do so; the parsimony requirement of Occam's razor can be applied to computer simulations. This parsimony does have a downside. Although parsimony helps to keep control of the model, if the assumptions themselves are too simple, the model's adequacy might suffer. Models of norms are a case in point, where it seems that overly simplistic assumptions about the agents lead away from truthfulness. Although one should not assume more than necessary, one should also not assume less than necessary to model a phenomenon. In the case of normative behaviour, this is particularly important as social norms are both so intuitive and so elusive.

The visible macro-phenomenon of normative behaviour is a behavioural regularity across a population. However, not every regularity is normative behaviour. We would for example not call the behaviour of the molecules in a ferromagnet 'normative' even though they display regular patterns. If we are very inclusive we might classify animal behaviour as normative, for example bird or fish formations, but even then we need to acknowledge that human social norms are considerably more complex than these animal counterparts. Even regularities in human societies might come about due to reasons other than normativity. For example, the pharmacy Boots is currently giving away free nappy bags to anyone who joins their Parenting Club. As a result almost every pram is adorned by one of those nappy changing bags. This phenomenon is a behavioural regularity but it does not come about normatively.

In this chapter we will argue that we will need to give up some parsimony to be able to model normative dynamics, in particular human normative behaviour, more truthfully.

10.2 A Social Embedding

The first criticism of the previously reviewed models is that their agents are not socially embedded. Agents either exist in arbitrary neighbourhoods (e.g. Epstein 2000; van Baal 2004), limiting interaction to a circle of neighbours or they interact with all other agents randomly (e.g. Epstein and Axtell 1996; Gatherer 2002; Epstein and Axtell 1996; Flentge et al. 2001). Some models implement social networks but use the embedding only to restrict agent interactions rather than have the network influence agents' behaviours directly. In Sect. 8 we saw that the interaction policies make a difference to the outcome of the simulation, both in the opinion dynamics models and in the model based on the theory of reasoned action.

Social embedding is potentially very important for social norms. One of the hallmarks of social norms is that adhering to them defines group membership and therefore social norms are inextricably tied to the concept of a group. Agents do not adhere to the majority behaviour of the overall population but to behaviours exhibited by relevant others. Neighbourhoods in simulations can sometimes be interpreted as indicating groups. But adaptation to a group is not the only dynamic underlying social groupings. A potentially more important dynamic is the selection of a group to belong to. Neighbourhoods do not support the idea of selection as they are geographically static.

In the next two chapters we discuss models which take the idea of embedding agents in social networks seriously. The first model uses dynamic social networks to simulate the influence of delinquent peers on agents. The second model uses feedback between group selection and assimilation to investigate the movement of opinions to extremes.

10.3 Compliance

In Sect. 2.2.4 we discussed the three kinds of normative behaviour, *conformity*, *obedience* and *compliance*, that are commonly distinguished in (experimental) social psychology. Agent-based models so far only capture the first two, conformity and obedience, which are relatively simple behavioural mechanisms. Compliance is a behaviour in which an agent actively chooses to adhere to a norm although it might contravene its personal beliefs and values. It is the normative behaviour touching on the *homo duplex*, the possibility of humans to forgo individual advantage for the greater good (Shilling and Mellor 1998). None of the models presented so far tackle compliance because their agents do not have the cognitive capacity to reason about behaviour in this more involved way.

In Sect. 2.2.4, we defined compliance as *public conformity whilst keeping personal values*. This implies two levels of conceptualisation, a private and a public one. The agent needs to have (a) knowledge of its personal attitudes, values and beliefs about the world; (b) a representation of the external world, including the understanding of normative rules and judgements; and (c) a way of combining those two by judging, choosing, integrating and juxtaposing the internal and external.

Compliance has not been covered as a type of normative behaviour in agent-based modelling, although it is the most interesting as it is uniquely human. Conformity and obedience fit into the paradigm of agent-based modelling of focussing on behaviour (rather than cognition). For conformity, it is sufficient to have a rule that a behaviour is changed if a different behaviour is displayed in more than a threshold number of other agents in a certain environment (neighbours, the whole population etc.). The agent needs a factual representation of the outside world to know when to change behaviour but it needs no normative knowledge whatsoever. For obedience, the behaviour of an agent changes when a behaviour is "punished". This needs a utility assigned to the violating behaviour with the punishment leading to a utility reduction. The agent calculates the utility of the behaviour by subtracting the punishment assignment from the behaviour assignment. The behaviour is changed if the utility becomes too low. In contrast, in order to achieve compliance, we need an agent that can make context sensitive decisions for which it needs to be able to reason about its own values and external normative demands.

There are two modelling approaches we shall consider in relation to compliance models, both detailed in earlier chapters. One is recent work on the feedback between society and individuals by norms in the EMIL project discussed in Chap. 9, the other is work on the learning of group norms discussed in Chap. 8. Summarising the salient points of the EMIL-A architecture (Andrighetto and Campenni 2007), there are agents with knowledge divided between factual (event) knowledge, stored on the event board, and normative (rule) knowledge. The agent has a normative interface with the world rather than just the factual one of a BOID agent. The agents also have a *normative frame* to infer and store rules from the event board. In addition agents are informed of norms that have emerged communally by the *normative board* where this common information is stored. The focus here is on how agents understand, learn and change norms by adaptation and invocation. As we noted in Chap. 9, Lorscheid and Troitzsch (2009) explore learning concepts for this new kind of information and test them in a norm invocation model. The authors identify reinforcement learning as one underlying mechanism but show that it is insufficient to model norms. They add normative learning which is learning from the normative invocation messages sent between agents. The mechanism of norm invocation messages incorporates a penitence level, a threshold for individual agents at which they change their behaviour, and a social hierarchy in which agents having more authority are able to enforce norms on those lower in the hierarchy.

In this model agents have a personal value and are confronted with public values in the form of norm invocations. The penitence level means that agents do not just conform blindly to public demands but delay behaviour change. Only when the pressure gets too great does an agent change its behaviour.

According to the EMIL-A architecture, this delay results in behavioural outputs which could take the form of two different kinds of normative actions: compliance/violation and norm-defence. This is because, while there is a decision-making process that consists of checking for potential obstacles in conforming to a norm (material impossibility and goal conflict), this checking takes place only when a norm has been recognised as such and adopted. At that stage, the action selected is either a result of instrumental reasoning or cooperative/normative disposition rather than situational. EMIL-A, therefore, seems to allow for a form of context-based reasoning about whether to conform to a norm (Conte et al. 2013), while EMIL-S (Lotzmann 2010) allows for a form of deliberation comparing the current situation to an earlier one in which the agent received a norm invocation. The similarity of the current and the former situations determines the cogency of alternative norms.

Despite the possibility of context sensitive normative behaviour, compliance requires the possibility of normative action irrespective of whether it is backed up by the normative belief—normative goal norm adoption process. The process underpinning compliance is one of comparison of personal to social values in a given situation, which could result in acting in accordance with, but not (necessarily) adopting, a norm. Therefore, we need to break away from the interconnections between beliefs and behaviour (and, thus, from the longstanding problem of linking attitude to behaviour) to focus instead on the interconnection between decision and behaviour.

The EMIL-A architecture models an interrelation of conformity and obedience, in that agents will adhere to a norm once norm invocations exceed their penitence threshold. This behaviour is not norm compliance because once the agent has succumbed to the majority norm (say "red"), it no longer has its original value (say "blue") to guide its behaviour.

In Sect. 8.3.2 we described a model for the learning of group norms. Agents decide on actions based on both their personal norms and what they think the group norms are (Verhagen 2001). Through feedback from the group they refine and adapt their view of group norms, with their personal norms remaining intact.

Although in this model there are two layers, a personal value sphere and the group norms (as perceived by the agent), this is also not a model of compliance. The action decision is not made by weighing up the internal values and external demands with behaviour being adapted case by case. The agent receiving feedback on its decisions using the combined decision tree can update what it understands the group norms to be. It does evaluate the group norms independently of its own norms, making a decision whether to comply with the group norms or follow its own personal benefit. However, this model, by virtue of it representing both the public and private spheres of norms and values (or in this case, utilities), can serve as a starting point for a model of compliance. What needs to be modified is the evaluation of the two decision trees to allow agents to deliberate between them (rather than calculate an overall utility).

10.3.1 Compliance Model Sketch

What do we need for a model of compliance? We need an agent architecture that is able not only to reason *with* norms as in both the EMIL-A architecture and the Verhagen model of norm learning, but also to reason *about* norms. Modelling compliance brings together the two questions we discussed separately at the beginning of the book: 'why do agents behave normatively' and 'why do agents violate norms' become the combined question, why did agent X display behaviour Y in situation Z. The agent has to be able to compare personal values with normative demands and make a decision in a specific situation. We discuss such a model of situational action in Chap. 13. The Verhagen model has an important underlying formalisation in that it models private/individual values and public/group values separately but currently agents do not decide whether to follow one or the other according to a specific situation but according to how independent of the group an agent is in its thinking. The EMIL-A architecture has an important feature, the normative board which allows the learning of norms by interaction with the outside world and can be the underlying 'database' of normative demands that an agent perceives. A model of compliance also needs something like a 'value board' as a database of personal values (morals) and the agent needs to be able to reason about both boards and their applicability to specific situations.

10.4 Conclusion

We discussed missing features of models of social norms. We started by noting the importance of the social embedding of agents. Social norms are partly defined by group membership and group membership is constituted by two social dynamics, adaptation and selection. Agent-based models either neglect group membership altogether (agents interact with arbitrary other agents) or only model the adaptation dynamic (agents situated in neighbourhoods).

We discussed a tripartite classification of normative behaviour derived from social psychology. Using the three categories of conformity, obedience and compliance, we contended that most agent-based models of normative behaviour only formalised conformity and obedience. We gave some examples of normative modelling which go beyond the conformity/obedience frameworks but argued that even they do not encapsulate compliance. The theoretical discussion of compliance has pointed out what is missing in the models so far and also suggests future developments, such as the incorporation of intentionality and context sensitivity.

In the following three chapters we discuss extending existing agent-based models to represent social embedding and compliance. First, in Chap. 11, we focus on a proper social embedding of normative behaviour as exemplified in a network model of juvenile delinquency. Secondly, in Chap. 12, we focus on the construction of shared knowledge and shared meaning for the emergence of groups and group norms. Again the agents are situated in social networks but, more importantly, the sharing of meaning that constitutes group membership is explored by implementing argumentation about opinions. Thirdly we focus on the moral dimension of normative behaviour in Chap. 13. Here an agent makes an action decision based on its values within a specific situation, modelling the context sensitivity of compliance.

References

Andrighetto, G., & Campenni, M. (2007). On the immergence of norms: A normative agent architecture. In *AAAI Symposium, Social and organizational aspects of intelligence*, Washington, DC.

Axelrod, R. (1997). *The complexity of cooperation: Agent-based models of competition and collaboration*. Princeton: Princeton University Press.

Conte, R., Andrighetto. G., & Campenní, M. (2013). *Minding norms – Mechanisms and dynamics of social order in agent societies* (Oxford series on cognitive models and architectures). Oxford: Oxford University Press.

Edmonds, B. (2004). How formal logic can fail to be useful for modelling or designing MAS. In *Regulated agent-based social systems* (Lecture notes in artificial intelligence, vol. 2934, pp. 1–15) Berlin: Springer.

Edmonds, B., & Moss, S. (2005). From KISS to KIDS – an 'anti-simplistic' modelling approach. In P. Davidsson et al. (Eds.), *Multi agent based simulation 2004* (Lecture notes in artificial intelligence, vol. 3415, pp. 130–144). Berlin: Springer.

Elsenbroich, C., & Xenitidou, M. (2012). Three kinds of normative behaviour: Minimal requirements for feedback models. *Computional and Mathematical Organization Theory, 18*(1), 113–127.

Epstein, J. (2000). *Learning to be thoughtless: Social norms and individual computing*. Technical report, Center on Social and Economic Dynamics Working Paper, No. 6.

Epstein, J. M., & Axtell, R. (1996). *Growing artificial societies: Social science from the bottom up*. Washington, DC: Brookings Institution Press.

Flentge, F., Polani, D., & Uthmann, T. (2001). Modelling the emergence of possession norms using memes. *Journal of Artificial Societies and Social Simulation, 4*(4), 3. http://jasss.soc.surrey.ac.uk/4/4/3.html.

Gatherer, D. (2002). Identifying cases of social contagion using memetic isolation: Comparison of the dynamics of a multisociety simulation with an ethnographic data set. *Journal of Artificial Societies and Social Simulation, 5*(4), 5.

Lorscheid, I., & Troitzsch, K. G. (2009). How do agents learn to behave normatively? Machine learning concepts for norm learning in the emil project. In B. Edmonds & N. Gilbert (Eds.), *Proceedings of the sixth conference of ESSA*. Guildford, UK: University of Surrey.

Lotzmann, U. (2010). Enhancing agents with normative capabilities. In A. Bargiela, S. A. Ali, D. Crowley, & E. J. Kerckhoffs (Eds.), *Proceedings of the 24th European conference on modelling and simulation*, Kuala Lumpur.

Shilling, C., & Mellor P. A. (1998). Durkheim, morality and modernity: Collective effervescence, homo duplex and the source of moral action. *The British Journal of Sociology, 49*(2), 193–209.

van Baal, P. (2004). *Computer simulations of criminal deterrence*. Australia: Annandale, The Federation Press.

Verhagen, H. (2001). Simulation of the learning of norms. *Social Science Computer Review, 19*(3), 296–306.

Xenitidou, M., & Elsenbroich, C. (2010). Construct validity of agent-based simulation of normative behaviour. *The International Journal of Interdisciplinary Social Sciences, 5*(4), 67–80.

Chapter 11
Delinquent Networks

... is evil just something you are or something you do?

Morrissey

In this chapter, we present an agent-based model of juvenile delinquency. The construction of the model is explained step by step and results are discussed in relation to criminologic al theories. This chapter describes how one might implement the first of the features identified as missing in existing models of social norms, a social embedding of agents.

So far in this book we have seen social norms from a variety of angles. We discussed theoretical approaches and agent-based modelling as a methodology to tackle social norms in the first few chapters. The advantage of agent-based modelling in comparison to other methods is that it can model the both the micro level of agents and the macro level of social phenomena. We have seen models of the emergence of cooperation, models of imitation and models that can reason with social norms. In the previous chapter we discussed some problems of existing models. We identified three main problems:

1. The lack of social structure.
2. Only conformity and obedience considered as ways of norm adherence.
3. Agents not able to act according to personal values as well as norms depending on context.

In this chapter we develop the first of three models that overcome these problems. It implements agents in a social structure, represented as a personal social network. We use the example of juvenile delinquency for this model.

C. Elsenbroich and N. Gilbert, *Modelling Norms*, DOI 10.1007/978-94-007-7052-2_11,

11.1 Networks of Juvenile Delinquents

Some of the most stable facts in criminology are about juvenile delinquency:

1. Young people are substantially more involved in crime than older people.
2. Young men are substantially more involved in crime and delinquency than young women.
3. Juvenile delinquents have a higher proportion of delinquent friends than non-delinquents.

We have seen in Chap. 3 that there are essentially three different approaches to criminality: the rational choice/environmental approach, the personality approach and the social influence approach. There is no explanation of delinquent clustering from rational choice, environmental theories or personality theories of crime. Any addition of homophily will be an extra assumption of those theories, for example stating that it is 'better' or 'beneficial' for delinquents to hang out with other delinquents (e.g. your friends will not 'grass you up') or that delinquents are particularly prone to homopholous relationships. The third approach, differentiating criminals from others by social factors, can elucidate the clustering phenomenon but it is not clear whether the clustering is a result of selection, i.e. juvenile delinquents gathering together (Social Bond Theory, see Sect. 3.4.2), or of social influence, i.e. befriending delinquents makes juveniles more delinquent (Differential Association Theory, see Sect. 3.4.1).

We present the construction of an agent-based model of the dynamics of juvenile delinquency in a social network for the analysis of the dynamics underlying the observed phenomenon of delinquent clustering.

Social networks have been recognised long ago as important for the explanation of juvenile delinquency(Sutherland 1947; Shaw and McKay 1931), making the lack of social network analysis in criminology rather surprising. One reason for this lack might be the precariousness of criminal data in general and criminal network data in particular (Brame et al. 2010). Early studies of juvenile delinquent networks used self-report questionnaires asking about the delinquency levels of participants and their friends. These data are somewhat unreliable due to the projection effects of one's own delinquency onto one's friends. Whilst non-response is a problem in all survey data collection, Chattoe-Brown and Hamill (2006) use simulation to show the particular sensitivity of relational data to low response rates. They furthermore suggest an agent-based simulation for the generation of criminal co-offending networks, building on the idea of trust and friendship. Quantitative data originate mainly from the criminal justice system. Judicial data come with their own caveats, in particular as one is then measuring not criminality but apprehended or solved criminal offences (Smångs 2008). The few existing social networks studies in criminology include Baerveldt (2000), Baerveldt and Snijders (2003), Sarnecki (1990), Sarnecki (2001) and Smångs (2008).

The work by Baerveldt and Snijders is based on self-report data of friendship networks in high-schools and delinquency scores from self-assessment and assessment of their friends. The data is longitudinal with three collections over 10 years. The analyses are a social network analysis in Baerveldt (2000) and a multi-level network analysis in Baerveldt and Snijders (2003). Their findings are that pupils with higher delinquency do indeed have friends of higher delinquency. There is evidence that similarity in delinquency promotes friendship formation, but also that the same similarity leads to faster dissolution of friendships, i.e. delinquent friendships are more transient. Similarity in other attributes, e.g. interest in sports, has been shown to be conducive to friendship but the faster dissolution of friendships is a novel finding (Baerveldt and Snijders 2003, p. 147).

Sarnecki uses criminal justice data on co-offending for a network analysis. The longitudinal datasets consist of 5 years of co-offending data from youths aged under 20 in Borlänge (Sarnecki 1990) and Stockholm (Sarnecki 2001). Each year is divided into two 6 month periods, leading to 10 social networks of co-offending. This study also shows transient relationships, although one has to be careful in extrapolating transient friendships from this data because they are about co-offending, which might be more transient than friendship. Although there is a central network of slightly less transient relationships, it cannot be described as an organised or even semi-organised "Underworld" (Sarnecki 2001, p. 159).

Smångs (2008) investigates the support of Sarnecki's social network data for social bond and differential association theory. Four hypotheses regarding delinquent networks, based on Granovetter's work on the strength of weak ties, are investigated.

1. In delinquent networks, local bridges are to a disproportionate degree weak ties.
2. The stronger the tie between two delinquents, the more contacts they have in common.
3. In delinquent networks, the proportion of all persons with ties to either or both of the actors and to whom they will both be tied by a strong or a weak tie is least when their tie is absent, intermediate when it is weak and most when it is strong.
4. In delinquent networks, the probability of a tie, whether strong or weak, between dyads, $P - O$, with one common contact, X, is lowest when X has weak ties to P and O; intermediate when X has one strong and one weak tie to P and O, and greatest when X has strong ties P as well as O.

(Smångs 2008, p. 9)

All four hypotheses are supported by the data. Weak bridges are not distributed randomly, the stronger the tie between actors, the larger the overlap of their social circles, and the kind of tie between actors influences their connections in common in the proposed way. Smångs concludes that the network data supports differential association theory (a social ability theory which sees the cause of delinquency in social association) and does not lend support to social bond theory (a social disability theory which sees the cause of crime in the weak social ties of delinquents).

The above network studies use different kinds of data. Baerveldt and Snijders use data on a social network of relationships over a range of delinquencies, while Sarnecki's data only includes co-offending relationships, i.e. no relationships to non-delinquents are considered. They both, however, report relatively similar general structural phenomena, such as the transience of criminal relationships.

In the following we present an agent-based model of social influence on criminality in a social network. We examine the effect that a personal social network has on the criminality of an agent, where criminality is an agent's disposition to commit crimes. We show that homophilous selection leads to the clustering of delinquents in the expected way, with and without social influence mechanisms. We also show, moreover, that our model results in delinquent clustering without a selection mechanism, i.e. by social influence alone. This is a surprising result that gives some support for differential association theories of delinquency.

11.2 A Model of Criminal Influence

Most crime simulations start from (bounded) rational choice and deterrence (see van Baal 2004), routine activity (see Groff 2007) or environmental criminology (see Groff and Birks 2008). In an earlier Chapter we discussed a rudimentary simulation of social influences on criminal behaviour from Bosse et al. (2009). There exists some social network research on social influence such as Steglich et al. (2009) which looks at peer influence on substance use. However, there have been no agent-based models of social influence on criminality.[1] This is surprising, in particular as it seems that peer and neighbourhood effects have been found to be important variables in other research into crime, e.g. in multi-level models (Wikström and Loeber 2000; Oberwittler 2004). We develop a model of juvenile delinquency as a social influence phenomenon using insights from opinion dynamics and social networks.

11.2.1 Opinion Dynamics

Our starting point is a model of social influence. We stipulate that changing one's criminality according to the criminality of others around is a similar mechanism to attitude change in opinion dynamics models (Hegselmann and Krause 2002; Deffuant et al. 2002). We implement an existing opinion dynamics mechanism for our model; the model was discussed in more detail in Sect. 8.2.2.

In this model of criminal influence we use the same bounded rationality assumption as is used in Deffuant et al. (2002). It seems likely that a highly delinquent youth will not influence someone completely not in favour of crime and vice versa. We replace 'opinions' by 'criminality', taken from the interval [0, 1] with 1 being high criminality and 0 low. 'Confidence' is renamed as 'susceptibility', i.e. some agents are more susceptible to social influence than others.[2]

---

[1] Although *Drugtalk*, discussed in Sect. 8.2.5, is a model of drug uptake, it is not a model of criminality as such because the illegality of drugs does not matter in the model.

[2] Cf. Bearden et al. (1989) for empirical research on susceptibility to social influence.

Table 11.1 Characteristics of social networks (For a more detailed analysis see Hamill (2010, p. 104, Table 3.3.3))

	Regular	Random	Small world	Scale-Free
Limited personal Network	✓	✓	✓	✓
Fat-Tail	✗	✗	✗	✓
High clustering	✓	✗	✓	✗
Low density	✓	✓	✓	✓
Short path	✗	✓	✓	Possibly
Assortative	✗	✗	✗	✗
Communities	✗	✗	✗	✓

There are different policies about who influences whom in each step. In Hegselmann (2001) all agents are influenced by all other agents. In Deffuant et al. (2002) an agent picks out a random other agent at each step. Urbig et al. (2008) show the influence of these interaction policies. Using either of these two policies will yield a population where all agents are equally criminal (consensus in the opinion dynamics model) or one set is highly criminal and the other completely non-criminal (polarisation in the opinion dynamics model). The model hardly ever preserves a range of opinions. This extreme polarisation does not correspond to the actual distribution of criminality. An opinion dynamics model is thus not sufficient to model criminal influence. What we need on top of the influence dynamics is some kind of social embedding.

11.2.2 Social Networks and Social Circles

There are several templates for the production of models of different networks structures, for example random networks (Newman et al. 2006, pp. 43–47), directed networks (Barabási 2002), small world networks (Newman et al. 2006, pp. 83–100) and preferential attachment networks (Barabási 2002, pp. 79–92). In all of these network models, the links are established or broken exogenously. In contrast, we focus on social influence through social networks generated from the micro-behaviour of agents, envisaged as resulting from accidental encounters, hanging out' together and choices about friendships.

Another problem with these models is that they do not display important features observed in social networks (Hamill 2010). Social networks are limited in size, have low network density, positive assortativity, and communities, that is closely connected clusters that are loosely or not at all connected to other nodes (see Table 11.1).

To construct the networks in our criminality model, we use the *social circles model* from Hamill and Gilbert (2009) and Hamill (2010). The social circles model was conceived to examine the uptake of communication technology. The model starts from an idea by Simmel that people are embedded in "social circles" (Simmel 1890). A person belongs to the local church, a workplace, a family, some old school

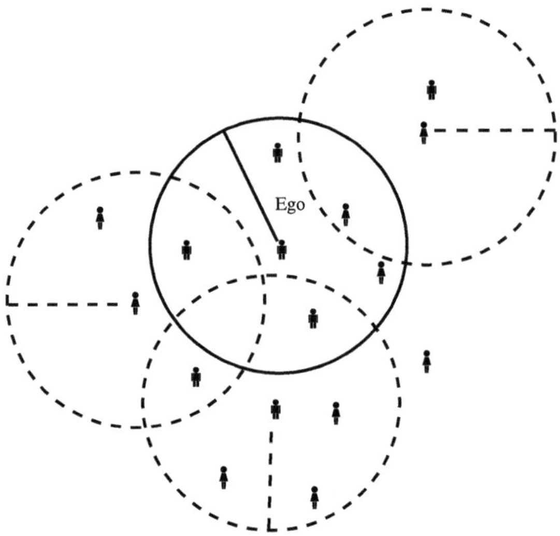

Fig. 11.1 Social circles. Ego has a personal radius *r* defining its social circle. All agents inside the circle influence ego

friends, a college alumni network, etc. Each one of those circles has some influence, making the person the product of their intersection. We adapt the circle idea but rather than defining the agent inside an intersection of circles each agent has an associated radius *r* defining its social circle (Fig. 11.1).

The social circles model produces personal (or ego-centric) networks that are:

- Are limited in size;
- Vary in size between individuals and can have right-skewed distributions of connectivity;
- Display high clustering;
- Can change over time.

It also produces social networks that:

- Have low whole network density i.e. most of the possible links do not actually exist;
- Are positively assortative by degree of connectivity i.e. well-connected agents tend to be connected to other well-connected agents
- Have communities i.e. there are groups of people that are closely connected to each other but not well connected to others;
- Can have short path lengths depending on the values chosen for certain variables.

In the simulation the social network is constituted by giving each agent a social reach (radius of the circle of influence) and all the agents within this circle influence the agents' criminality.

11.2.3 Dynamic Friendships

So far we have a static network of delinquents but our main interest is in the dynamic development of clustering. To make the network dynamic we make the agents move. In agent-based models, agent movement can either be undirected or directed. A completely undirected movement (e.g. random moves) does not give us any clustering of delinquents.

We choose to have directed movement. The interpretation of the space is social, i.e. distances in space represent social distances. For the direction of movement we use movement towards a social target. We test two types of movement, one towards the most similar agent in the network, the other towards the *centroid*, the 'centre of gravity', of the network. The first movement type represents the hypothesis of the selection of similar agents, the second one represents the idea of being part of an ever more tightly knit friendship circle.

For the first type of movement we choose to measure similarity by *maximal overlap*. This means that an agent does not necessarily move towards an agent with the most similar criminality to itself, but rather to the most influential or malleable agent with respect to its own criminality and susceptibility. For the second movement the agents move to the geometric centroid of their social circle. This movement means that social circles become more and more tightly knit, one assumption in differential association theory.

Implementing either type of movement gives a model in which agents' social circles evolve dynamically. We now have a model of dynamic social influence on criminality in which we find the clustering, i.e. the generation of groups, characteristic of juvenile delinquency. There remain two problems. First, after a few steps the simulation runs becomes static, meaning the groups become completely dissociated from each other and no further influence takes place. Second, we do not find a correlation between the criminality of the people in the same group, i.e. criminals do not have more criminal friends. This brings us to the last addition to the model.

11.2.4 The Leader of the Pack Model

The model now has a dynamic development of criminal influence through networks, which are constructed from the idea of social circles. Agents move through social space either towards the most similar agent or to the 'centre of gravity' of their social circle. The problem is that the social structure reaches equilibrium too quickly and loses its dynamics. Also, with neither selection nor centroid movement is there any criminality correlation.

Again we look to Simmel for the solution. In his analysis of fashion (Simmel 1957), Simmel analyses the 'push and pull' consisting on the one hand of those wanting to follow fashion, i.e. imitating others, and on the other hand those wanting to be special, to distinguish themselves from others. We transfer this idea to the setting of criminal influence by saying that agents can either move towards or away from certain social targets. For the case of selection movement, moving away means that the agent goes away from the maximally overlapping agent and for the centroidal movement, away from the centre of gravity, the centroid.

It might seem that we are now contradicting our initial assumption that criminals are only socially different rather than different in personality. Are we not saying now that criminals are different by making them move away from their social setting? We are not. The maximal criminal' here is a relative notion, relative to the criminality of the social network the agent is in. Rather than saying that criminals are different, there might be a tendency to move away from your friends if they are all less criminal than you. For example, being maximally criminal might lead to boredom with your social circle.

It might also seem that this movement is highly arbitrary. We do not have solid evidence for the assumption that relative maximal criminality leads to any movement whatsoever. As stated above, we use Simmel's theoretical account of a social push and pull' as a background with softer evidence that juvenile delinquents change friends more often than others. Using the movement away from the centroid for relatively maximal agents results in a model that no longer generates a static equilibrium. We keep the social influence dynamic going all through the simulation.

In summary, we now have a model of criminal influence, modelled on opinion dynamics, embedded in a social network setting where the networks are constructed from the social circles around an agent and made dynamic by a movement with relation to some feature of the social network. This movement can be uniform for all agents or those agents that are the most criminal (relative to their social network) can move differently from others. In the next section we discuss some results and observations from the model.

11.3 Results and Observations

We have described a model of the social influence on criminal tendencies of juvenile delinquents. It is based on a model of opinion dynamics together with a model for constructing social networks, the social circles model. We managed to recreate some of the general social features of juvenile delinquency, such as the clustering of delinquents, without the population splitting into criminals and non-criminals.

The initial research question for this model was to see whether we can replicate the clustering of delinquent agents through some simple mechanisms. We built the model by integrating existing models of opinion dynamics and network structures. Using existing models has two advantages. Firstly, the model has some external validation through the validation of its parts, with the caveat that there is no guarantee that the assembly of the different sub-models does not undermine essential parts of the originals. Secondly, by building the model in the step-by-step way we described above, we can see which parts contribute in what way to the overall outcome. For example, we had the surprising fact that the selective movement of agents, without the 'leader of the pack' model, did not lead to delinquent correlation. By the same token, the centroidal movement leads to correlation. The reason for this is that in order to develop the clustering we need to keep the dynamics going. Without these dynamics, groups build too quickly and become independent, leading to no more social influence. This is expressed in the Grannis factor which measures the extent to which a society is connected (Grannis 2010). If the factor is less than one, the society comprises disconnected groups. Because we assume that people are influenced by only a small number of others, the Grannis factor is always low in our model.

The model allows a theoretical exploration of criminological theories. If we run the model with maximal criminals moving away from their social circle, the selective movement, and the opinion dynamics turned off we obtain a high correlation between transience and criminality. If the movement is centroidal, the correlation persists but is weakened. On the other hand, if we turn the opinion dynamics on, i.e. run it as a social influence model, there is almost no correlation.

11.4 Conclusion

We have presented a model of juvenile delinquency clustering using existing models of opinion dynamics and social networks plus some social movement dynamics. The model was explained step by step to show exactly what each existing sub-model contributes to the overall model of criminal influence between agents. Although a simple model, it recreates some dynamics observed in juvenile networks, like clustering and the correlation of transient friendships with criminality. Furthermore it helps explore criminologic al theory. Both the implementation of Hirschi's Social Bond Theory, using the selective movement, and Sutherland's Differential Association Theory, using social influence, produce correlations between an agent's criminality and the criminality of its friends. However, the implementations differ when it comes to the social abilities of criminals and non-criminals. The results concerning the correlation of criminality and transience of relationships correspond with Hirschi's prediction of higher transience of friendships for delinquents. The non-centroidal selection is meant to mirror Hirschi's theory and is the movement producing a strong correlation. That the correlation does not persist for the case of social influence fits well with Sutherland's differential association theory where criminal networks are the same as non-criminal networks. It is not the structures that differ but the moral values transmitted within those structures.

References

Baerveldt, C. (2000). Pupil's networks in high schools. Network sampling, program and some results from a theory-oriented research project on petty crime of pupils. Paper for the 2nd international network sampling workshop, Maastricht, 2–4 March 2000.

Baerveldt, C., & Snijders, T. A. B. (2003). A multilevel network study of the effects of delinquent behaviour on friendship evolution. *Journal of Mathematical Sociology, 27*, 123–151.

Barabási, A.-L. (2002). *Linked: the new science of networks*. Cambridge: Perseus Publishing.

Bearden, W. O., Netemeyer, R. G., & Teel, J. J. E. (1989). Measurement of consumer susceptibility to interpersonal influence. *Journal of Consumer Research, 15*, 473–481.

Bosse, T., Gerritsen C., & Klein, M. C. (2009). Agent-based simulation of social learning in criminology. In *International conference on agents and artificial intelligence*, Porto.

Brame, R., Turner, M., & Paternoster, R. (2010). Missing data problems in criminological research: Two case studies. In *Handbook of quantitative criminology*. New York/London: Springer.

Chattoe-Brown, E., & Hamill, H. (2006). It's not *who* you know—it's what you know about people you *don't* know that counts. *British Journal of Criminology, 45*, 1–17.

Deffuant, G., Amblard, F., Weisbuch, G. & Faure, T. (2002). How can extremism prevail? A study based on the relative agreement interaction model. *Journal of Artificial Societies and Social Simulation, 5*(4) 1, http://jasss.soc.surrey.ac.uk/5/4/1.html.

Grannis, R. (2010). Six degrees of 'Who cares?'. *American Journal of Sociology, 115*(4), 991–1017.

Groff, E. R. (2007). Simulation for theory testing and experimentation: an example using routine activity theory and street robbery. *Journal of Quantitative Criminology, 23*, 75–103.

Groff, E. R., & Birks, D. (2008). Simulating crime prevention strategies: a look at the possibilities. *Policing: A Journal of Policy and Practice, 1*(0), 1–10.

Hamill, L. (2010). *Communications, travel and social networks since 1840: a study using agent-based models*. Ph.D. thesis, University of Surrey.

Hamill, L., & Gilbert, N. (2009). Social circles: A simple structure for agent-based social network models. *Journal of Artificial Societies and Social Simulation, 12*(2), 3.

Hegselmann, R. (2001). Verstehen sozialer strukturbildungen. In M. Wink (Ed.), *Vererbung und Milieu* (pp. 355–379). Heidelberg: Springer-Verlag.

Hegselmann, R., & Krause, U. (2002). Opinion dynamics and bounded confidence: Models, analysis and simulation. *Journal of Artificial Societies and Social Simulation, 5*(3), 2. http://jasss.soc.surrey.ac.uk/5/3/2.html.

Newman, M., Barabasi, A.-L., & Watts, D. (2006). *The structure and dynamics of networks*. Princeton/Oxford: Princeton University Press

Oberwittler, D. (2004). A multilevel analysis of neighbourhood contextual effects on serious juvenile offending: The role of subcultural values and social disorganization. *European Journal of Criminology, 1*(2), 201–235.

Sarnecki, J. (1990). Delinquent networks in Sweden. *Journal of Quantitative Criminology, 6*, 31–50.

Sarnecki, J. (2001). *Delinquent networks: Youth co-offending in Stockholm*. Cambridge Studies in Criminology. Cambridge/New York: Cambridge University Press.

Shaw, C. R., & McKay, H. D. (1931). Social factors in juvenile delinquency: A study of the community, the family, and the gang in relation to delinquent behaviour. Report of the national commission on law observance and enforcement, causes of crime II(13). Washington, DC: U.S. G.P.O.

Simmel, G. (1890). *Über Soziale Differenzierung: Sociologigische und Psychologische Untersuchungen (On social differentiation)*. Leipzig: Duncker & Humbolt.

Simmel, G. (1904/1957). Fashion. *The American Journal of Sociology, LXII*(6), 541–558.

Smångs, M. (2008). Differential associations, control theory, and the strength of weak ties—linking criminological theories with social network theory. Paper presented at the annual meeting of the American Sociological Association, Sheraton Boston and the Boston Marriott Copley Place, Boston, MA.

Steglich, C., Snijders, T. A. B., & Pearson, M. (2009). *Dynamic networks and behavior: Separating selection from influence*. Technical report, ICS Interuniversity Center for Social Science Theory and Methodology.

Sutherland, E. H. (1947). Principles of criminology. In *The sociology of crime and delinquency* (4th ed.). New York: Harper and Row, Publishers Inc.

Urbig, D., Lorenz, J., & Herzberg, H. (2008). Opinion dynamics: The effect of the number of peers met at once. *Journal of Artificial Societies and Social Simulation, 11*(2), 4.

van Baal, P. (2004). *Computer simulations of criminal deterrence*. Australia: Annandale, The Federation Press.

Wikström, P.-O. H., & Loeber, R. (2000). Do disadvantaged neighbourhoods cause well-adjusted children to become adolescent delinquents? A study of male serious juvenile offending, individual risk and protective factors and neighbourhood context. *Criminology, 38*, 1109–1142.

Chapter 12
Social Construction of Knowledge

If you can't change the world, change yourself.

The The

This chapter presents a model which focuses on the intra-group radicalisation of opinions.[1] In the previous chapter we saw a model in which criminality was transmitted through a social network. We used this as an example of extending simulations of social norms by adding a social structure, a friendship network. The network was constituted by a spatial proximity measure, the social circle (cf. Hamill and Gilbert 2009; Hamill 2010) and a movement dynamic towards or away from the centroid of the social circle depending on similarity criteria. This spatial implementation of a social network resulted in reasonably realistic clustering of delinquents, i.e. the establishment of social groups.

Here we approach the idea of groups from a different perspective. Rather than using spatial proximity, we use the idea of shared opinions resulting from a social construction of knowledge as the starting point for group formation and group radicalisation. This model also sits within the tradition of opinion dynamics (e.g. Deffuant et al. 2002; Hegselmann and Krause 2002; Urbig et al. 2008) but rather than having a passive assimilation of opinions, agents actively engage in opinion exchange.

In order to do this, agents need not only to hold opinions but also to reason about other agent's opinions. Currently, agent-based models focus largely on behavioural rather than cognitive agents. The exceptions are the models discussed in Chap. 9, which have an underlying architecture that allows reasoning with normative facts. Much can be gained when examining phenomena like opinion dynamics by explicitly modelling the communicative interactions and influences between agents, in particular when opinion dynamics are used as an underlying mechanism to explain

[1]This chapter is based on a collaboration with Piter Dykstra, Wander Jager, Rienke Verbrugge and Gerard R. Renardel de Lavalette and uses parts of our publications Dykstra et al. (2009, 2013).

C. Elsenbroich and N. Gilbert, *Modelling Norms*, DOI 10.1007/978-94-007-7052-2_12,

other social phenomena, in our case group formation and group radicalisation. Whereas behaviour alone might be enough for inter-group dynamics (such as the delinquent network model in Chap. 11), more complex reasoning is necessary for intra-group dynamics, e.g. radicalisation. In this chapter we develop a model in which agent communication is based on influencing group opinion by winning arguments.

In the next section we briefly discuss some background theory on social influence and group formation in which to position the model. We then describe the model and its results. We only discuss the baseline model as presented in Dykstra et al. (2009).[2]

12.1 The Social Construction of Knowledge

Some of the theoretical background we have already discussed in previous chapters. The theory of reasoned action (Ajzen 1985), reviewed in Sect. 2.3.1, is one of the foundations of the model as it directly addresses group influences on an agent's opinion. General social influence research discussed in Sect. 2.2.4 also feeds into this model.

In addition we take the idea of *social constructuralism* as promising for the kind of intra-group dynamics we set out to model (Carley 1986). Constructuralism exposes the double-dynamics of opinion formation and group formation. Opinion dynamics shows how an agent's opinion is influenced by other agents' opinions. This way opinions in a group assimilate. However, a social group is not an arbitrary aggregate. Agents choose their social groups depending on how close they feel to others in their opinions.

> Constructuralism is the theory that the social world and the personal cognitive world of the individual continuously evolve in a reflexive fashion. The individual's cognitive structure (his knowledge base), his propensity to interact with other individuals, social structure, social meaning, social knowledge, and consensus are all being continuously constructed in a reflexive, recursive fashion as the individuals in the society interact in the process of moving through a series of tasks. [...] Central to the constructuralist theory are the assumptions that individuals process and communicate information during interactions, and that the accrual of new information produces cognitive development, changes in the individuals' cognitive structure. (Carley 1986, p. 386)

Theories supporting the group selection phenomenon are Festinger's Social Comparison Theory (Festinger 1954) and Merton's Value Homophily (Lazarfeld and Merton 2002). It has been argued that these homophily phenomena are themselves not a result of choice but of environmental circumstances (clustered living, stratified education etc.) (McPherson et al. 2003). Recent research on homophily on social networking sites shows, however, that the phenomenon seems to be fundamental rather than a derivative of other social forces. Thelwall (2009) uses

---

[2]An implementation in NetLogo of the baseline model is available at: http://www.math.rug.nl/~piter/essa/index.html

data from the social networking site MySpace where environmental and social class factors do not apply, or apply much less than in the physical world. Although friendship networks on the web still bear some resemblance to the physical friendship networks of people, the networks are so large that this resemblance often becomes minimal. The virtual friendship networks on MySpace displayed very similar, i.e. very strong, homophily to traditional friendship networks, supporting the idea of social constructuralism that social groups are the outcome of a homophilous selection process as well as opinion assimilation.

12.2 A Model of Social Cognition

Common ways for an agent to start a communication in a simulation model are to either communicate with all agents simultaneously (Hegselmann and Krause 2002) or pick another agent at random (Deffuant et al. 2002). In contrast to these random one-to-one communication strategies, the agents in this model make announcements that are heard by all agents within a certain range. Announcements travel with varying *loudness* which decreases as the message travels through space. The transmission of the message stops when the loudness falls below an audibility threshold.

Agents try to convince each other of their opinions. Opinions are their only source of knowledge (i.e. knowledge is purely socially constructed) and the truth and falsity of a statement is decided by vote. In order to spread an opinion, agents need to communicate, i.e. utter their opinions. Other agents can attack an utterance and an argument ensues. To resolve the argument, the winner is decided by public vote of the surrounding agents. Winning an argument solidifies a particular opinion within a group and raises the reputation of the winning agent. Defining a high reputation as an agent goal means agents have an incentive to argue. If an agent's opinion diverges too much from the accepted opinion in the group, an agent can either assimilate or leave to find a more appropriate group.

The social interactions of the agents are based on an *argumentation game.* Kamlah and Lorenzen (1973) introduced this type of argumentation to define a construction for the concept of *logic al truth.* For Kamlah and Lorenzen, a proposition φ is logically true if and only if a proponent of φ has a *winning strategy* for a *formal dialogue* about φ (i.e. the proponent is always able to prevent an opponent from winning). A formal dialogue is one in which no assumption about the truth of any propositions is made. Hence Kamlah and Lorenzen (1973) define a tautology as a proposition which, if stated, can never lose in an argumentation game. We adapt this argumentation game for our purposes. As we do not model tautologies but opinions and we want to model the social construction of knowledge, we replace the idea of a *winning strategy* by the group vote.

An agent, the proponent, that announces a statement enables another agent, the opponent, to attack that statement and an argument is the consequence of these two actions. A game is a sequence of alternating actions by the proponent and the opponent. With the initial announcement the proponent states how convinced it is of the statement. This is operationalised by agents putting a wager of their reputation on statements, stating what amount of reputation they are expecting to gain on winning the argument and how much they are willing to forego in case they lose. Since arguments are decided by group vote, agents need to be in tune with the surrounding opinions to assess how much they should gamble.

12.2.1 The Argumentation Game

The argumentation game is played as follows: An announcement is a triplet consisting of a statement S and two values of reputation points (RP) p, r between 0 and 1, representing what the agent is expecting to win (p) or lose (r) depending on the eventual outcome. An announcement of (S, p, r) by agent A, means 'A believes in S expecting to win p reputation points or lose r points'. The proponent may specify any amount p it is prepared to pay in case of losing, and any amount r it wants to receive in case of winning the dialogue. Agreeing with a statement is cost-free.

The p/r-ratio reflects an agent's belief in the chances of winning the dialogue. If an agent A believes it will win the dialogue about a statement S in $2/3$ of cases, it might consider offering $p_a = 2$(RP) and $r_a = 1$(RP) as the least ratio that is still reasonable. For an agent B who disagrees with a proposition S with values p_b and r_b, attacking that proposition is a rational thing to do. $p_b/r_b < p_a/r_a$ assigned to S means that opponent B expects to win a dialogue about S more often than the proponent A. Agents simply infer their odds from their degree of belief in a statement S. Their degree of belief is a tuple (e, i) consisting of the evidence e an agent has for S and the importance i that A attaches to S. We discuss these concepts in the next section as well as a mechanism for their update.

12.2.2 Updates for Socially Constructed Beliefs

In order to win arguments, agents must stay in tune with their surroundings, meaning they must update their beliefs by listening to announcements and considering the winning arguments. We use the values p and r to define the epistemic notions of the *evidence* for and the *importance* of a statement S to define the belief update mechanism. The higher the value for e, the more an agent A is convinced of a statement S. The higher the value for i, the more important the statement S is for A.

Definition 12.2.1. Let $e, i \in [0, 1]$.

$$e = \frac{p}{p+r} \qquad i = \frac{p+r}{2}$$

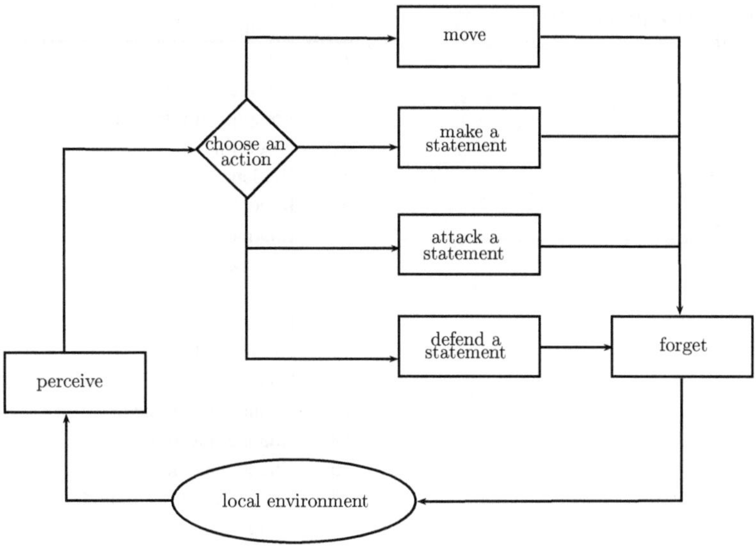

Fig. 12.1 Flowchart of agent actions taken from Dykstra et al. (2013)

An agent can compute its (p,r)-values for any statement S from an (e,i)-pair:

$$p = 2 \cdot e \cdot i \text{ and } r = 2 \cdot i \cdot (1 - e).$$

Each announcement of S modifies an agent's e and i incrementally. If an agent is in agreement with a proposition S, repeated utterances of the same message count as evidence but make the statement less important. If it disagrees, repeated utterances detract evidence in favour of S but raise the importance of S. In order to preserve a belief in S an agent can move away from a place where $\neg S$ (not S) is announced repeatedly.

12.2.3 The Simulation

A simulation based on these principles has been implemented to demonstrate the effect of argumentation. The main loop of the program performs a cycle in which the agents have the opportunity to act in random order. The action possibilities are shown in Fig. 12.1.

Initially the environment is a neutral space. When an opinion is uttered on a patch, it and its neighbours (with decreasing intensity) take on the opinion making the environment an *opinion space*. Agents are initially randomly distributed in space, and have a random allocation of their degree of belief in statements, i.e. random values for *evidence* and *imporatance* (Parameters 3 & 4 from Table 12.1) for each one of the statements A, B, C, D, E. The initial distribution of RP is

Table 12.1 Input parameters in the program

	Parameter	Range
1	Number-of-agents	0–100
2	Number-of-propositions	0–5
3	Force-of-argumentation	0–1
4	Force-of-norms	0–1
5	Evidence	0–1
6	Importance	0–1
7	Loudness	0–20
8	Stepsize	0–10
9	Visual-horizon	0–100
10	Forgetspeed	0–10
11	Undirectedness	0–45
12	Chance-walk	0–100
13	Chance-announce	0–100
14	Chance-question	0–100
15	Chance-attack	0–100
16	Chance-learn-by-neighbour	0–100
17	Chance-learn-by-environment	0–100
18	Chance-mutation	0–100
19	Neutral-importance	0–0.99

calculated from the evidence importance for each statement. An agent can announce a statement, attack and defend announcements and move in the opinion space, for example in the direction of an area closest to its own opinion (within its visual horizon).

The likelihood of an announcement, a defence or an attack is determined by Parameters 12–14. The higher the value, the more 'opinionated' the agents are, i.e. the more likely they are to argue. The reach of an announcement is determined by its *loudness* (Parameter 6). How loud an agent can shout out its opinion is determined by its reputation points: the more points, the louder the agent and the more reach it has. An agent can only attack a statement it can hear, i.e. where there is an intersection between the announcement's reach and the agent's visual horizon (Parameter 8). The visual horizon together with *chance-walk* (Parameter 11) also determine whether an agent will move in space, with *undirectedness* determining whether they move towards agents that are closer to them in their opinions; *stepsize* (Parameter 7) determines how fast agents move about. Agents will update their opinions depending on the values of Parameters 15 & 16, learning from their neighbours or from lingering information in the opinion space itself. Agents will forget what they have heard depending on the *forgetspeed* (Parameter 9). Forgetting only happens if a statement is not uttered for a while. Opinions can randomly change if we allow mutations (Parameter 17). After each round, i.e. when every agent has had its turn to act, the reputation is normalised keeping the sum of reputation points constant. To increase its accordance with its environment, an agent has to utter a statement that is not attacked or win an argument. Previously uttered statements are forgotten unless repeated. The loudness of an agent's utterance is a random number between 0 and the maximal loudness multiplied by the agent's reputation points.

Parameters 1, 4 and 5 are static parameters used only in the setup. All other parameters are variable and can be changed during the simulation. When all variable parameters are set to zero nothing happens. Adding the chance of announcements and some loudness produces agents that shout out their opinions but nobody listens. All statements just coexist, like Speaker's Corner in London's Hyde Park before the public comes along. Adding the possibility of attacking an uttered statement produces a proper Speaker's Corner with agents shouting out their opinions and other agents heckling them. Agents change their opinions by assimilating their neighbours' opinions or by using environmental information.

So far we have a simulation in which agents announce and attack statements and win arguments but do not move. In order to get some group formation we need to add some physical dynamic. This is done by allowing the agents to (a) find other agents with similar opinions within their visual-horizon and (b) by giving them the chance to walk (chance-walk) and a "speed" (stepsize). The larger the visual-horizon, the more other agents can be checked for similarity. It might seem that the visual horizon should really be called an 'audial horizon' as similarity is assessed by comparing utterances. However, in order to move towards another agent, this agent has to be "seen" not only heard. Due to its loudness, an utterance has a reach over many patches, whereas the position of an agent only has the extension of one patch. Using both assimilation of opinions through argumentation and selection of agents with similar opinions, the model implements the parallel dynamics of the social construction of knowledge.

12.3 Results and Observations

The model sets out to investigate the influence of argumentation on group formation and radicalisation. Argumentation is formalised with an argumentation game in which agents try to maximise their reputation points (*RP*). The influence of argumentation is measured by how these reputation points are allocated. Two methods for the computation of the *RP* values have been implemented:

1. (*Force of norms*): At each round, the *RP* value of an agent is incremented or decremented by a value proportional to the gain/loss in similarity with its environment. The *RP* value reflects its success of being in conformity with the environment.
2. (*Force of argumentation*): The *RP* value is determined by the outcome of arguments. On winning an attack/defence of a statement the *RP* value is incremented by respectively the p/r amount of the attacked/defended statement. On losing an attack/defence *RP* is decremented by respectively the r/p value of the statement.

The two calculations produce very different outcomes for both group formation and the radicalisation of opinions. If reputation status is calculated as a function of an agent's similarity with its environment, its conformity, the simulation results in strong polarisation of opinions and a number of segregated groups. The *RP* are relatively equally distributed and there are no opinion leaders. If, on the other hand, reputation status is calculated as a function of an agent's individual argumentation performance, opinions become much less polarised. However, the distribution of *RP* is much more skewed, with a small number of agents holding all the *RP*. This means that the other agents can no longer announce their opinions because having no *RP* means they have no *loudness*.

There are some interesting interaction dynamics that can be observed in this simulation. The first is the interaction of loudness and visual horizon: If the visual horizon is quite large (100) then, if loudness is small, agents all join one block after a while and opinions align completely. If the visual horizon is large and the agents are also loud, groups form and opinions stay much more varied. If the visual horizon is small and the loudness is small, many local clusters develop.

Two dynamics are of particular interest. The first is that agents can accumulate 'kudos' (RP) on one proposition, say *A*, and then use it to convince their surrounding agents of another proposition, say *B*. The second is that agents can convince other agents of opinions that they themselves are not fully convinced of. This means that opinion leaders that do not have extreme opinions can develop.

12.4 Conclusion

In this chapter we have presented another model in which agents are socially embedded. This time agents either adapt their opinion to their surroundings or they move away to find agents that are more similar to them. Agent's opinions are constructed solely through their social surroundings.

Agent communication is based on dialogues. A dialogue is a game in which agents gamble reputation points (*RP*) on their opinion being accepted by their surrounding agents. Agents start to argue in order to gain reputation points, trying to convince other agents of their views. Conflicts are resolved by appeal to surrounding agents in such a way that the more supported statement wins the dialogue. Agents can move to find other agents more in accordance with their opinions or they can assimilate to their environment.

Two dynamics have been simulated, group formation and group radicalisation. Two different mechanisms of social interaction have been implemented, the force of norms mechanism in which an agent gains status by conforming to its environment and the force of argumentation mechanism in which status is gained by winning arguments. The force of norms mechanism led to a strong segregation of groups with radical opinions but agents relatively equal in status. The force of argumentation mechanism also led to groups, but the groups were less radical in their opinions and status was distributed very unequally, with some agents becoming opinion leaders.

References

Ajzen, I. (1985). From intentions to actions: A theory of planned behaviour. In J. Kuhli & J. Beckmann (Eds.), *Action—control: From cognition to behaviour* (pp. 11–39). Heidelberg: Springer.

Carley, K. M. (1986). Knowledge acquisition as a social phenomenon. *Instructional Science, Elsevier Science Publishers B.V., Amsterdam, 14*(4), 381–438.

Deffuant, G., Amblard, F., Weisbuch, G., & Faure, T. (2002). How can extremism prevail? A study based on the relative agreement interaction model. *Journal of Artificial Societies and Social Simulation, 5*(4), 1. http://jasss.soc.surrey.ac.uk/5/4/1.html.

Dykstra, P., Elsenbroich C., Jager, W., de Lavalette, G. R., & Verbrugge, R. (2009). A dialogical logic-based simulation architecture for social agents and the emergence of extremist behaviour. In *Proceedings of the European social simulation association annual conference 2009*. Guildford, UK: University of Surrey.

Dykstra, P., Elsenbroich, C., Jager, W., Renardel de Lavalette, G., & Verbrugge, R. (2013). Put your money where your mouth is: DIAL, a dialogical model for opinion dynamics. *Journal of Artificial Societies and Social Simulation, 16*(3), 4. http://jasss.soc.surrey.ac.uk/16/3/4.html.

Festinger, L. (1954). A theory of social comparison processes. *Human Relations, 7*(2), 117–140.

Hamill, L. (2010). *Communications, travel and social networks since 1840: A study using agent-based models*. Ph. D. thesis, University of Surrey.

Hamill, L., & Gilbert, N. (2009). Social circles: A simple structure for agent-based social network models. *Journal of Artificial Societies and Social Simulation, 12*(2), 3.

Hegselmann, R., & Krause, U. (2002). Opinion dynamics and bounded confidence: Models, analysis and simulation. *Journal of Artificial Societies and Social Simulation, 5*(3), 2. http://jasss.soc.surrey.ac.uk/5/3/2.html.

Kamlah, W., & Lorenzen, P. (1973). *Logische Propädeutik*. B.I.-Wissenschaftsverlag, Muñchen, Wien, Zuřich.

Lazarfeld, P., & Merton, R. K. (2002). Friendship as a social process: A substantive and methodological analysis. In M. Berger, T. Abel, & C. H. Page (Eds.), *Freedom and control in modern society*. New York: Van Nostrand.

McPherson, M., Smith-Lovin, L., & Cook, J. (2003). Birds of a feather: Homophily in social networks. *Annual Review of Sociology, 27*, 415–444.

Thelwall, M. (2009). Homophily in myspace. *Journal of the American Society for Information Science and Technology, 60*(2), 219–231.

Urbig, D., Lorenz, J., & Herzberg, H. (2008). Opinion dynamics: The effect of the number of peers met at once. *Journal of Artificial Societies and Social Simulation, 11*(2), 4.

Chapter 13
Morality

Everything in nature acts according to laws. Only a rational being has the power to act according to his conception [representation] of a law, i.e. according to principles....

Immanuel Kant

In Chap. 11 we saw the use of social networks for modelling juvenile delinquency. In Chap. 12 we introduced a model of group formation by shared knowledge and meaning. In this chapter we discuss a final extension to models of normative behaviour to add the previously discussed context sensitivity of compliance.

Words like 'moral malaise' are still used in the discussion of crime, see for example the August 2011 Riots in England.

> Whatever the reasons, a moral malaise has gripped a minority of young Britons, a subgroup that is nevertheless big enough to terrorise and humiliate the country. (The Economist, 13/08/2011)

However, morality is no longer a central concept in the social sciences. This is in contrast to the early days of sociology when it was seen as the 'science of morality' (Durkheim 1974, also see Sect. 2.1.1). Nevertheless, there has been some resurgence of the concept in the past two decades, mainly in discussions of modernity (e.g. in works of Bauman 1993 and Giddens 1991; see Shilling and Mellor 1998 for an overview).

In criminology, concern with morality has become muted, despite the intuitive entanglement of the concepts of crime and morality. As discussed in Chap. 3, criminology focusses on individual risk factors such as behavioural difficulties or biological differences, measurable offender variables, such as gender, class and race, and the influence of the physical environment on crime. The economic analysis of crime made committing a crime a matter of choosing the action with the highest utility to the agent, dispensing with ideas that the criminal is at all different from others and that the criminal is a passive 'victim' of external circumstances. However, morality as a concept in criminology is not entirely dead.

C. Elsenbroich and N. Gilbert, *Modelling Norms*, DOI 10.1007/978-94-007-7052-2_13,

> The Criminal Law assumes that 'man' is a moral agent who is responsible for his actions. Economists further assume that these actions can be altered by appropriate structuring of incentives... (Pyle 2000, p. 86)

In this quote, Pyle explicitly states that there is a moral dimension to actions. An operationalisation of morality within rational choice theory can be found in Paternoster and Simpson (1996). The authors collect data on attitudes and behaviour towards corporate crime using questionnaires relating to specific corporate crime scenarios. The decision to commit a corporate crime was strongly determined by personal cost-benefit factors such as career advancement. It seems, however, that sanctions and factors, such as colleagues recently being caught in a similar act, had relatively little influence on the decisions to commit a crime. The most interesting feature of this study is the finding of the importance of personal morality in the decision process. The definition of a moral norm used in the study is different from the outcome orientated factors of rational choice theory. A moral norm is deontological, rather than evaluated by its consequences. The authors found that the moral evaluation of an act was the best predictor of whether a crime was executed or not and that rational choice criteria took over only when morality decayed.

Although the authors state that they want to enrich rational choice theory with a notion of morality, their study does not corroborate rational choice theory overall. Clearly, rational choice theory does not capture the idea of a deontological influence on choices. This means there must be some other feature in an agent's reasoning that accounts for the salience of morality. The authors recommend that morality should be exploited more in the corporate world.

> Finally, we have evidence to suggest that moral appeals may be an especially powerful source of corporate social control. (Paternoster and Simpson 1996, p. 579)

However, rather than shedding light on the problem of morality, this study opens up a host of questions about traditional approaches in criminology that do not pay any attention to what constitutes morality and how it influences an agent's decision making.

Pyle believes that moral actions are achievable by a simple restructuring of incentives. Can an action resulting from personal utility maximisation within a pro-social incentive structure be seen as a moral action? In this chapter we want to resuscitate morality and make it part of the analysis of normative behaviour and crime. For this we investigate a theory in which crime is explicitly modelled as moral decision making. Crime is defined as 'a breach of a moral norm (as defined in law)' and the agent as making a choice about this breach in particular situations.

13.1 Theories of Moral Action

Describing theories of moral action would require a book in itself. In the following we do a quick listing of some formal approaches to questions of normative, value and moral reasoning. We then turn to a social science theory of moral action applied to crime which we use as the background for our final agent-based model.

13.1.1 Formal Approaches

There are some formal approaches that will be useful to underpin a model of moral reasoning. There exists a host of deontic logics, that is logics concerned solely with processing normative statements. Deontic logics are usually a form of modal logic conceptualising reasoning about permission and obligation. The original deontic logic was conceived by von Wright (1951). Recently the literature on deontic logics has exploded. Although the research into deontic logics for multi-agent systems can offer some useful conceptualisations and reasoning mechanisms for simulations, there is also criticism that it has become self-serving (Edmonds 2004). Input/Output logic (Makinson and van der Torre 2000) is a kind of meta-logic distilling the reasoning of deontic logics into a general framework. However, it cannot be applied in a simulation itself.

Atkinson and Bench-Capon (2008) and Atkinson and Bench-Capon (2009) develop an implementation of moral reasoning using an abstract argumentation framework. The authors argue that values, whether moral or otherwise, can conflict without one value being less than the other. Perfectly rational agents can thus still advocate different courses of action, leading to conflicts which need to be resolved.

> We can be coercive about what is the case, but need to be persuasive about what should be the case. (Atkinson and Bench-Capon 2009, p. 63)

When it comes to deciding actions, to transform the world into what it 'should be', agents will need to juggle conflicting values. Given the equality of the different values, it is impossible to put them into a simple partial ordering of importance. Instead they can be represented as an Value based Argumentation Framework where the supporting and attacking relationships between values can be clarified and a winning argument and thus the right course of action determined.

These logics show how agents reason about what inferences can be drawn from normative statements. This is important for the representation in a model of, for example, the private and public values needed to implement compliance. In addition, these logics can be assessed with respect to belief-revision tools and tricks developed from Alchourrón et al. (1985) (by, for example Hansson 1999) on how to deal with possible inconsistency. Together with the EMIL-A architecture, discussed in Chap. 9, these logics might open the door to the design of an agent that can reason not only with norms (as EMIL-A can) but also about norms so that it can make decisions with regard to context, either according to private values or public norms.

Rather than working on a new highly cognitive agent-architecture, we will approach morality from a more agent-based modelling perspective. As we saw before, agent based models are particularly good at implementing social theory. In the next section we discuss a theory of crime as moral decision making which lends itself quite naturally to an agent-based implementation.

13.1.2 Crime as Moral Decision Making

In Chap. 3 we observed a dichotomy in the literature between conceptualising crime from an offender perspective and from an environmental perspective. However, neither treating crime as pathological nor as purely environmental accounts for the fact that most people commit crimes at some points in their lives and that even criminals do not commit crimes most of the time.

Recently, Wikström has developed a theory of crime to bridge the dichotomy between individual and environmental explanations of crime, and, more importantly, to give a causal theory of crime, *Situational Action Theory* (Wikström 2010). In his view most criminology confuses the causes of crime with the "causes of the causes of crime" (Wikström 2011). Situational Action Theory is a theory of criminal action based on the idea that crime is a breach of a moral norm (as defined in law). The cause of a crime is the decision of an agent in a specific situation to breach a moral norm. He argues that what is traditionally seen as causes of crime, such as class, gender, race, family background, education (the list is almost endless), are at most causes of the cause of crime. In Situational Action Theory, criminal behaviour becomes a special case of moral action.

Wikström argues that the analysis of crime using crime correlates has become an unintelligible bulwark where "everything seems to matter" (Wikström 2011). Much of social science is based on the analysis of correlations. In criminology correlations fulfil the function of finding the regularities that explain crime, for example, most crime is committed by men meaning that gender and crime are correlated. However, Wikström (2011) points out that (a) too many correlations are found for them to be explanatory and (b) many correlations seem to be completely irrelevant to the explanation of crime. Crime is correlated with ethnicity, educational attainment, gender, family income, age, personality, alcohol and drug use, intelligence, and mental health, to name but a few. Given the number of correlates it is difficult to consider any one of them as explanatory. Correlation does not suffice for a causal relationship between two variables, for example, both could be caused by a third, a *common cause*. The explanatory irrelevance of correlates is another, related, problem. Although there is a strong statistical correlation between committing a crime and being male, being male cannot possibly be seen as an explanation of someone committing a crime. Instead of a correlation analysis, Wikström proposes an explanation resting on agency, i.e. a mechanism explanation in which we have agents and situations as entities resulting in action decisions to commit a crime or not.

Wikström proposes that:

i *Situational Action Theory intends to be a general theory of moral action and the causes of crime.* It achieves this by focusing on explaining what all crimes, in all places, and at all times have in common, the breach of a moral rule (defined in law).

ii *Situational Action Theory aims to offer an alternative to rational choice theory in the study of moral action and the causes of crime.* While the theory accepts that rationality and self-interest at times [see further point (iv) below] play a role in guiding human action, it reasons that on a more fundamental level humans are rule-guided actors (and that the social order is essentially based on shared moral rules).

iii *Situational Action Theory is developed to overcome the common (but unfruitful) divide between individual and environmental explanatory approaches to the causes of crime.* It accomplishes this by proposing a situational mechanism (a perception–choice process) that links the person and his or her environment to his or her actions. People engage in acts of crime because they (i) come to see such acts as viable action alternatives and (ii) choose (habitually or deliberately) to carry them out.

iv *Situational Action Theory further aims to integrate behaviouristic and voluntaristic approaches to the explanation of crime.* It does so by recognising that human behaviour (including law-abidance and acts of crime) is predominantly caused by processes of either habit or rational deliberation (two different kinds of perception–choice processes).

v *Situational Action Theory seeks to bridge macro and micro, and situational and developmental approaches in the study of crime.* It addresses this problem by stressing the need to carefully distinguish between the causes and the causes of the causes in the analysis of crime causation, arguing that macro (structural, systemic) factors and (individual) developmental factors are best analysed as causes of the causes, while micro and situational factors are best analysed as causes.

(Wikström 2010, p. 216/217)

Actions are a result of a specific agent in a specific situation. Situational Action Theory distinguishes between a *setting*, i.e. the environment accessible to the agent (via perception) and a *situation*, i.e. the agent's awareness of action alternatives. Different agents in the same setting can become aware of different action alternatives leading to different choices. Agents can also be in the same situation, i.e. see the same actions alternatives, but make different decisions about which one to act on. Wikström distinguishes between habitual behaviours and those resulting from deliberated decision. In Situational Action Theory, both the environment and the agents play a role in the genesis of criminal behaviour. The theory stipulates four ingredients at work in the commission of a crime (see Table 13.1).

Traditional parameters of criminology such as deterrence and self-control are integrated into the decision to commit crime. Neither weak deterrence nor lack of self-control are themselves causes of crime but they support the agent's decision. Figure 13.1 is the action-tree of an agent's decision to commit a crime. The first step is situating the agent in the environment and making it decide whether there is a temptation or not (Motivation). If there is no motivation, no crime will be committed. Most people would simply walk past a car with a handbag on the passenger seat but some are tempted to snatch it. In case of temptation the next level influencing the decision is activated, the Moral Filter. The decision now depends on the interaction between the setting's rule guidance and the agent's morality. If the setting rules and the agent's morality are congruent, two cases have to be distinguished. If the setting encourages crime and the agent's morality is low, a crime will be committed. If the setting discourages crime and the agent's morality is high, no crime will be committed. If the setting rules and agent morality are congruent, the next level influencing the decision is activated, the Controls. If the

Table 13.1 Elements of situational action theory (Wikström 2010, p. 219, Fig. 12.1)

Element	Definition
Person	Body, biological and psychological make-up, experiences, agency (power to make things happen intentionally)
Setting	Part of the environment to which the individual is directly exposed and reacts; configuration of objects, persons and events accessible to the person through his or her senses (incl. any media present)
Situation	Perception of action alternatives and process of choice as the result of the person's interaction with a setting
Action	Bodily movements under the person's guidance

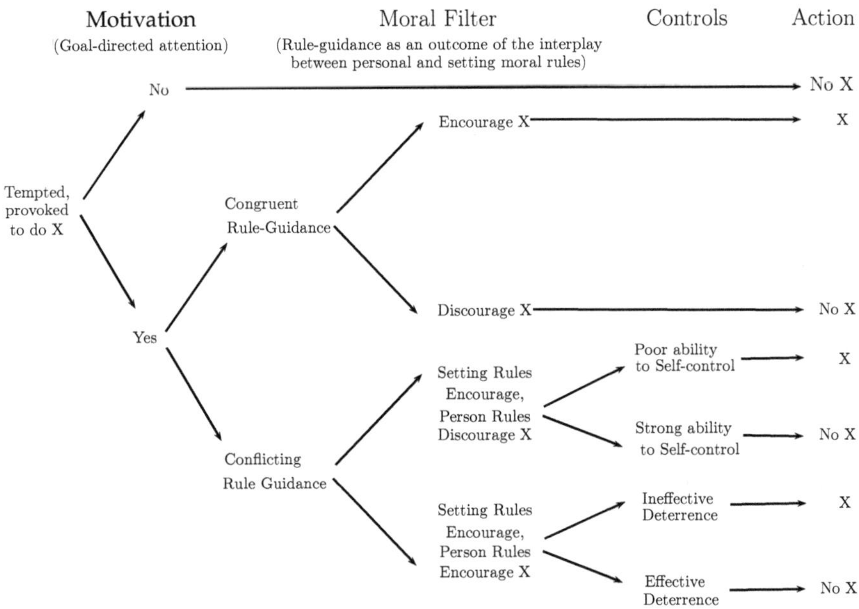

Fig. 13.1 The roles of motivation, moral filter and controls with regards to action decisions in situational action theory (Wikström 2010, p. 234)

setting encourages and the agent's morality discourages crime, it depends on the agent's self-control whether a crime is committed. If the setting discourages and the agent's morality encourages crime, it depends on the external deterrence.

13.1.3 The Peterborough Adolescent and Young Adult Development Study

The Peterborough Adolescent and Young Adult Development Study (PADS+) is an ongoing longitudinal study of juvenile delinquency in Peterborough, a medium sized town in the East Midlands, UK. So far it consists of five waves of data collection between 2003 and 2008. The cohort is roughly one third of the population aged 11 in 2002. Individuals were asked to participate in 45 min structured interviews, and fill out questionnaires covering individual-level variables including morality and self-control, psychometric measures and a self-report on crime frequency in the last year. They were also asked to provide a space-time budget, asking young people to provide hourly information on their geographic location (area), the place (e.g. school, home), who they were with (e.g. peers, family) and their activity (e.g. socialising, playing tennis) over a 4 day period each year. In addition the space-time budget asked about acts of crime, substance abuse, and victimisation in the time period. A community postal survey was conduced across the whole study area to assess the differences in the social environment using the smallest administrative units, output areas, to generate a fine grained differentiation.

The individual interviews and personality questionnaires provide data on crime propensity. The community postal survey provides information about the settings such as their collective efficacy, or how much they encourage or discourage acts of crime. The space-time budgets provide information about the interaction between setting and person as well as actions performed in particular settings. They give details of agents' exposure to crime and whether they spend time supervised or unsupervised with peers alone.

In Wikström et al. (2010) the data are presented in detail and related to Situational Action Theory. Although routine activities play a role in whether young people commit crimes or not, the data show that the commission of crime depends most on a person's crime propensity. Agents with crime averse morality and high levels of self-control are almost *situationally immune*. This gives support to the person-setting interaction approach of Situational Action Theory.

13.2 A Model of Crime as Moral Decision

As we have noted in Chap. 4, an agent-based model consists of three ingredients: agents, an environment and some kind of dynamic interaction between the agents and the environment. Situational Action Theory provides a specification for agents and an action theory that describes the interaction between the environment and the agent. It also provides some indirect specification of the environment, proposing that there are areas more conducive to crime and that agents are provoked/tempted into committing crime. The final decision whether to commit a crime is a result of the interaction of the environment and the agent's moral rules and ability to self-control.

In order to create a model, one needs to make some assumptions (that is, assumptions not dictated by Situational Action Theory) about the 'geography' of the environment and the initial states of the agents. Once the model has been formulated, one can then test to see whether these assumptions are critical to the behaviour of the model, using a sensitivity analysis.

For this model of Situational Action Theory, we have chosen young adults as agents and to represent the environment as a 33×33 torus of locations ('patches')

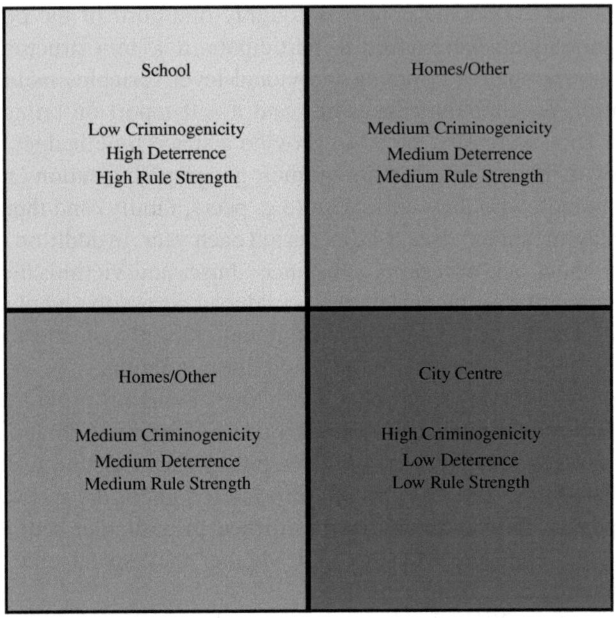

Fig. 13.2 The geography of the environment

representing the settings. The toroidal grid is divided into four squares, one square representing the city centre, one square representing a school and two squares, representing any location outside of school and the city centre (e.g. agents' homes) (Fig. 13.2). Each patch within the squares has a degree of:

1. Temptation, i.e. the extent to which a setting offers a criminal action alternative (how criminogenic the setting is).
2. Rule-strength, i.e. how much the setting encourages a moral rule.
3. Deterrence-strength, i.e. how much the setting deters crime.

The squares differ in the values of these parameters. The school has high rule-strength, high deterrence and low temptation. The city centre has low rule-strength, high deterrence (there is usually plenty of security around shops) and high temptation. The two other squares have medium values for all parameters. This classification of locations is chosen following categories in the PADS+ dataset in which, for example, the space-time budgets of agents are categorised into time at school, in the city centre, at home, and in and outside the urban area being researched. Agents have two characteristics, following Situational Action Theory:

1. Morality, normally distributed with mean 0 and standard deviation 10. The higher its morality, the less likely the agent is to commit a crime.
2. Self-control, also normally distributed with mean 0 and standard deviation 10. The higher its self-control, the less likely the agent is to commit a crime.

Table 13.2 Percent time spent awake at some key locations by crime propensity, derived from the PADS+ dataset (Wikström et al. 2010, p. 76)

	Crime propensity		
Location	Low	Med	High
Home	47.7	45.7	44.2
School	31.1	28.9	22.4
Best friends	1.6	2.9	5.6
City and local centre	3.2	4.2	5.3
Elsewhere in study area	7.7	11.3	16.0
Elsewhere outside study area	8.7	7.0	6.6
Total (%)	100	100	100
Total hours	30,732	137,990	31,385

An agent's crime propensity is a function of its morality and self-control, again resulting in a normal distribution. Agents are divided into three types, those with low, medium and high crime propensity. Low and high crime propensity agents are those with crime propensity more than one standard deviation away from the mean. An agent's crime propensity influences the first decision of whether a situation is perceived as a temptation. It also influences the distribution of its time between locations, see Table 13.2. For example, a more crime prone agent spends only 22 % of its time at school whereas a less crime prone agent spends nearly 31 % of its time there. These data have been obtained from the PADS+ survey, and so accurately reflect the behaviour of youth in Peterborough.

There are three global parameters that apply equally to all agents:

1. Control threshold: if an agent's self-control is less than this threshold, and the setting encourages crime, but the agent's morality discourages it, the agent succumbs to the temptation.
2. Deterrence threshold: if the amount of deterrence in a setting exceeds this threshold, an agent is deterred from committing a crime.
3. Temptation threshold: if the temptation of the patch is greater than this threshold, a patch is tempting. Then, if the crime propensity of an agent is greater than the temptation of the patch, a crime is considered by the agent.

One step (tick) of the simulation represents one time unit. At each step, an agent can commit a crime if the Situational Action Theory decision procedure (Fig. 13.1) so dictates. This decision procedure implies the following agent rules: The first check is whether the agent's crime propensity is higher than the temptation of the patch. If so, crime is seen as an option. The next check is whether the moral setting of the patch and the agent are congruent or not. This means that both agent morality and patch rule-strength are positive or both negative; both being negative leads to the commission of a crime. If morality and the setting's rule-strength are not congruent there are two cases to consider:

1. If the agent's morality is positive and the patch's rule-strength is negative, the agent commits a crime if the agent's self-control is lower than the overall control threshold.
2. If the agent's morality is negative and the patch's rule strength is positive, the agent commits a crime if the patch's deterrence strength is below the overall deterrence threshold.

Initially, agents are scattered randomly on the grid. Depending on their crime propensity, they spend time in the different squares, informed by the space-time budgets of PADS+ (Table 13.2). Once an agent has exhausted its time allocation in one square, it moves to another, randomly chosen square.

13.3 Results and Observations

The implementation of Situational Action Theory as an agent-based model is an exercise in modelling that is both data and theory driven with a minimum of arbitrary assumptions. It thus differs from the models discussed in Chaps. 11 and 12, which were mostly theory driven. Given the deterministic nature of Situational Action Theory, an agent-based model can be implemented deterministically, although some factors in the commission of crime have a random element, such as the exposure of agents to criminogenic settings as they move randomly around and spend time in certain areas according to their crime propensity.

Taking the space-time budget data together with crime propensity, the model recreates the situational exposure of agents. The specifications of patches provide the interaction of the agents with more or less crime inducing environments. We can recreate approximately the proportion of crimes committed at certain locations (Table 13.3) with reasonable parameter settings.

Setting the temptation threshold at −2 means we exclude low propensity agents almost completely from committing crime. This matches the PADS+ data:

Table 13.3 Comparison of simulated and actual proportions of crime at selected locations with 100 agents, Temptation = −2 and Deterrence = 6. The PADS+ proportions are derived from Wikström et al. (2010, p. 76)

Percent time spent at	School	City centre
PADS+ Data (%)	18	12
Best fit run	18.22	11.31
Mean (25 runs)	16.82	11.42
St. Dev.	2.04	1.02

> However, just as important as the finding that crime-prone young people tend to offend in response to criminogenic settings is the finding that young people with a low crime propensity appear (situationally) to be largely immune to the criminogenic features of a setting. Regardless of whether they are in a criminogenic setting or not they practically never offend. (Wikström et al. 2010, p. 80)

In fact, in the 20 day period of data collection, only one low crime propensity agent committed a crime (Wikström et al. 2010, p. 80, footnote 33).

By implementing Situational Action Theory we are able to explore the theory. Although there are some uncontroversial findings such as the increased criminal behaviour of youths with high criminal propensity in a tempting setting and the near immunity of low propensity youths in the same setting, agent-based modelling lets us explore whether the proposed mechanism is indeed sufficient to create the observed behaviour.

We have implemented Situational Action Theory as an individualistic causal theory of crime commission. In the current version, an agent's morality and self-control are static. In future work it would be interesting to implement a dynamic version in which an agent's morality and self-control can change according to both previously successful criminal behaviour and the influence of its social network.

13.4 Conclusion

We have presented an agent-based implementation of Situational Action Theory, a theory that takes into account the interplay of environmental influences and personal characteristics on a person's decision. The focus on this interplay makes it a particularly good theory for an agent-based implementation. The initial formalisation of the notions of person and setting characteristics yields a static model of Situational Action Theory. In order to obtain dynamics we calibrated the model against the space-time budget data from the PADS+ study, which provide information about how much time particular agents spend in different settings. Running the model we can replicate the numbers of crimes committed in two special settings, school and the city centre.

Situational Action Theory sets out to provide a causal explanation of crime where crime is defined as a breach of a moral norm (as defined in law). In this theory an agent makes a decision to adhere or breach a norm depending on the situation. Although its moral values remain the same, agents will behave differently in different situations. This situational sensitivity makes action decisions in Situational Action Theory a case of compliance, as discussed in Sect. 10.3.

References

Alchourrón, C. E., Gärdenfors, P., & Makinson, D. (1985). On the logic of theory change: Partial meet contraction and reveision functions. *Journal of Symbolic Logic, 50*, 510–530.

Atkinson, K., & Bench-Capon, T. (2008). Addressing moral problems through practical reasoning. *Journal of Applied Logic, 6*(2), 135–151.

Atkinson, K., & Bench-Capon, T. (2009). Abstract argumentation and values. In I. Rahwan & G. R. Simari (Eds.), *Argumentation in Artificial Intelligence*. Dordrecht/New York: Springer.

Bauman, Z. (1993). *Postmodern ethics*. Cambridge: Polity Press.

Durkheim, E. (1974). *Sociology and philosophy*. Glencoe, Illinois: Free Press.

Edmonds, B. (2004). How formal logic can fail to be useful for modelling or designing MAS. In *Regulated agent-based social systems* (Lecture notes in artificial intelligence, vol. 2934, pp. 1–15). Berlin: Springer.

Giddens, A. (1991). *Modernity and self-identity*. Cambridge: Polity Press.

Hansson, S. O. (1999). *A textbook of belief dynamics, theory change and database updating*. Dortrecht: Kluwer.

Makinson, D., & van der Torre, L. (2000). Input/output logics. *Journal of Philosophical Logic, 29*, 383–408.

Paternoster, R., & Simpson, S. (1996). Sanction threats and appeals to morality: Testing a rational choice model of corporate crime. *Law and Society Review, 30*(3), 549–583.

Pyle, D. (2000). Economists, crime and punishment. In N. G. Fielding, A. Clarke, & R. Witt (Eds.), *The economic dimensions of crime*. New York: Palgrave.

Shilling, C., & Mellor P. A. (1998). Durkheim, morality and modernity: Collective effervescence, homo duplex and the source of moral action. *The British Journal of Sociology, 49*(2), 193–209.

von Wright, G. H. (1951). Deontic logic. *Mind LX*, (237), 1–15.

Wikström, P.-O. H. (2010). Explaining crime as moral actions. In S. Hitlin & S. Vaisey (Eds.), *Handbook of the sociology of morality* (Handbooks of sociology and social research). New York: Springer.

Wikström, P.-O. H. (2011). Does everything matter? Addressing the problem of causation and explanation in the study of crime. In: J. M. McGloin, C. J. Sullivan, & L. W. Kennedy (Eds.), *When crime appears: The role of emergence*. New York: Routledge.

Wikström, P.-O. H., Ceccato, V., Hardie, B., & Treiber, K. (2010). Activity fields and the dynamics of crime: Advancing knowledge about the role of the environment in crime causation. *Journal of Quantitative Criminology, 26*, 55–87.

Chapter 14
We-Intentionality

Everything is moral, only morality is no longer moral.

Robert Musil

Although agent-based modelling adds to strict individualism by showing the emergence of social phenomena, it does not quite do justice to what in Sect. 10.3 we called the *homo duplex*. The *homo duplex* describes the pull between selfish behaviour and moral or pro-social conduct in human beings. For Durkheim this duality was at the heart of sociological enquiry and sociology was to be the methodology of a moral science (Giddens 1984, also see Sect. 2.1.1).

All the models so far discussed in this book rely on strong individualism. Agents have their own beliefs, desires and intentions and behave accordingly. Beliefs and desires might be influenced by their social surroundings, as in the models discussed in Chaps. 8, 11, and 12, but their intentions are formed by maximising their own utility. Although humans sometimes behave in an individualist, selfish way, for example in many economic exchanges, they do not do so in most situations. A host of empirical and experimental evidence shows that humans do not conform to the principles of utility maximisation. Violations to utility maximisation are most vividly shown in experimental findings for the Ultimatum Game. The Ultimatum Game consists of two players, *A* and *B*. *A* is allocated a sum of money, say £10, and is asked to allocate some of it to *B*. If *B* accepts the offer, it receives the allocated amount and *A* keeps the remainder. If *B* rejects the offer, neither *A* nor *B* receive anything. The rational decision for *B* is to accept whatever *A* offers as the utility of £1 is greater than the utility of nothing. Experimental studies have found, however, that people generally do not accept low offers, thus punishing what is seen as unfair distributions at their own expense. Thus, rather than behaving rationally, they seem to behave according to a norm of fairness.

These violations of utility maximisation in experimental economics have led to the supposition that norms, rather than utility calculations, influence behaviour. The proposal of 'normative framing' is used as an explanation of this fact

C. Elsenbroich and N. Gilbert, *Modelling Norms*, DOI 10.1007/978-94-007-7052-2_14,

(Bicchieri 2006). Another influential idea to resolve these experimentally exposed irrationalities is 'team thinking' (Bacharach 2006). The idea of team thinking is that agents do not use expected personal utility as the predictor of another agent's choice, but what an invisible manager would recommend both players to do. So, games in which individually maximising decisions lead to overall detrimental outcomes (e.g. the prisoner's dilemma) are resolved by both agents thinking that the advice would be to cooperate.

In this chapter, we shall explore the possibility of replacing the strong atomism of current modelling by a weaker individualism in which agents are able to share intentions. We start from the vantage point of a social agent and propose that situations are framed as cooperative rather than adversarial in the first place. This cooperative framing is the cognitive result of the capacity of agents for *we-intentions*, or their *we-intentionality*.

Before going into a detailed discussion of we-intention(ality), it needs to be distinguished from imitation. One could contend that imitative behaviour is sufficiently social to model human sociality. After all, if I imitate another agent's behaviour, I join in with its behaviour, thus contributing to the other agent's intention. However, this is not necessarily the case, as the following examples highlight:

1. Agent A wants to stand out from the crowd by wearing extraordinary items of clothing. Other agents imitating join A's behaviour but do not contribute to its goal, indeed they are in direct opposition to its goal of 'standing out'.
2. Agent B is colouring in a painting-by-numbers painting. C sees it colouring a patch with red. C picks up a brush and imitates A's behaviour, painting another arbitrary patch red. C is joining B's behaviour but does not contribute to its intention of colouring in the painting by numbers.

And there are some things that we-intentionality can explain that imitation cannot:

1. Improvement of tools: Only if an agent understands the intention behind a tool can it be improved.
2. Cultural objects such as money: Joining in with another agent's intentions means to understand the meaning of its behaviour and to interpret it.

In this chapter we look to the future and explore the possibility of extending the ontology of agent-based modelling to model genuinely social agents rather than collections of *homines economica*. What we need to capture is the other side of the *homo duplex*, the side that behaves according to moral values. This means that pro-social behaviour is no longer seen as an emergent feature of society, but a property of the human itself. Conceptualising the human with this duality enables us to do justice to society as an entity. But rather than using society as the originator of moral behaviour as Durkheim does, we will use the intrinsic sociality of the human being as a starting point. This conception thus remains true to individualism with the individual as the source of society, but an intrinsic sociality or morality weakens the strong individualism of 'only the individual for the individual' into an individual that has the ability of 'being *for* the other' as in Bauman's (1993) theory of moral action.

14.1 Intention in Agent-Based Models

We have seen that intention plays a major role in agent specifications in agent-based models (see Chap. 4). Although some agent systems use very simple agents, as soon as any sort of planning, even at the most rudimentary level, comes into play, agents can be modelled using the Belief-Desire-Intention (BDI) framework (Bratman 1987). Agents have desires, or goals, beliefs about the world, and intentions, which are plans towards the goals constructed from their beliefs. In models of normative behaviour, the starting point is usually a BDI agent as simpler agents can not behave normatively. We have seen a range of foci for models of normative behaviour. One focus is on cooperation and punishment (see Chap. 6). Here the goal of an agent is to maximise individual utility and the intention is to defect when cooperation is detrimental for this goal. Another focus is an agents' adaptation to a social environment using imitation or memetics (see Chap. 7). Here agent behaviour is socially determined, and the goal is to "fit in" with others. The intention is to change one's behaviour depending on the social circumstances. Other models discussed in the book focus on more complicated social influences on individuals' intentions (see Chaps. 8 and 9).

We classed agent-based models of norms into five categories: environmental models, game theory models, diffusion models, social influence and learning models and finally cognitive models of norms. Two important aspects of normative systems have not been touched on by agent-based models. One is the high complexity and abstraction of human normative social systems, the existence of abstract objects such as money and wedding rings, and complex institutions like the judiciary system. The other is the dynamics of changing norms, e.g. the change from shaking hands to hugging as a greeting, the change from smoking as "cool" to smoking as an outcast activity.

In what follows we argue the problem of current models of normative behaviour is that they start from a strongly individualist paradigm. We propose that the concept of we-intentionality should lie at the heart of theories of human social interaction. Only shifting our starting point from strong individualism to a weaker position using the intrinsic disposition of agents to share intentions will allow us to start modelling human society properly in its unique complexity and abstraction. The price we pay in parsimony of modelling is worth paying for the increase in veracity.

The concept of we-intentionality could be a valuable starting point for future work on agent-based modelling of norms. The uniqueness of the human social world (in complexity and abstraction) implies that there must be a unique feature of humans that brings it about. We will argue that we-intentionality is this unique feature. We will then discuss how we-intentionality might be operationalised in agent-based models of normative behaviour.

When it comes to explaining the cultural and social complexity of the human world, there are two standpoints: (a) the complexity simply emerges from the basic properties that also explain animal behaviour or (b) humans have a unique feature which explains why their social world is different from that of animals.

Standpoint (a) is the usual starting-point for models of normative behaviour. It might be possible, in time, to devise a model that can generate the emergence of complex institutions from very simple assumptions, but given the low level of complexity reached by existing models it is likely that simple behavioural models will not be able to do so. In contrast, we opt here to explore the second standpoint. Let us briefly discuss a hierarchy of intentionalities before turning to we-intentionality.

14.2 Intentionality

In this section we discuss different layers of intentionality. Figure 14.1, taken from Searle (1995), will help to guide us through the different kinds and levels of intentionality.

The first level is the set of intentional facts. These can be split into three kinds. Individual intentionality is the most basic form where an individual's actions are directed towards a goal and action steps are planned towards achieving this goal. This kind of intentionality is operationalised in the BDI agents discussed in Sect. 4.1.2.

An individual displays second order intentionality if it recognises other individuals as intentional agents, i.e. agents whose actions are directed towards a goal. This means a person has a theory of mind. Second order intentionality has been explicitly operationalised in cognitive agent models such as Bosse (2007) and is at the heart of many simulations. Any game theoretic interaction presupposes that the interaction partner is behaving intentionally, e.g. Axelrod (1986). Simulations, such as Lorscheid and Troitzsch (2009) and Conte et al. (2013) that model social interactions explicitly (e.g. via norm invocation) have an underlying assumption of a theory of mind. Second order intentionality accounts for social coordination.

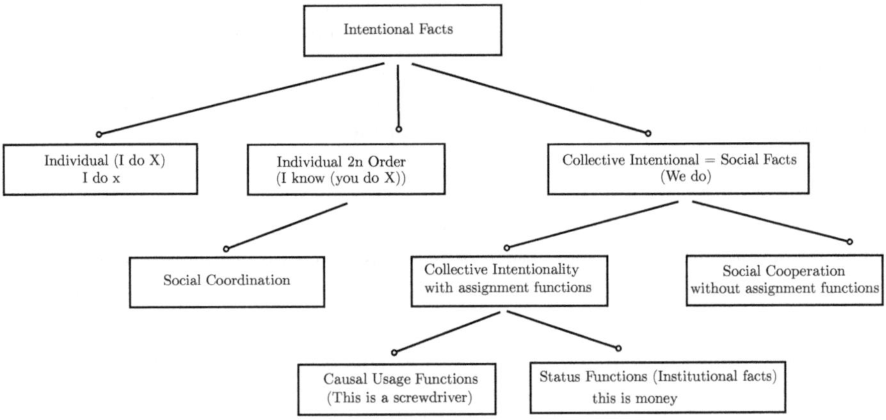

Fig. 14.1 Layers of intentionality (Searle 1995)

The final kind of intentionality to be distinguished is collective intentionality, we-intentionality or shared intentionality. The hypothesis is that collective intentionality lies at the heart of human social behaviour. It is the underlying capacity that leads to proper social cooperation (in contrast to the social coordination resulting from the theory of mind) and to the assignment of usage/status functions (e.g. this piece of wood is the queen in a game of chess, this piece of paper is money).

14.3 We-Intentionality

We-intentionality has been investigated in various disciplines, in particular in psychology (e.g. Tomasello et al. 2005; Tomasello 2009; Plotkin 2003), the philosophy of psychology (e.g. Dennett 1987; Searle 1995), computer science and AI (Bratman 2006, 2009) and the philosophy of sociality (e.g. Gilbert 2009; Tuomela 2007). The idea is that human beings not only behave following their own intentions, but also join intentions with other agents.

In what follows we discuss some reductive and non-reductive accounts of we-intentionality and assess their usefulness for agent-based models. We start with the experimental evidence for we-intentionality. We focus on the ontogeny work by Tomasello et al. on attention and intention sharing. Their research strongly suggests that we-intentionality is a fundamental feature of human cognition. We then discuss a reductive position, i.e. a position that acknowledges that we-intentionality is a feature of human sociality but contends that it can be reduced to individual intentions. Such a reductive position is presented in Bratman (2006) and Bratman (2009). Also early work by Tuomela and Miller (1988) is often seen as a reductive account but later on, in Tuomela (2007), he distances himself from reductionism and develops a non-reductive account based on a layering of intentions. We finish in the field of philosophy of sociality and discuss Searle's position on shared intentionality (Searle 1995) and Gilbert's principled account of non-reductive we-intentions (Gilbert 2009). The reason for discussing the different accounts is that they lead to different ways of modelling collective, shared or we-intentionality.

14.3.1 Experimental We-Intentionality

Tomasello and his colleagues have been investigating shared attention and intention for almost two decades. They contend that there is a unique human feature they call 'we-intentionality' that none of our primate cousins have. We share a large part of our cognitive skills with other primates, such as the folk psychological specification of human action captured by the BDI agent. In humans, there is something in addition to recognising intentions in others. This 'something' is recognising other agents' understanding of one's own intentions, resulting in "shared attention" (intentional perception) as well as homing in to other agents' intentions, resulting in "shared intention". This triadic interaction of me-object-you starts from about 1 year of age.

The experimental research shows that children at around their first birthday can distinguish intentional from non-intentional actions, thus experimentally establishing that 1 year olds have a theory of mind. Chimpanzees also have a theory of mind (Tomasello et al. 2005). For example they understand when experimenters point them towards food and react by focusing their attention and moving there. Chimpanzees can also be trained to point and thus share attention with an experimenter. They do not, however, use pointing either in a natural habitat or between themselves. This means that although the understanding of other agents as intentional is present, the sharing of attention or intention is not.

Another experiment, reported in Tomasello et al. (2007), is on the reaction of toddlers towards intentional and non-intentional action. If an experimenter intentionally drops an object, toddlers are not inclined to help picking the object up whereas, if the drop is accidental, the toddlers help significantly more often. These experiments not only show that toddlers have a theory of mind, but also show that they have a ready capacity to help others. The toddlers not only recognise the other's intentions but also start to participate in the intentions. This shared intention can be seen as social cooperation, distinct from social coordination present in other animal species.

Piaget (1932) argued that pretence play starts as an individual pasttime before becoming a social interaction. In contrast, Rakoczy (2009) argues that pretence play is social from the start. In order to pretend, i.e. to assign a different identity or function to something, an understanding of the original identity or function must be present. For this reassignment to be understood socially, not only the understanding of the original identity or function must be shared, but also the intention behind the reassignment. Rakoczy concludes that we-intentionality must be the foundation of pretence play.

These experiments suggest that we-intentionality is a capacity of humans.

14.3.2 Non-Reductive We-Intention and We-Intentionality

The experimental evidence discussed in the previous section suggests that humans are capable of joining or sharing intentions. There are different accounts of shared intention and intentionality. Two distinctions have to be made: (a) whether shared intentions can be reduced to individual intentions or become new entities in their own right and (b) whether shared intentions are the result of an explicit joining of intentions or whether they come about implicitly.

We first discuss a reductive account from Bratman (2009) who defines shared intentions in such a way that agents explicitly agree to achieve a goal together. Non-reductive accounts of shared intentionality have prevailed in recent literature, (for example Roth 2004; Tuomela 2007; Schmid 2008). We discuss Gilbert (2009) as an

Table 14.1 The difference between we-intention and we-intentionality

	Non-reductive	Reductive
We-intention (explicit)	We-intention as something over and above the linking of individual intentions. (e.g. Gilbert, later Tuomela)	We-intention as an explicit add on to or a contract between intentions. (e.g. Bratman, early Tuomela)
We-intentionality (implicit)	The disposition to represent or conceptualise a situation as collective. (Searle, Tomasello)	

explicit non-reductive account of we-intention and Searle (1995) as a non-reductive account of we-intentionality. The distinction between we-intentionality and we-intention is an important one. Traditionally, intentionality is the capacity of the mind to direct thoughts at something, to be *about*, to represent objects, properties, or states of affairs (Searle 1983; Dennett 1987, e.g.). Intention refers to the orientation of an action towards an outcome. Intention is the hallmark of agency, of acting with a purpose, a goal (Anscombe 1957). In line with this distinction, we-intentionality is the capacity to conceptualise a situation as *collective, shared, together*, whereas we-intention is the deliberate aligning of goals, the conjunction of purposes (see Table 14.1).

14.3.2.1 Bratman's Joining of Intentions

As the father of the Belief-Desire-Intention agent it might not be surprising that Bratman also developed a theory of shared intention (Bratman 2009). Nor is it a surprise that he starts from individual intention to build up his theory. At the root of all social behaviour lies the individual intention, where an individual intention is defined as a plan of action to achieve a goal. Shared intention means more than one individual has the same plan of action to achieve a (common) goal.

However, just having the same intention is not sufficient for a shared intention. We might both have the intention to paint a house and both set off armed with a paintbrush and roller. The first possibility is that we both paint all walls, i.e. double paint everything. This is not only not a shared intention but not even a coordinated one. The second possibility is that we coordinate, say by observing what the other is doing and at least not double painting or bumping into each other. This is coordinated action and we might say that we shared the experience, but it certainly does not result from shared intentions, as neither knew about the other's intention at the start. What is missing from the scenario is some cognitive state that makes an action result from shared intentions rather than coordinated or uncoordinated individual intentions. Bratman gives several other examples of large-scale coordinated behaviour, such as many people opening their umbrellas on the street when it starts raining. He also cites the applause after a concert, but rather than seeing it as simple coordinated behaviour reacting to a common stimulus (like the opening of umbrellas on the onset of rain), he classifies it as shared behaviour.

> Again, given a sufficient common understanding of the circumstances, an audience at a Yo Yo Man cello recital may more or less spontaneously arrive at a shared intention to applaud together at the end of the performance as they all recognise to be and recognise that they all recognise to be wonderful. When they applaud they do not merely each individually applaud at the same time. Rather they intentionally applaud together. (Bratman 2006, p. 7).

Bratman's theory is derived from the following six axioms and a Dependency Principle (DEP).

Definition 14.3.1. Agents A and B have a shared intention to φ iff

1. Intentions on the part of each in favour of activity φ
2. Agent A knows that agent B has the intention to φ (and vice versa)
3. Both have intentions in favour of meshing subplans to achieve φ
4. Beliefs about the joint efficacy of the relevant intentions
5. beliefs about interpersonal intention-interdependence
6. (DEP) agent A continues to intend to φ if and only if agent B continues to intend to φ (and vice versa)
7. Common knowledge of (a)–(f) and (DEP).

According to this position, shared intentions derive from individual intentions plus some connecting conditions linking intentions between agents. These conditions are about knowing of the other's intention, agreeing to find ways to achieve a common goal and both seeing the possibility to achieve joining intentions, i.e. plans to achieve the common goal. In addition there are some conditions about persistence and continuation and the public knowledge of the connectedness of the intentions. This account relies on the assumption of an independent standpoint available to judge whether the conditions are met. Other reductive accounts can be found for example in Kutz (2000) and Zaibert (2003).

14.3.2.2 Gilbert's Plural Subject Account of We-Intention

Margaret Gilbert (2009) develops an explicit, non-reductive account of we-intention. Against Bratman, she develops a plural subject account of shared intentions. In short, shared intentions create a 'plural subject', i.e. a body, a new single entity, consisting of those agents sharing intentions, rather than the purely relational account of joint individual intentions put forward by Bratman. Gilbert's plural subject account has parallels to Durkheim's idea of society as the cause of moral behaviour. Gilbert argues that her account more faithfully represents our intuitive understanding of we-intention. The main points are connected to joint commitment and breach of commitment. Agents that have joint intentions also have joint sub-plans and reneging on a sub-plan constitutes a breach of commitment. Gilbert states criteria for we-intentionality which the plural subject account satisfies but which the joint individual intention account by Bratman does not. She identifies criteria to assess whether a situation is the result of we-intentions and presents a principled account for a non-reductive version of we-intentions. The joining of intentions creates a new entity, the plural subject, in which the individuals act and to which the individuals are committed in a more involved way than in Bratman's reductive account. By virtue of constituting a new entity with a single intention, we-intentionality in Gilbert's account is not reducible to individual intentions.

Although her account is non-reductive in the sense of we-intentions being something over and above the set of individual intentions, it might be accused of being reductionist in the sense that it does not allow for the emergence of we-intentions. As every agent has to partake actively in the joint intention there is no space for partially overlapping intentions or the partial sharing of meaning. Most of our social life does not involve this kind of commitment, however. We do not actively agree that a particular object is a hammer of that paper issued by the Bank of England is money. We do not actively agree with each other that we do not bump into each other in the street, even though we expect that most people will not do so. We have to distinguish between an account of we-intentionality as an underlying disposition of complex social interaction and an account of the instantiation of we-intentions.

14.3.2.3 Searle's Collective Intentionality

Searle calls the extension of his account of individual intentionality to a system with multiple agents sharing intentions an account of "collective intentionality" (Searle 1995). Humans exercise collective intentionality by assigning functions to objects or events leading to constitutive rules of action. The pretence play discussed above exemplifies that understanding of status functions of objects, the shared meaning of status functions and the ability to playfully forego the functions. Other examples are the assignment of the function of a hammer to a heavy piece of metal (or other hard material) attached to the top of a stick and the assignment of currency to a piece of paper issued by the Bank of England to be used in market transactions. The first is the assignment of a usage function, i.e. this object is for hammering nails into the wall, the second the assignment of a status function, i.e. this object is money. Searle acknowledges that many people avoid a non-reductive account of we-intentionality as it seems to commit us to an ontology of almost Hegelian proportions in which a collective spirit is housed along with individuals (Searle 1995, p. 25). For Searle there is, however, no contradiction between we-intentionality and methodological individualism. Clearly, mental states only exist in individuals' minds; however, one kind of individual mental state is a we-intention. For Searle, collective intentionality is the distinguishing feature of human beings for the establishment of institutional facts or complex social norms. He distinguishes observer-relative facts (e.g. "The moon looks beautiful tonight") from brute facts (e.g. "The moon causes the tides"). The moon will still cause the tides if no one is looking, but the first sentence makes no sense without an observer. From this distinction Searle invokes collective intentionality to get from observer relative to institutional facts. Through collective intentionality we can collectively assign a function to an object (e.g. the function of value storage and exchange currency for a piece of paper) and a set of constitutive rules that make the object fulfil the function (e.g., to be issued by the Bank of England). In a way, collective intentionality is the enabler for shared meaning, since language is the underlying construction of a social fact, as Searle explicitly acknowledges. The capacity for we-intentionality is however prelinguistic as Tomasello's work shows (see Sect. 14.3.1).

14.4 We-Intentionality in Agent-Based Models

In this section we briefly relate the different conceptions of we-intention and we-intentionality to agent-based models. This discussion is meant to prepare the ground for modellers to start implementing we-intentionality.

For a reducible notion of we-intentionality we can keep the existing BDI architecture. Looking at Bratman's account the important features of we-intentionality are:

1. The agents' agreement on a shared goal
2. The merging of sub-plans towards the achievement of the goal
3. The common commitment to the goal and plans, and
4. That both stop the activity when one drops out.

Agents form individual goals and intentions and join them in a kind of contract. Goals are simple statements like "spend a weekend in New York", "paint the house" or "get married". In an implementation, agents can choose common goals from a set of possibilities or from the intersection of their respective existing goals and agree on one of them. Common commitment can also be modelled with relative ease, even though it will not be descriptive of what happens in real life. Let common commitment be given as a binding contract that agents 'sign'. Defaulting on the contract might lead to punishment. To effect this, the BDI agent would have the sharing of goals and the (contractual) commitment to sub-plans added to its behavioural repertoire.

Because adding reductive we-intention is a behavioural extension to the BDI agent, any model using this architecture can be extended by adding such behaviour components. The main problem with the reductive account of we-intentionality is that it adds normative behaviour (in the form of cooperation contracts) explicitly to a model. It is thus not possible a model the emergence of norms using this explicit account of we-intention.

But just treating we-intention as non-reducible will not lead to an emergentist account of normative behaviour either. If we take Gilbert's non-reductive plural subject account of we-intentions, we still conclude with agents bound to explicit we-intentions. There is no space for the non-explicit joining into common meaning.

An emergentist account can only be achieved by implementing we-intentionality as an agent disposition. This means we need not only to make the agents behave according to shared intentions, but also the agent architecture itself has to incorporate the capacity for shared intentions. An idea we might want to use as groundwork to achieve this is language evolution for the emergence and evolution of shared meaning. A language is a structure of shared meanings. Social norms can be seen as shared meanings established in a similar way to a lexicon. Social norms would be a lexicon of social structure, just like a language lexicon is of natural structures. The simulation developed in Hutchins and Hazlehurst (1995) explores the emergence of a shared lexicon. The authors define a lexicon as "a consensus on a set of distinctions" (Hutchins and Hazlehurst 1995, p. 6). The simulation replicates the dynamics between external objects/situations, the internal cognitive state of an agent and the communicative social actions. This point is also explored in Salgado (2012) who takes into account any symbolic communication, one kind of which are social norms can be seen as one kind (see Sect. 8.3.3). Salgado explicitly connects the evolution of language, shared intentionality and socialisation (Salgado 2012, Chap. 3).

Building on the emergence of shared meaning captures Searle's theory of the social construction of reality in which meaning is generated by collective ascription of a function to an entity or situation, thus exemplifying shared intentionality. Simulations of language emergence or the emergence of shared meaning can also be directly related to the simulation of we-intentionality because their starting point is the assumption that agents will communicate with each other, similar to the joint attention discussed in Tomasello et al. (2005).

Some models of normative behaviour can be adapted to model we-intentionality. One of the most sophisticated models of normative behaviour is the model of norm invocations developed in Lorscheid and Troitzsch (2009). In this model, agents have the goal to colour the world a specific colour (some agents have blue, and some have red as their goal). They move about a grid colouring the patches they stand on. In addition to colouring they can send norm invocation messages to other agents. For example, if a blue agent sees an agent painting patches red it can send a message asking it to change its colouring to blue. In the original model agents change their colouring behaviour gradually towards the requested colour. In this scenario it is a possibility to replace simple norm invocation by shared intentionality, i.e. agents sharing a colouring intention.

Adding we-intentionality to the agent complicates the BDI architecture. The standard BDI architecture is, however, not able to model adequately many dynamics of normative behaviour, such as the feedback between social norms and individual behaviour or the change of norms over time. Although parsimonious, the BDI architecture is insufficient for the modelling of all but the most basic dynamics of normative behaviour. It seems that any model wanting to go beyond the most basic patterns of social norms to model *human* normative behaviour needs to extend its set of assumptions beyond the basic BDI architecture to support we-intentionality.

Despite this additional complication, including we-intentionality in agent specifications enables us to respond to issues and questions that cannot be tackled without it, such as modelling the dynamic change of social norms or the fact that human normative systems are very complex. The non-reductive account of we-intentionality also gains validity from the ontogenetic work of Tomasello and colleagues which strongly suggests we-intentionality as a fundamental property of human beings.

We hope this discussion of we-intentionality will inspire other agent-based modellers to depart from the paradigm of strong individualism towards an intrinsically social agent. Although the question of why norms exist in the first place becomes trivial with such an agent, it does open up the possibility of research into complex norms and norm change.

References

Anscombe, G. E. M. (1957). *Intention*. Boston, MA: Harvard University Press.

Bacharach, M. (2006). *Beyond individual choice: Teams and frames in game theory*. Princeton: Princeton University Press.

Bauman, Z. (1993). *Postmodern ethics*. Cambridge: Polity Press.

Bosse, T., Gerritsen, C., & Treur, J. (2007). Grounding a cognitive modelling approach for criminal behaviour. In S. Vosniadou, D., Kayser, & A. Protopapas (Eds.), *Proceedings of the second European cognitive science conference, EuroCogSci'07*, Delphi (pp. 776–781).

Bicchieri, C. (2006). *The grammar of society: The nature and dynamics of social norms*. New York: Cambridge University Press.

Bratman, M. E. (1987). *Intention, plans and practical reason*. Cambridge: Harvard University Press.

Bratman, M. E. (2006). Dynamics of sociality. *Midwest Studies in Philosophy, 30*(1), 1–15.

Bratman, M. E. (2009). Shared agency. In C. Mantzavinos (Ed.), *Philosophy of the social sciences: Philosophical theory and scientific practice*. Cambridge/New York: Cambridge University Press.

Conte, R., Andrighetto. G., & Campenní, M. (2013). *Minding norms – Mechanisms and dynamics of social order in agent societies* (Oxford series on cognitive models and architectures). Oxford: Oxford University Press.

Dennett, D. (1987). *The intentional stance*. Cambridge: Bradford Books/MIT.

Giddens, A. (1984). *The constitution of society: Outline of the theory of structuration*. Berkeley: University of California Press.

Gilbert, M. (2009). Shared intention and personal intentions. *Philosophical Studies, 144*, 167–187.

Hutchins, E., & Hazlehurst, B. (1995). How to invent a lexicon: The development of shared symbols in interaction. In N. Gilbert & R. Conte (Eds.), *Artificial societies: The computer simulation of social life*. London: UCL Press.

Kutz, C. (2000). Acting together. *Philosophy and Phenor erzologicaRlesearch, LXI*(1), 1–31.

Lorscheid, I., & Troitzsch, K. G. (2009). How do agents learn to behave normatively? Machine learning concepts for norm learning in the emil project. In B. Edmonds & N. Gilbert (Eds.), *Proceedings of the sixth conference of ESSA*, Guildford, UK: University of Surrey.

Piaget, J. (1932). *The moral judgement of the child*. London: Kegan Paul, Trench, Trubner and Co.

Plotkin, H. C. (2003). We-intentionality: An essential element in understanding human culture? *Perspectives in Biology and Medicine, 46*(2), 283–296.

Rakoczy, H. (2009). Collective intentionality and the root of human societal life. In L. S. Röska-Hardy & E. Neumann-Held (Eds.), *Learning from animals?* Hove/New York: Psychology Press.

Roth, A. S. (2004). Shared agency and contralateral commitments. *The Philosophical Review, 113*(3), 359–410.
Salgado, M. (2012). *More than words: Computational models of emergence and evolution of symbolic communication*. Ph.D. thesis, Department of Sociology, University of Surrey.
Schmid, H. B. (2008). Plural action. *Philosophy of the Sociel Sciences, 38*(1), 25–54.
Searle, J. (1983). *Intentionality: An essay in the philosophy of mind*. Cambridge/New York: Cambridge University Press.
Searle, J. R. (1995). *The construction of social reality*. London: Penguin.
Tomasello, M. (2009). *Why we cooperate*. Cambridge: MIT.
Tomasello, M., Carpenter, M., Call, J., Behne, T., & Moll, H. (2005). Understanding and sharing intentions: The origins of cultural cognition. *Behavioural and Brain Sciences, 28*, 675–735.
Tomasello, M., Carpenter, M., & Lizskowski, U. (2007). A new look at infant pointing. *Child Development, 78*, 705–722.
Tuomela, R. (2007). *The philosophy of sociality: The shared point of view*. Oxford/New York: Oxford University Press.
Tuomela, R., & Miller, K. (1988). We-intentions. *Philosophical Studies, 53*, 367–389.
Zaibert, L. A. (2003). Collective intentions and collective intentionality. *American Journal of Economics and Sociology, 62*(1), 209–232.

Chapter 15
Conclusion

The rules of morality are not the conclusion of our reason.

David Hume

Margaret Thatcher's "There is no such thing as society" was one of the defining statements of her premiership, describing a world in which only individuals exist and everyone needs to take responsibility for their own actions. We have seen that the spirit of individualism also pervades the social sciences, starting with microeconomic theory but further invading other social sciences in the form of rational choice, exchange and game theory. It is futile to ask which came first, the individualisation of society or the victory of individualism in the social sciences. They feed back into each other like most social phenomena.

If people are selfish, why do we find so much pro-social behaviour? The world around us is full of social norms, institutions and pro-social actions. We linked the questions of cooperation and normative behaviour to the question of why people commit crimes. Both are questions asked in the social sciences but they are investigated separately. We combined them as the question of why people behave as they do in relation to norms (where norms can be social, legal or moral). In Chaps. 2 and 3, we discussed theoretical approaches to this question. We saw that overly structural approaches, that treat social norms as causing human action are too restrictive of human agency. We also saw that individualism, putting human agency first, cannot explain many features of the human social world. In comparing the study of norms and crime we discovered that, although the subject matters are so closely related, the approaches differ markedly, with norm analysis focussing mostly on institutions or individuals and much crime analysis focussing on the environment. The problem for both is to explain social macro phenomena from individual micro assumptions.

In Chap. 4 we proposed agent-based modelling as a method to go beyond individualism by showing the emergence of anti- or pro-social behaviours. Agent-based modelling was identified as a particularly useful methodology for questions relating

C. Elsenbroich and N. Gilbert, *Modelling Norms*, DOI 10.1007/978-94-007-7052-2_15,

to normative behaviour as it allows the specification of micro-behaviours (at the agent level) and the generation of macro-phenomena from repeated interaction of many agents with each other and their environment.

In Chap. 5 we looked at environmental models of normative and criminal behaviour. Whereas the theoretical analysis of social norms does not take the physical environment into account, it features a lot in agent-based models of norms. We concluded that environmental models can mimic some interesting dynamics of social norms but that they remain at a rather basic level.

In Chap. 6 we discussed models using deterrence and punishment for modelling social norms and crime. Game theoretic models were some of the first models of normative behaviour, investigating the conditions under which cooperation might emerge in a society of purely selfish agents. We discussed models which implement punishment to reduce the success of an uncooperative strategy as well as models which use the possibility of punishment, i.e. deterrence, as the major influence on behaviour. We concluded that game theoretic models are limited to the investigation of the emergence of social norms.

In Chap. 7 we reviewed diffusion models of social norms relying on either simple behavioural imitation or the transmission of cultural units called memes. These models can produce many normative macro-phenomena, such as local conformity to one norm whilst retaining global diversity of different norms. We concluded that although diffusion models can generate interesting macro-phenomena, given their simplicity, they are insufficient to model the complexity of the human social world.

In Chap. 8 we discussed more involved micro mechanisms for the transmission of social norms. Starting with social influence mechanisms, we considered models based on different theories of social influence, such as the theory of reasoned action and social impact theory. We turned to model a yet more complex kind of norm transmission using the idea of social learning. We concluded that both social influence and social learning produced models of social norms that produces some plausible underlying dynamics.

In Chap. 9 we described the currently most complex models of social norms, modelling not only the emergence and diffusion of social norms, but also the feedback between norms and an individual.

In Chap. 10 we discussed what we see as missing features in existing models. We identified two major omissions: (a) a failure to embed the agents in relevant social structures and (b) the lack of models of compliance, which is the third kind of norm adherence identified in social psychology in addition to conformity and obedience, which have been modelled extensively.

In Chaps. 11–13 we presented three models tackling these missing features. The first was model of juvenile delinquency implementing a social embedding of socially influenced agents. The second was a feedback model of group assimilation and selection and its influence on the radicalisation of opinions. The third model was an implementation of compliance using a context sensitive (or situational) theory of crime commission.

Chapter 14 discussed the main positions on we-intention and we-intentionality, explicit, reductive, explicitly non-reductive and dispositional, and related them to agent-based modelling of social norms. An implementation of we-intentionality leads to less parsimonious agent-based models. Either we-intentionality is added as a behavioural component to a purely individualistic agent (Bratman) or we-intentionality is added as a disposition to the agent architecture (Searle, Tomasello). We argued that any model that wants to go beyond simulating the most basic patterns of normative behaviour (e.g. diffusion) needs to go beyond a simple BDI agent.

One important overall conclusion has to be that agent-based modelling is most successful when implementing theories that propose mechanisms such as social network theory, the social construction of knowledge and Situational Action Theory, and that draw on detailed qualitative observations. Such models can be validated against statistical data resulting from empirical research. Although agent-based models not relying on theoretically or empirically backed mechanisms can produce dynamics that might be seen as similar to social phenomena (e.g. the models discussed in Chaps. 6 and 7), validation becomes much more of a problem (see also the discussion on thought experiments and agent-based modelling in Sects. 1.3.3 and 4.1.3).

Author Index

C. Elsenbroich and N. Gilbert, *Modelling Norms*, DOI 10.1007/978-94-007-7052-2,

Subject Index

C. Elsenbroich and N. Gilbert, *Modelling Norms*, DOI 10.1007/978-94-007-7052-2,

MIX
Papier aus verantwortungsvollen Quellen
Paper from responsible sources
FSC® C105338
FSC
www.fsc.org

If you have any concerns about our products,
you can contact us on
ProductSafety@springernature.com

In case Publisher is established outside the EU,
the EU authorized representative is:
Springer Nature Customer Service Center GmbH
Europaplatz 3, 69115 Heidelberg, Germany

Printed by Libri Plureos GmbH
in Hamburg, Germany